Pelican Books

A Farewell to Marx

Da
Lo
Sch
wh
wh
Mi
so

A

DATE DUE

nd Conway was born in Liverpool in 1917. He grew up in
London where he attended St Olave's and St Saviour's Grammar
School

A Farewell to Marx

An Outline and Appraisal of His Theories

David Conway

Penguin Books

For my Father and Mother

Penguin Books Ltd, Harmondsworth, Middlesex, England
Viking Penguin Inc., 40 West 23rd Street, New York, New York 10010, U.S.A.
Penguin Books Australia Ltd, Ringwood, Victoria, Australia
Penguin Books Canada Ltd, 2801 John Street, Markham, Ontario, Canada L3R 1B4
Penguin Books (N.Z.) Ltd, 182–190 Wairau Road, Auckland 10, New Zealand

First published 1987

Copyright © David Conway, 1987
The Acknowledgements on pp. 229–31
constitute an extension of this copyright page
All rights reserved

Typeset, printed and bound in Great Britain by
Hazell Watson & Viney Limited
Member of the BPCC Group
Aylesbury, Bucks
Typeset in 10/12 Linotron 202 Bembo

Contents

Contents

Preface

There are several people who have helped me greatly in the writing of this book and whom I should like to thank.

First and foremost, I should like to thank Ted Honderich whose idea it was that I write this book, and who has given me enormously helpful criticism, advice and encouragement throughout every stage of writing it.

Second, I should like to thank Gerald A. Cohen, partly for the encouragement he has given me despite his having little sympathy with what I was writing, but mainly for his various writings on Marx which have done so much to illuminate Marx's thought and which have served me – as I am sure they have served many others – as a paradigm of lucid and rigorous philosophical discussion of Marx.

I should additionally like to thank Peter Ayre, Renée Danziger, Geoffrey Goldkorn, Richard Jeffries, and Stephen Torrance for their criticism of drafts. I have been greatly helped by their comments even though I have not always followed their advice.

I must emphasize that none of the above-mentioned bears any responsibility for any of the views expressed in this book other than those which are explicitly attributed to them.

I should like also to thank Middlesex Polytechnic for a term's leave in 1983 to work on the book.

Finally, I should like to thank my wife, Diana, for all her support and patience during the time I have been working on this book. What she has had to endure has given her much reason to be glad to be saying at last a farewell to Marx.

1 Introduction

'A spectre is haunting Europe – the spectre of Communism.' These are the opening words of the *Communist Manifesto*. They ring as true today as when Marx first wrote them in the winter of 1847–8, just before a widespread outbreak of political revolution in Europe. What else in Marx's writing is true? This is the question which the present work seeks to answer. How we feel about the spectre will depend on our answer to that question.

Whatever the reasons for its presence in Europe in the 1840s, since Marx's time one of the prime reasons for the presence of the spectre both there and throughout the rest of the world has been Marx's writings themselves. As a general world-view and ethic, Marx's writings have had an appeal second to none. The only systems of ideas that compare with Marx's in terms of their influence are the major world religions.

Once accepted, Marx's ideas can be a heady brew. They can impel people to do things they would not otherwise have done. They can make people react and feel towards things very differently from how they would otherwise feel and react. Because of his ideas, people are willing to stand outside London Underground stations on cold and wet winter mornings selling Marxist newspapers to generally uninterested, if not distinctly hostile and disdainful commuters. Because of his ideas, people will march on demonstrations and organize petitions, strikes, and sit-ins at work or college. People will join picket-lines in industrial disputes. And, in very rare and extreme but nonetheless very important cases, because of his ideas, some people are prepared to plant bombs, kidnap and shoot people.

Many people who become Marxists do so without ever having

subjected Marx's views to critical scrutiny. They become Marxists in the same way that young people often become smokers: that is, through imitation or cultural osmosis. Equally, many non-Marxists – often Marx's most vociferous opponents – reject Marx's views out of nothing more than emotional revulsion and without ever having conducted a serious examination of what he had to say.

Marx's views, however, purport to be at worst philosophy and at best science. They are based, for Marx, on hard historical and economic fact and rigorous rational argument. They are, therefore, amenable to rational debate. They demand critical and dispassionate examination before being accepted or rejected.

Some Marxists would deny this. They will say that it is a person's class interests that determine what he or she believes. In the end, such people would claim, whether or not one accepts Marx is not a matter of rational persuasion. Rather, it is a matter of one's interests as a member of a particular economic class. Marx himself, however, was a living refutation of this claim. For he was throughout his life thoroughly, if not typically, bourgeois or middle-class. Moreover, the claim is contrary to Marx's own stated view. For Marx explicitly acknowledged that non-working-class individuals are capable of embracing communism out of theoretical appreciation of its ultimate validity. His views and theories may, perhaps, be incapable of final proof or disproof. But nevertheless it is possible to come to reasoned convictions about them.

Marx called his views 'scientific'. He marshalled much empirical evidence and advanced complex arguments in support of them. The present work sets out to determine what precisely Marx's views were as well as to discover the arguments he advanced in support of them. It aims, then, to evaluate these arguments. At the end of the investigation, we shall be able to judge whether we have any good reason to accept Marx's theories. The practical importance of forming an opinion on this issue need hardly be emphasized. No one can be indifferent to the spectre of communism, given the contemporary national and international political situation.

The majority of citizens of Western democracies nominally

reject Marxism; they do so by voting for non-Marxist candidates. None the less, Marxist activists continue to exert considerable influence within socialist parties and within trade unions. As a polarization of political attitudes continues to take place in society, individuals are increasingly forced to give explicit consideration to the ideas of Marx and to decide where they stand in relation to them.

Committed Marxist activists of the kind who sell Marxist newspapers outside high-street supermarkets at weekends do not attempt to offer the public at large Marx's *arguments* for his conclusions. Instead, they present the conclusions themselves as they see them applied to contemporary events. Marx's arguments are rarely examined in depth in schools, while at centres of higher education the discussion is often far too technical and abstruse for the non-expert to follow. Those who approach Marx's writings unaided are soon forced to stop in their tracks. Apart from the *Communist Manifesto* and one or two other texts, Marx's writings are often very difficult to understand. His arguments are all too often presented in a very inaccessible and forbidding idiom. They are cast in the language of nineteenth-century Hegelian and post-Hegelian philosophy. They invoke concepts drawn from classical political economy. And they employ ideas introduced by early nineteenth-century French socialists. Marx's ideas need to be 'translated' into the idiom of our day to make them accessible to the non-specialist. The academic establishment has largely failed to meet this need. The late twentieth century has witnessed in the West an enormous flowering of interest in the thought and writing of Marx. In the wake of this growth of interest, there has followed a vast plethora of tests giving the general reader overviews of Marx's theories. Of these, many are vitiated as introductions by their adoption of a partisan stance. They are written less as introductions to the thought of Marx than as calls to action. Other works, again written from a committed stance, suffer by being written in a terminology that presupposes familiarity with Marx's ideas. In both cases, there is a tendency on the part of many writers on Marx to give lengthy and convoluted explanations of why some other equally impenetrable interpretation of Marx is mistaken, rather than give an explanation of Marx's own ideas.

Some recent introductory works on Marx, however, are very good indeed.[1] But even the best introductory works have hitherto been primarily expository rather than critical.

As a result of the upsurge of interest in Marx in the West, particularly since the late 1960s, Marx's ideas have become part of the general intellectual *Zeitgeist*. Today, a nodding acquaintance with such distinctive Marxian notions as those of alienation, ideology and so on is as much part of the intellectual equipment of the educated Westerner as is a smattering of Freudian terminology. In both cases, however, the level of misconception and distortion has built up as the distance from the author's writings has increased. The present work aims to dispel misunderstandings of Marx's thought.

Suppose one were asked to say in a nutshell what Marx's most important contribution to thought has been. The answer would be that Marx has been responsible for the widespread acceptance of two fundamental doctrines. The first is that capitalism is vastly inferior to socialism as a form of organization of modern society. The second is that sooner or later capitalism is destined to be replaced by socialism. Doctrines such as these are not without momentous practical significance. Just as he may be deemed responsible in a large measure for the prevalence of these two beliefs throughout many parts of the world today, so he may be deemed responsible for what has been done in the name of these doctrines. This means that Marx may be deemed indirectly responsible in considerable measure for nothing less than the entire socio-political complexion of the world today. For half the world professes itself to be socialist, while in the remaining half the single most important political division is between those who do and those who do not wish to see socialism established there. This is not to suggest that all who are socialists are so by virtue of Marx's influence upon them. It is only to say that to date it has been Marxists who have been the most active and influential socialists. It is Marxists who have been responsible for establishing socialism in those countries which are socialist. And it is Marxists within the non-communist countries who are the most vocal opponents of capitalism and the most enthusiastic supporters of socialism. Our object is to understand what led Marx to propound this pair of doctrines and to consider whether he made out a convincing case for them.

It is possible to identify in Marx's writings three supporting reasons offered for the thesis that capitalism is inferior to socialism. The first is the claim of Marx that capitalism morally and spiritually deforms and stultifies people. It is alleged that communism would enable human beings to flourish fully. The name that Marx gave to the debased condition to which, so he claims, capitalism reduces human beings is *alienation*. There are many people today, especially in the affluent capitalist societies of the West, who accept what Marx said on this matter. They believe that capitalism is less conducive to human well-being than communism because capitalism creates alienation while communism overcomes it.

The second of Marx's reasons for supposing capitalism to be inferior to socialism is that capitalism is a system that is based on *exploitation*. On this view, the vast majority of members of society, who earn their living by selling their labour, are exploited by the comparatively small minority whose main source of income is derived from their owning the means of production. Precisely what Marx meant by 'exploitation' is a matter of some debate, as is the question of what Marx believed to be wrong with it. But there is no question that Marx believed that capitalism involves exploitation and that he regarded exploitation as evil.

The belief that capitalism necessarily involves the exploitation of the workers is especially prevalent in socialist countries and in the non-industrialized world. But it is also widely held in capitalist countries. No claim of Marx's has done more than this one to arouse antipathy towards capitalism.

The third of Marx's reasons for claiming capitalism to be inferior to socialism is that capitalism, on Marx's view, is destined to undergo unavoidable periodic economic fluctuations. These fluctuations necessarily create unemployment among workers and economic insecurity. The occurrence within the present century of two major world recessions – one in the 1930s and one today – certainly has given this contention of Marx much contemporary relevance.

Marx's second great teaching is that capitalism is destined to be replaced by socialism. This doctrine is part of a much larger theory of human history that Marx advanced. This is the theory known as *the materialist conception of history* or *historical materialism* for short. This theory of history provides two things. First, it provides a synoptical overview of human history from its dawn to the present and beyond. Second, it provides a theory of society and social change which explains why history has taken the course it has. According to historical materialism, any form of economic organization of society such as capitalism only lasts for as long as it can make full use of society's productive resources. When it ceases to do so, the form of economic organization of society changes. A new form of organization arises that is able to make full use of productive resources. Historical materialism holds that capitalism is destined to be replaced by socialism because the economic fluctuations to which capitalism is subject reveal that capitalism is incapable of maintaining full use of the resources of an advanced industrial society.

The order in which the various theories of Marx will be examined here will be the order in which they came to be advanced by Marx. Accordingly, we begin by considering Marx's claim that capitalism creates alienation. Marx formulated his theory of alienation in 1844 in his *Economic and Philosophical Manuscripts*. This text remained unpublished until the present century and was not widely known of until after the Second World War. This theory, as well as the related theory of human nature on which it is based, is the subject of Chapter 2.

Towards the end of 1845, Marx, working closely with Friedrich Engels, formulated the materialist conception of history. Again, the theory was initially formulated in a work, the *German Ideology*, that remained unpublished until the present century. However, this theory of history was to become widely known during Marx's lifetime, since Marx published works in which the theory was outlined or employed. The most notable of such works is the *Communist Manifesto*, published in 1848. This theory forms the subject of Chapter 3.

The claim that capitalism involves exploitation and the claim that it is prone to economic fluctuations belong to Marx's mature economic theory. This was set out in Marx's most important work, *Capital*. The first volume of this work was published in 1867. Marx's economic theory is examined in Chapter 4.

Having completed our survey of his economic theory, we shall then examine Marx's attitudes to politics, revolution and the state in Chapter 5. After that, in Chapter 6, we shall consider Marx's theory of ideology and his contention that such systems of ideas as classical political economy, morality and religion are instances of ideology.

It is to be the central thesis of this book that none of Marx's claims about capitalism nor his theory of history stands up to critical scrutiny. Marx fails to make a valid case either for the contention that capitalism is inferior to socialism or for the contention that capitalism is destined to give way to socialism. People who accept such beliefs on the authority of Marx lack warrant for their political outlook. Their hostility towards capitalism is without rational foundation. In the last analysis, a person's convictions are his or her own. Every thinking person forms his or her political, religious, philosophical and moral views for him or herself. However, they can often be helped to form their opinions by thinking through the arguments of other people. This book represents the results of the author's own efforts to come to terms with Marx. It is offered to the public in the hope that it may serve as a stimulus to others to determine for themselves their attitudes to this most challenging of philosophical thinkers.

2 Philosophical Anthropology

1. Communism and Socialism Before Marx

Although Marx is by far the most famous communist, he is by no means the first. Marx became a communist in 1843 when he was twenty-five years old. By that date, a rich and varied body of communist and socialist thought had grown up in Europe. It is impossible to single out any one individual as being the originator of the idea of communism. One notable figure in the formation of communist doctrine was the Frenchman Gracchus Babeuf. In 1796, he formed the Conspiracy of Equals. This short-lived and ill-fated organization was set up with a view to seizing political power and establishing a society of strict equality based upon communal ownership of property. Babeuf's conspiracy was crushed at its inception. However, his ideas were to receive a fresh lease of life after the publication in 1838 of a book about him, entitled the *Conspiracy for Equality*. The book's author, Philippe Buonarotti, had been a former associate of Babeuf's. The insurrectionary ideas that Babeuf had advanced were to be taken up by August Blanqui, who led an abortive coup in Paris in 1839.

By that time, many other less extreme and violent forms of socialism had been proposed. There were three thinkers in particular around whose ideas socialist movements had grown up in the early decades of the nineteenth century. Marx was to call these thinkers 'Utopian' socialists in view of the fact that they hoped to institute their ideal societies through peaceful persuasion of everyone rather than by militant working-class revolutionary action. The first of these was Henri Saint-Simon, leading apostle of the new industrial era. Saint-Simon proposed that political power should pass from those whom he called the 'unproductive classes' – landowners, politicians and the idle rich – to the productive classes. The latter were business men, bankers, engineers, and workers. Saint-Simon was no egalitarian. People differed markedly in their natural aptitudes, and they should be differentially rewarded accordingly. His ultimate objective was the replacement of political rule by the administration of production and material things rather than people. A rational order of society, directed towards production, would remove the causes of social conflict and thus eliminate the need for the state. He also advocated a new form of Christianity based upon the idea of brotherly love.

The second major Utopian thinker was another Frenchman, Charles Fourier. In contrast with Saint-Simon, Fourier was an opponent of the industrial society. It was Fourier's view that the entire course which Western civilization had taken was a mistake. The mistake had consisted in trying to organize society in opposition to human nature. His goal was the replacement of modern civilization with a state of what he called 'harmony'. Harmony would prevail when society had been so organized that all the passions of every individual would be permitted full gratification. This was to be accomplished through the creation of a network of what Fourier called *phalansteries*. These were economically self-sufficient communes of approximately 1,700 members each. Fourier's ideas were grounded upon a detailed conception of human nature. Human beings were viewed as possessing a complex set of drives. The relative strength of these drives varied from individual to individual. These drives fell into three groups. The first group of drives were called by Fourier 'the luxurious passions'. These were the source of desires for sensuous gratification. The second group were the so-called 'group passions'. Included here were desires for respect, friendship, love and parenthood. Finally, there were what Fourier called 'the serial passions'. This group included the passions for making arrangements, for intrigue, and for variety. The phalansteries were to be so organized that each of the different passions of each individual was to be given scope for full gratification in a way that was socially useful, or at least not harmful. The passion for variety, the so-called 'butterfly passion', would be catered for by means of rapid job rotation. It was proposed that members of the phalanstery would change the task that they were doing every hour. The result would be that all work would be done with enjoyment. Even the seemingly most distasteful jobs, such as manuring fields, were deemed capable of being done with enjoyment. The 'natural penchant of children for filth' would make children positively relish such tasks. Social conflict and antisocial behaviour arose in civilization because it suppressed the passions, which returned in perverse forms. Even sadistic and aggressive impulses were thought to be capable of being allowed socially useful gratification. People in whom they were powerful were to be given the task of being community butcher. Fourier was not averse to unearned income. Phalansteries were envisaged as being financed by private investment. In contrast with Saint-Simon, Fourier was against the abolition of inheritance. His followers tended to minimize the inegalitarian aspect of his work and to stress the element of communism in it.

The third major Utopian socialist had somewhat more practical experience of founding such ideal societies than Fourier had. This was the Englishman, Robert Owen. Owen was a self-made business man, who, during the Napoleonic wars, had come to amass a fortune through his cotton-spinning factory in New Lanark, Scotland. At the time, this factory was the most important cotton-spinning factory in the country. For Owen, its importance lay in the way in which, through considerate treatment of the workers, he had been able to turn them into model workers and citizens. On the basis of his experience at New Lanark, he formed the idea of a world-wide system of 'villages of unity and mutual cooperation'. Like Fourier, but unlike Saint-Simon, Owen displayed a marked preference for the agrarian as opposed to the industrial way of life. He argued in favour of a gradualist approach to the creation of these new forms of association, hoping that they would spread by example. He believed that the workers' demand for universal suffrage was an irrelevance.

Each of these three thinkers had his own band of enthusiastic supporters. And there were other groups of communist and socialist thinkers too. Socialist and communist movements proliferated during the 1830s and early 1840s in France and England. The importance of these movements had been drawn to the attention of the German public with the publication in 1842 of a book entitled *Socialism and Communism in Present Day France*. This book by Lorenz von Stein asserted that socialist revolution was immanent in society, and foretold that it would be carried out by the disaffected labouring poor of the industrial cities.

Marx was not merely *not* the first communist thinker, but he was also left decidedly lukewarm after his first encounter with communist ideas. Marx came into contact with communist ideas in 1842, when, having completed his university education and failing to obtain the university teaching post for which he had hoped, he embarked on a career of journalism. The paper he joined was the *Rheinische Zeitung*. This had been set up a short time previously, backed by Rhineland business men and professional people, with the aim of promoting business, trade, and commerce in that region. The paper had quickly been taken over by a group of young radical German intellectuals who had studied together at the University of Berlin and who now made the paper a mouthpiece for their own ideas. The Paris correspondent of the paper was a German communist, Moses Hess, who periodically submitted reports on various communist factions within that city.

Initially, Marx expressed grave reservations about communism. In October 1842, he became editor-in-chief of the paper. His first editorial took the form of a defence of the paper against the charge levelled by a Cologne rival paper of its having espoused communist ideas. Marx wrote in this editorial that 'The *Rheinische Zeitung* . . . does not admit that communist ideas in their present form possess even *theoretical reality*, and therefore can still less desire their *practical realization*, or even consider it possible.'[1] Twelve months later Marx had overcome his earlier scruples. He was now extolling proletarian communist revolution. What happened to lead Marx to change his mind about communism? We shall investigate this matter in the next section.

2. Marx's Route to Communism

Marx was led to become a communist by the conviction that nothing less than communism could possibly enable human beings to live fully human lives. This conviction grew steadily during the course of 1843 as Marx became more and more disillusioned, first with his own Prussian government, then with the idea of constitutional monarchy as such, and finally with all forms of political liberalism.

It had not always been so. When Marx arrived at the *Rheinische Zeitung* in March 1842, he had not yet become an enemy of the established order. In one of his early articles for the paper, published in May 1842, Marx had written that 'Laws are in no way repressive measures against freedom . . . Laws are positive, clear, universal norms in which freedom has acquired an impersonal, theoretic existence independent of the arbitrariness of the individual. A statute book is a people's bible of freedom.'[2]

A few months later Marx was still writing approvingly of Hegel's idea of the state as 'the great organism, in which legal, moral and political freedom must be realized, and in which the individual citizen, in obeying the laws of the state, only obeys the natural laws of his own reason, of human reason.'[3]

What led Marx to abandon support for this view of the state? The answer is a steadily growing realization that the state was simply incapable of overcoming and remedying the egoism and selfishness that he saw to be rampant in commercial society. For Marx, selfishness and egoism were not just morally reprehensible. They were the very antithesis of what it was appropriate for a human being to feel. In thinking this, Marx had been deeply influenced by the views of a former associate of his from his student days in Berlin. This was the philosopher, Ludwig Feuerbach, who, in 1839, had published his seminal *Essence of Christianity*. The main purpose of this work of Feuerbach's had been to argue the case for atheism, or, at least, for a purely secular religion in which the human species itself was to receive the veneration formerly reserved for deity. Feuerbach's basic thesis was that what people had previously conceived of as God was nothing other than the human species in an alien form. The antithesis between the human and the divine only marked the distinction between the individual aware of all his or her limitations and imperfections and his or her idea of the species as a whole in which every humanly conceivable excellence could be found. 'The divine being is nothing else than the human being, or rather, the human nature purified, freed from the limits of the individual man, made objective – i.e. contemplated as another, a distinct being.'[4] Religious belief, for Feuerbach, constituted a theoretical error that had baneful practical consequences. In ascribing all excellence to the postulated divine being, the religious man impoverished himself in his own eyes. It was the aim of philosophy to unmask this error. 'The work of self-conscious reason in relation to religion is simply to destroy an illusion: an illusion, however, which is by no means indifferent but which, on the contrary, is profoundly injurious in its effects on mankind, which deprives man as well of the power of real life as of the genuine sense of truth and virtue.'[5]

Marx was to be deeply influenced by Feuerbach's idea that man could be adversely affected by creations of his own that had assumed an independent existence in his own eyes. It formed the basis of his idea of alienation. By the time that he became a communist Marx had come to believe that the state and the institution of private property figured pre-eminently among such impoverishing human creations. But Marx also derived from Feuerbach another idea no less important than that of self-estrangement or alienation. This was the idea that egoism and self-centredness are attitudes that are less than fully human. For Feuerbach, what distinguishes human beings from other species of animals is that human beings possess a consciousness of being members of a species. Animals, by contrast, have at most only a consciousness of their individual selves. 'The essential difference between man and the brute . . . is consciousness in the strict sense . . . present only in a being to whom his species, his essential nature, is an object of thought.'[6] The fact that the possession of species consciousness is the distinguishing characteristic of man had, for Feuerbach, ethical implications. 'He who lives in the consciousness of the species as a reality, regards his existence for others, his relation to society, his utility to the public, as that existence which is one with the existence of his own essence . . . He lives with his whole soul, with his heart, for humanity. How can he hold in reserve a special significance for himself, how can he separate himself from mankind.'[7]

Since, for Feuerbach, what makes an individual human is

consciousness of the species, a person is more fully human the more fully conscious he or she is of their species. But consciousness of one's species, says Feuerbach, necessarily results in an attitude of 'other-regardingness' towards members of the species. Therefore, the more fully human a person is the more other-regarding that person is, and conversely. Marx took over this inference from Feuerbach's writings. It formed the basis both of his initial enthusiasm for the state and of his eventual disenchantment with it. It initially aroused his enthusiasm for the state because he perceived the state to be a vehicle for the expression and development of that universal concern for others that he took to be an appropriate attitude for human beings to possess. It became the basis of his rejection of the state as he became increasingly sceptical of the pretensions of the state to serve as such a vehicle.

The process of disillusionment with the state began in late 1842 when Marx began to write articles for the *Rheinische Zeitung* about the way in which the Prussian state treated, or rather failed to treat, the poor. The first of these articles was written in October 1842. It took the form of a commentary on the proceedings of the Rhine Province Assembly of the previous year. The debates in question were concerned with a recently promulgated law prohibiting the gathering of fallen branches in Rhine forests. Getting fallen branches for firewood had previously been a customary right of the poor. Growth in the numbers of poor exercising this customary right had led to damage to saplings. To put a stop to the damage to live trees, the gathering of dead branches had been banned. The debates in the Assembly about which Marx wrote had been addressed to the question of what penalty should be imposed upon those caught gathering branches or damaging trees. Marx condemned the Assembly for failing to adopt the truly universal and impartial attitude that was morally demanded of a legislature. Instead, both the law and the penalties being proposed were merely a defence of the selfish interests of landowners at the expense of the poor. Marx wrote that 'The true legislator should fear nothing but wrong, but the legislative interest knows only fear . . . of the evil-doers against whom laws are made . . . Private interest is always cowardly . . . How could the selfish legislator be human when something inhuman . . . is his supreme essence.'[8] Marx concluded the article by saying that it had shown how 'the Assembly degrades the executive power, the administrative authorities, the life of the accused, the idea of the state, crime itself, and punishment as well to the *material means of private interest*'.[9]

In a later article written in January 1843, Marx returned to the same theme of the inability of the state to adopt a truly universal and human attitude towards the poor. The poor in question this time were the impoverished vintners of the Moselle valley who had been suffering since the 1830s from a protracted depression in their industry. Marx's strictures this time were directed against the bureaucracy. In theory, the bureaucracy was meant to embody the universal point of view of the state, rising above all partial and sectional interests to concern itself with the public good. In practice, so Marx argued, the very nature of bureaucracy prevents the bureaucrat from being able to acknowledge that the regions over which he has authority could be administered any better than he is administering them. In the eyes of the bureaucrat, poverty is either unavoidable and nothing can be done to treat it, or it is the fault of the poor themselves and nothing should be done about it. Once again, in Marx's eyes, the state had been found unable to rise to a human level.

By May 1843, Marx had become firmly convinced that the Prussian monarchy was beyond redemption. In a letter of that month to Arnold Ruge, a fellow associate from his student days at Berlin, Marx wrote: 'Human beings – that means men of intellect, free men – that means republicans . . . The principle on which monarchy in general is based is that of . . . *dehumanized man*.'[10] By this time, Marx had been obliged to resign from the *Rheinische Zeitung*. His editorial line had proved too uncompromising and provocative for the proprietors, who feared – rightly as it turned out – that the authorities would order closure of the paper. This period of retirement gave Marx the opportunity to reflect in more abstract terms upon the nature and adequacy of the state. Marx left the paper in March 1843. In that month, he began a detailed study of the account of the state given by the philosopher Hegel, whose views up to this time had dominated

Marx's thinking as well as that of his Berlin associates. Until his death in 1831 Hegel had been professor at Berlin and his philosophy had continued to dominate that university when Marx was a student there between 1837 and 1841. Between March and August 1843, Marx undertook a detailed critical study of Hegel's *Philosophy of Right*. This latter was a work in which Hegel had set out to portray the Prussian state, or at least something closely approximating to it, as rational. Fundamentally, Hegel had done this by showing how the institutions of the state served to provide a necessary corrective to the unbridled egoism that prevailed in the no less equally necessary and rational sphere of commerce. Following the eighteenth-century British philosopher and political economist, Adam Smith, Hegel had called the latter sphere *civil society*. According to Hegel, the state was intended to overcome the selfish preoccupations of civil society and to establish a realm in which universal social concern prevailed.

According to Hegel, a modern rational state would be found to possess three basic institutions. The first is the Crown, which was to be placed above faction by being made hereditary. The second was the civil service, called by Hegel the bureaucracy. The bureaucracy is charged with the task of carrying out the policies of the state. Members of the bureaucracy formed what Hegel called the *universal class*. He meant by this that they were identified in their daily life with the good of society as a whole. This distinguished them from the two remaining social classes which Hegel identified as present in a modern society. The first was the agricultural class, landowners and peasants, steeped in local community and tradition. The second was the business class, immersed in the pursuit of self-interest. The third and final major state institution was the legislature. This was to be composed of all elements in society. The Crown was represented in person; the bureaucracy was represented through its heads – the ministers of state. The remaining social classes (the agricultural and business classes) were to be represented in the parliament or Estates Assembly. As in Britain, the parliament was to consist of two houses. The members of the upper house were to be drawn from the landed aristocracy. Because their land was a hereditary possession and could not be sold, the landowning aristocracy were deemed to have the resources to enable them to participate actively in the Estates Assembly. Because of their economic security, they were deemed able to do so in an impartial spirit. The lower house gave representation to the business classes. Its members were not to be elected directly, since Hegel argued that the gap between the private citizen and the state was too great. Rather, the members of the lower house were to be appointed representatives of various trade and professional guilds and corporations. By representing a corporation, members of the lower house would be elevated above their purely private concerns, thereby becoming eligible to participate in state affairs.

Marx's 'Critique of Hegel's *Philosophy of Right*' was designed to show that Hegel had failed to demonstrate his form of constitutional monarchy to be rational. All he had in fact done was to offer a rationalization of the German status quo, which, in actuality, was permeated with egoism and selfishness at all levels. The bureaucracy, for example, the so-called universal class, merely treated the state as their private property.[11] As Marx analysed it, the state was unable to overcome the egoism endemic in civil society. 'The state . . . is not realized power. It is *supported* impotence; it represents not the power over these supports but the power of these supports.'[12] What was ultimately responsible in Marx's opinion both for the impotence of the state and for the selfishness of civil society was the very separation of the two domains of the state and civil society. 'The atomism into which civil society is plunged . . . is a necessary consequence of the fact that the community, the communistic entity in which the individual exists, civil society, is separated from the state . . . This atomistic point of view . . . returns in the political state just because the latter is an abstraction from the family and civil society.'[13] The separation of the two spheres could only be dissolved, he argued, through the establishment of what he called *true democracy*. This involved more than just universal suffrage. True democracy was not just formal, political democracy. Some North American states had achieved democracy of this kind but had not overcome the separation of civil society and state.[14] For Marx, truly human existence was possible only where there had taken place a complete fusion between the universal concerns of the state and the economic life of civil society, transforming both in the process. As things stood, civil society was a realm of selfishness because public concern had been assigned to the separate sphere of the state. What was needed was a reabsorption of public concern within the domain of civil society.

Marx made this point more forcefully in an article, 'On the Jewish Question', composed towards the end of 1843. Marx's article took the form of a response to an article of his former philosophy teacher and mentor from Berlin, Bruno Bauer. Bauer had argued that Jews should not be supported in their demands for equal civil rights. Such rights had been granted by Napoleon but rescinded in Prussia in 1816. By continuing to practise their religion, Jews deliberately maintained a separate identity which cut them off from the mainstream of society and history. While they practised their religion, they failed to identify with the general good of society as a whole. Their religion thus prevented them from being able to participate fully in the life of the state. Were Jews to be serious about wanting full liberty, argued Bauer, they must first give up their antiquated religion which prevented them from being able to assume citizenship of a modern rational state. Marx responded to Bauer by drawing a sharp distinction between what he called political and human emancipation. Political emancipation had been attained in North America and France through their respective revolutions of 1776 and 1789. These revolutions had created states which accorded all citizens equal rights to life, liberty, and property, as well as freedom of conscience in the matter of religious belief. The practice of religion was thus fully compatible with full political emancipation. North America was proof of this fact since there diverse religions flourished alongside political emancipation. All that political emancipation did was to perfect the state as an entity given over to the protection and support of the pursuit of self-interest in the domain of civil society. The only rights protected in liberal states were those of the egoistic man of civil society. Marx contrasted the modern liberal states of France and North America with the pre-revolutionary regimes which had represented the society of feudalism. In feudal society, property, family and work had all had a political character. But in feudalism, the affairs of the state as such were not the affairs of the people. The political revolution had overthrown the feudal order. In so doing, it had turned the affairs of the state into the affairs of the people, but at the cost of separating civil society and state. Matters of universal concern had been separated from civil society and assigned to the separate realm of the state. In a liberal democratic state – that is, in a political as against a true democracy – the good of the citizens is made the supreme end of the state. But the sort of individual whose good is sought by the state is the self-centred egoistic man of civil society. The state, thus, fails to be a genuine locus for what Marx called *species-being*, that is, man conscious of and concerned for others as well as self. Marx wrote: 'Political democracy . . . regards man – not just one man but all men – as a *sovereign* and supreme being; but man in his uncultivated, unsocial aspect, man in his contingent existence, man just as he is, man as he has been corrupted, lost to himself, sold, and exposed to the rule of inhuman conditions and elements by the entire organization of society – in a word, man who is not yet a *true species-being*.'[15] For Marx the political implications were clear. 'Only when real, individual man resumes the abstract citizen into himself and as an individual man has become a *species-being* in his empirical life, his individual work and his individual relationships, only when man has recognized and organized his own forces as *social forces* so that social force is no longer separated from him in the form of *political* force, only then will human emancipation be completed.'[16]

Marx had now arrived at the idea of communism as that form of human association alone adequate to man's nature as a species-being. By this time, Marx had moved to Paris, the centre of communist and socialist thought and activity. His subsequent meetings there with communist workers and intellectuals quickly led Marx to the opinion that the proletariat, the disaffected poor of industrial society, would be the agents who would bring communism into being through revolution.

Marx made these views plain in an article intended as an introduction to his critique of Hegel's *Philosophy of Right*. Marx began this 'Introduction to the Critique of Hegel's *Philosophy of Right*' by pointing out that the criticism of religion begun by Feuerbach and by other German philosophers such as Bauer had by now been completed. The time had now come to criticize the social conditions that had made recourse to such comforting illusions necessary. 'The criticism of religion ends with the doctrine that *for man the supreme being is man*, and thus with the *categorical imperative to overthrow all conditions* in which man is a debased, enslaved, neglected and contemptible being.'[17] These conditions will be overthrown by the class which is most oppressed by them. This is the proletariat who possess no property of their own. By overthrowing the established order and instituting communism, the proletariat will make universal their own relation to private property.

Marx's 'Introduction to Hegel's *Philosophy of Right*' and 'On the Jewish Question' were published in Paris in February 1844 in a Franco–German yearbook that Marx co-edited with Arnold Ruge. This publication also contained another article which was to have great influence upon Marx. This was 'A Critique of Political Economy', composed by Friedrich Engels. In this article, Engels had criticized both capitalist economic practice and the economic theory that had uncritically analysed this practice, partly on the grounds of their condoning selfishness. Engels's article served to arouse Marx's interest in the subject of economics. In the spring and summer of 1844, Marx turned his attention from politics to the study of political economy, the forerunner of modern economics. In his writings of this period, Marx developed his first critique of capitalism. The most famous of these writings is his *Economic and Philosophical Manuscripts*, unpublished until 1932. As well as condemning capitalism for fostering selfishness and egoism, Marx finds other reasons for regarding capitalism to be inimical to human well-being. These other reasons reflect the effects of Marx's exposure to the various forms of socialist thought with which he had come into contact in Paris. The following sections examine this critique of capitalism developed by Marx in 1844.

3. The Human Essence

The central political issue of our time is undoubtedly how far society should tend in the direction of capitalism or socialism. As this issue is normally debated, it is envisaged as being primarily about which of the two forms of organization of society better secures for its members the things they are presumed to want. Members of a society are rightly presumed to want a variety of things. Thus, people are presumed to want such non-material goods as personal dignity, justice and freedom, as well as the more tangible but no less important goods such as freedom from poverty and disease, economic security, educational opportunity for their children and, last but not least, a large disposable personal income. Opposing political parties and affiliations within Western-style democracies recommend themselves to voters on the grounds of being better able than their opponents to supply these goods or to supply a better mix of them. Similarly, outside these countries, the alternative forms of society are variously recommended and condemned largely in terms of how they fare in providing the things wanted by those whose political allegiance is being sought.

In 1844, a preliminary study of economic theory convinced the twenty-five-year-old Marx that communism is a vastly superior form of societal organization to capitalism. His primary reason, however, was not that communism was better able than capitalism to supply members of society with the various things they wanted, although he undoubtedly thought this to be the case. It was, rather, that communism produces as members of society human beings possessed of better wants and superior accomplishments than capitalism does. It had become Marx's conviction – and he was never to abandon it – that members of a communist society would have a different and vastly superior psychology to that which members of capitalist society possess. Communist man and woman, on Marx's reckoning, are far less acquisitive and selfish than their capitalist counterparts. They are thus more altruistic and cooperative. They are reckoned to be more aesthetically sensitive as well as more versatile and creative. Marx thought that communist man and woman would enjoy an incomparably greater degree of personal autonomy than people do in capitalism. It was his belief that communism would produce finer human beings that led Marx to embrace communism and become a life-long opponent of capitalism.

Marx's belief that communism would produce finer human beings than capitalism did was grounded upon an assumption made by Marx which he was never to renounce. This assumption is that human psychology – what people are like psychologically – is to a large extent a product of the social and economic structure of their societies. According to Marx, the wants and powers people have are largely a function of how their societies are organized. In particular, they are primarily a function of their mode of production. For Marx, there is no such thing as an immutable human nature. This is not to say that Marx believed that men and women were complete ciphers. Rather, what Marx believed was that human beings by nature possess a set of potentialities that are unique to members of the human species. Different forms of society facilitate the actualization of these potentialities in varying degrees. Those human potentialities whose fullest actualization Marx thought most desirable were those that he considered unique to human beings. This set of potentialities constituted what Marx called the *human essence*. The more fully these potentialities were actualized in human beings the more fully human did those individuals become. To the extent that the social and economic arrangements of a society prevented these distinctively human potentialities of its members from becoming actualized, the more dehumanized would those members be. In Marx's view, capitalism was an extremely dehumanized and dehumanizing form of society. This was because its central constitutive economic institutions militated against the actualization of the distinctively human potentialities of its individual members. These potentialities are only able to achieve their maximum degree of actualization within the framework of a communist society. Communism, for Marx, enables its individual members to be fully human. We thus find Marx writing that 'Communism is . . . the true *appropriation* of the *human* essence through and for man; it is the complete restoration of man to himself as a . . . human being.'[18]

Before we begin to consider what Marx took to be the specific effects of capitalist and communist economic institutions upon what he took to be the human essence, we must first examine what Marx took the human essence to consist in. Marx regarded the ideal condition of human beings to be one of the maximum possible actualization of those potentialities that are unique to members of the human species. Three such potentialities of human beings were of paramount concern to Marx. The first is a potentiality for autonomous action, that is for being self-determining in one's activity. The second is a potentiality for sociality. The third is a potentiality for aesthetic enjoyment. How Marx conceived of each of these potentialities requires some explication, which will now be given.

Marx believed that human beings were, alone of all animals, capable of autonomy. By *autonomy* I mean being self-determining, the conscious author of one's acts. The autonomous agent is one whose actions are the product of conscious, deliberate choice. It is true of the members of every species that, in order for them to obtain their means of subsistence, they must engage in certain characteristic forms of activity. Marx called such forms of activity the *life-activity* of a species. Marx took the life-activity of human beings to be different from that of all other animals by being – potentially, at least – autonomous. He writes: 'The whole character of a species, its species-character, resides in the nature of its life-activity, and free conscious activity constitutes the species-character of man.'[19]

In describing the life-activity of human beings as being free, Marx intended to convey the thought that human beings are capable of engaging in productive activity without being driven to it, as are the non-human animals, by physical want or need. 'Animals . . . produce only when immediate physical need compels them to do so, while man produces when he is free from physical need and truly produces only in freedom from such need.'[20] A man who is driven to pick an apple from a tree from a desire to exercise his faculties in some way is free, for Marx, in a way in which a man driven to pick an apple by pangs of hunger is not. Marx imputes to man a need to exert himself, to be active in some way. This need to be active is not a physical need and when he acts from it, according to Marx, a man acts freely. Marx writes: 'The individual in his normal state of health, strength, activity, skill facility . . . needs a normal portion of work, and of suspension of tranquillity.'[21] When motivated to engage in some activity by this need to be active, the agent fully identifies himself with what he is doing. The act he does is not one which the agent is doing only for the sake of what doing it achieves. The act is done for the sake of doing it. Even where the activity has as its goal the production of future means of subsistence, the activity is free and the agent autonomous in his action so long as the need to be active is what it is that is being satisfied by the activity. When the need to be active is being satisfied by some activity, Marx writes, 'the external aims become stripped of the semblance of merely external natural urgencies, and become posited as aims which the individual himself posits – hence as self-realization, objectification of the subject, hence real freedom.'[22] In order for the productive activity of a person to be such that it is capable of satisfying the need of that person to be active, the activity must have a certain character. Marx writes of a person that 'the less he is attracted by the nature of the work and the way it has to be accomplished, and the less, therefore, he enjoys it as the free play of his own physical and mental powers, the closer his attention is forced to be.'[23] A man who does not enjoy what he is doing is forced to attend to what he is doing. His activity is, thus, not free. Marx believed that a man's work is only free when it is intellectually stimulating and physically non-arduous. He writes: 'The work of material production can only achieve the character [of really free working and the individual's self-realization] . . . when it is of scientific and at the same time general character, exertion . . . as activity regulating all the forces of nature.'[24]

Human beings are capable of autonomous action only by virtue of having the capacity to be *conscious* of what it is they are doing. By being conscious of what they are doing, the activity of humans is capable of being intelligent and reflective in a way in which the activity of non-human animals is not. 'The animal is immediately one with its life activity . . . Man makes his life activity itself an object of his will and consciousness . . . It is not a determination with which he directly merges. Conscious life activity directly distinguishes man from animal life activity.'[25] Marx regarded artistic creation as a paradigm of truly human activity because it embodied reflective purposiveness in such a high degree.

That human beings possess a potentiality for sociality is an idea which Marx derived from Feuerbach. In his early writing, Marx sometimes expressed this idea by speaking of man as a species-being. Marx wished to convey at least two ideas by using this expression. The first is that all distinctively human activity has a social dimension: it is made possible only by virtue of the individual agent's membership of some human society. Marx wrote: 'Even if I am active in the field of science, etc. – an activity in which I am seldom able to perform in direct association with other men – I am still *socially* active because I am active as a *man* . . . The individual *is* the *social being*. His vital expression – even when it does not appear in the direct form of a *communal* expression, conceived in association with other men – is therefore an expression and confirmation of *social life*. Man's individual and species-life are not two *distinct* things however much . . . the mode of existence of individual life is a more *particular* or a more *general* mode of the species-life.'[26]

The second idea which Marx wished to convey by using the expression 'species-being' to refer to man is that human beings have a capacity unique to members of the human species for empathizing and cooperating with fellow members of the species. Like Feuerbach, Marx believed that the possession by human beings of this potential had important ethical implications. It implied that compassion for the suffering of others and conscious cooperation with others were more human attitudes than selfish indifference and hostility to others. In Marx's view, egoism is unworthy of a human being.

The final potentiality which Marx took to be unique to members of the human species is that for the aesthetic enjoyment of nature and works of art. Aesthetic appreciation of an object involves adopting towards it an attitude of disinterested contemplation. This is an attitude of which only human beings are capable. Marx writes: 'The *human* eye takes in things in a different way from the crude non-human eye, the human *ear* in a different way from the crude ear, etc., . . . The senses . . . relate to the *thing* for its own sake . . . *Sense* which is a prisoner of crude practical need has only a *restricted* sense. For a man who is starving the human form of food does not exist, only its abstract form exists; it could just as well be present in its crudest form, and it would be hard to say how this way of eating differs from that of *animals*.'[27]

Capitalism was originally condemned by Marx because he believed it prevented the actualization of these three distinctively human potentialities to any significant degree. We shall now examine why he thought this.

4. Why Capitalism Produces Alienation

It was Marx's view that capitalism prevents the distinctively human potentialities of its individual members from being actualized to any significant degree. Private ownership of the means of production, production for profit, and wage-labour all militate against human living. The condition to which human beings are reduced in capitalism as a result of its constitutive economic institutions preventing the actualization of the distinctively human potentialities was called by Marx *alienation* or *self-estrangement*. In capitalism, human beings are alienated or estranged from their human essence.

The two philosophers who had most formative influence upon the young Marx were Hegel and Feuerbach. Each had employed a notion of alienation in their accounts of human life. In the case of these two philosophers, however, the condition had been equated with some mistaken form of consciousness. Very roughly, for Hegel, an individual suffers from alienation when he or she fails to identify him or herself with the natural world and with the institutions of their society. On this view, alienation is overcome by the individual learning to conceive of him or herself and their natural and social world as manifestations of the world Spirit in process of development. For Feuerbach, a person is alienated when he or she subscribes to a belief in the existence of any extra-human spiritual entity, no matter whether these entities be some traditional religious deity or Hegel's Spirit. For these two thinkers, alienation is overcome through a person freeing him- or herself from intellectual error. In sharp contrast, Marx considered alienation to be an actual objective condition of a person. It was a condition, therefore, that could not be removed by any number of transformations of consciousness. Individuals suffer alienation, according to Marx, not because they succumb to intellectual error, but because their basic social institutions obstruct the actualization of their human potentialities. Removing alienation requires getting rid of these disabling institutions and replacing them with more convivial ones. Hence Marx's famous slogan, 'The philosophers have only *interpreted* the world in various ways; the point is to *change* it.'[28]

Although, as Marx conceived it, alienation is an objective condition, it is not one lacking subjective manifestations in the thoughts and feelings of those who suffer from it. A human being who is unable to live a human life is hardly going to be able to sustain either a sense that life has meaning or a sense of self-worth, unless by resorting to illusions about his or her condition that hide the truth from him- or herself. Pre-eminent among such illusions is religious faith. It has been rightly held, therefore, that, for Marx, low self-esteem, a sense that life lacks meaning, or the acceptance of religious beliefs are all symptomatic of the condition of alienation.[29] As Marx put it, 'Religion is the self-consciousness and self-esteem of man who has either not yet won through to himself or has already lost himself again . . . Religion is the general theory of this world . . . its universal basis of consolation . . . It is the *fantastic realization* of the human essence since the human essence has not acquired any true reality . . . It is the *opium* of the people.'[30]

What were Marx's reasons for regarding capitalism as so inimical to human flourishing? In order to answer this question, we shall now consider the account that Marx gave of what becomes of each of the distinctively human potentialities in capitalism. We begin by considering the potentiality for autonomy.

Marx identifed two different ways in which capitalism prevents human beings from achieving autonomy. The first way concerns the fact that capitalism is a market economy. This means that it is reliant upon market forces to determine production rather than central planning. According to Marx, reliance upon the market as a mechanism for determining what gets produced and how it gets produced causes the productive activity of members of capitalist societies to be governed by factors other than their own conscious decisions about what to produce and how to produce it. Workers must do as they are instructed by their employers. In turn, the employers must do what market forces bid them to. It is the impersonal forces of the market that determine economic activity in society, not conscious decision. Admittedly, market forces result from a mass of separate and uncoordinated decisions taken by members of society in their individual capacities as buyers and sellers of goods and services. However, despite market forces being the result of a mass of human micro-decisions, the productive activity that comes to be governed by these forces escapes being regulated by the conscious decisions of members of society. They are subjected to control by forces which are of their making but which dominate their creators. The clearest expression of this view of Marx is to be found in the *German Ideology* composed in 1845–6. Here Marx writes as follows: 'As long as man remains in naturally evolved society, that is, as long as a cleavage exists between the particular and the common interest, as long, therefore, as activity is not voluntarily, but naturally, divided, man's own deed becomes an alien power opposed to him, which enslaves him instead of being controlled by him . . .The social power . . . which arises through the cooperation of different individuals . . . appears to these individuals, since their cooperation is not voluntary but has come about naturally, not as their own united power, but as an alien force existing outside them, of the origin and goal of which they are ignorant, which they thus are no longer able to control, which on the contrary [becomes] the prime governor of . . . the will and action of man . . . [T]rade, which after all is nothing more than the exchange of products of various individuals and countries, rules the whole world through the relation of supply and demand.'[31]

The second way in which, according to Marx, capitalism prevents human beings from attaining autonomy concerns the nature of the sort of productive activity or work it causes to be demanded of human beings. It is Marx's view that capitalism causes productive activity to become as intrinsically unpleasant, monotonous, and soul-destroying as it is possible for such activity to become. Because the purpose of production in capitalism is profit, capitalists seek to minimize their costs of production. This leads them to adopt those techniques of production that maximize the productivity of their labour force. Capitalists have recourse to two techniques to improve the productivity of labour. Each technique impoverishes the character of work. Their combined effect is devastating. The first of these techniques is the division of labour or job specialization. By dividing up and breaking down the number of separate tasks to be undertaken, and by assigning an individual to each task permanently and exclusively, much more can be produced by a given group of workers than can be produced by each attempting to perform all the operations by themselves. Capitalism carries out the division of labour to the furthest possible extent. In so doing, the jobs to which individuals are assigned become ever more narrow and specialized. The scope for developing a wide range of skills that would make work interesting becomes ever narrower.

The second technique resorted to by the capitalist to enhance the productivity of labour is the mechanization of industry, the introduction of machines to perform operations previously performed manually. When mechanization is combined with the division of labour, it makes productivity activity for the vast majority as monotonous and unattractive as work can possibly be. Some of Marx's most impassioned passages are concerned to lay emphasis upon the extreme unpleasantness of the work demanded of people in capitalism. Marx never ceased to be preoccupied with this aspect of capitalism. Thus, in *Capital*, a comparatively late work, Marx wrote: 'Within the capitalist system of production all methods for raising the social productivity of labour are put into effect at the cost of the individual worker; all the means for the development of production . . . become means of domination . . . of the producers; they distort the worker into a fragment of a man, they degrade him to the level of an appendage of a machine, they destroy the actual content of his labour by turning it into a torment; they alienate from him the intellectual potentialities of the labour process in the same proportion as science is incorporated in it as independent power; they deform the condition under which he works.'[32]

When work acquires the unpleasant character it does in capitalism, all direct incentive for the worker to perform it is destroyed. Such work is not of a kind that can satisfy the need to be productively active. Consequently, as Marx says of the worker in capitalism, 'he does not confirm himself in his work, but denies himself, feels miserable and not happy, does not develop free mental and physical energy, but mortifies his flesh and ruins his mind . . . His labour is therefore not voluntary but forced, it is *forced labour*. It is therefore not the satisfaction of a need but a mere *means* to satisfy ends outside itself.'[33]

Turning now to the potentiality for sociality, the first point to observe is that Marx did not wish to deny that human beings are social beings in capitalism. Capitalism is, for Marx, a form of society. Its individual members stand in relations of mutual dependency upon one another. Yet, for all that, capitalism is not a form of genuine society. The characteristic form of social intercourse in capitalism is the act of exchange. Two individuals each possess something that the other wants. Each gives the other what he wants but only for the sake of receiving from the other something that the giver wants in return. The social bond that unites individuals in capitalism is, therefo , one of mutual self-interest. Individuals regard one another only as means to their own private ends. People do not make the well-being of fellow members of society part of their own end. The community that develops in capitalism, therefore, fails to reflect man's species-character. Marx speaks of the society founded upon exchange between self-seeking individuals as 'a caricature of a true community'.[34] Where it is only mutual self-interest that serves to unite individuals, according to Marx, a state of latent hostility obtains between them. Marx writes that capitalist society 'tears apart all the species-bonds of man, substitutes egoism and selfish need for those bonds and dissolves the human world into a world of atomistic individuals confronting each other in enmity'.[35] Marx believed this because he was convinced that the pursuit of self-interest necessarily involves selfishness and complete indifference towards others. 'The intention to *plunder*, to *deceive*, inevitably lurks in the background, for, since our exchange is self-interested on your side as well as on mine, and since every self-interested person seeks to outdo the other, we must necessarily strive to deceive the other.'[36] Capitalism, thus, prevents the formation of bonds of genuine cooperation and concern between people. In their place stand covert antagonism and hostility.

Marx mentions two other ways in which capitalism opposes the development and actualization of the potentiality for sociality. The first of these two ways leads to the workers' alienation; the second to the capitalists'. The first of these ways is that the unpleasant nature of the work that workers are obliged to perform leaves them ill-disposed towards their capitalist employers, who are perceived by the workers as responsible for making them perform such work. The result is that deep social rifts and hostility between classes develop in capitalism. Marx writes of the worker in capitalism: 'If he relates to his own activity as unfree activity, then he relates to it as activity in the service, under the rule, coercion and yoke of another man.'[37] Just as the worker is estranged from the capitalist, so the capitalist – especially the *rentier* – is estranged from the workers. 'He looks upon the slave labour of others, their human *sweat* and *blood*, as the prey of his desires, and regards man in general – including himself – as a futile and sacrificial being.'[38]

The human potentiality for aesthetic enjoyment fares no better in capitalism, according to Marx, than the other two distinctively human potentialities do . Two reasons are given by Marx. These attitudes preclude the adoption of that attitude of disinterested contemplation that is a necessary condition for the apprehension and enjoyment of aesthetic qualities. 'Private property has made us so stupid and one-sided that an object is only *ours* when we have it, when it exists for us as capital or when we directly possess, eat, drink, wear, inhabit it, etc., in short when we *use* it . . . Therefore, all the physical and intellectual senses have been replaced by the simple estrangement of all these senses – the sense of having.'[39] This process is carried to its extreme for Marx in the phenomenon of saving: 'The less you eat, drink, buy books, go to the theatre, go dancing, go drinking, think, love, theorize, sing, paint, fence, etc., the more you *save* and the greater will become that treasure which neither moths nor maggots can consume – your *capital*. The less you *are*, the less you give expression to your life, the more you *have*, the greater is your *alienated* life and the more you store up of your estranged life . . . All passions and all activity are lost in *greed*.'[40] Second, capitalism imposes upon everyone a constant or near-constant preoccupation with making a living that precludes the aesthetic attitude. 'The man who is burdened with worries and needs has no *sense* for the finest of plays; the dealer in minerals sees only the commercial value, and not the beauty and the peculiar nature of the minerals.'[41]

Before proceeding to consider Marx's account of the fate of the distinctively human potentialities in communism, it is worth mentioning two other important ways in which Marx alleges that capitalism damages the aesthetic sensibilities of human beings.

First, the quest for profits on the part of capitalist manufacturers causes them to stimulate in consumers unhealthy and base appetites and desires. '[T]he expansion of production and needs becomes the *inventive* and ever *calculating* slave of inhuman, refined, unnatural and *imaginary* appetites – for private property does not know how to transform crude need into *human* need . . . [The manufacturer] places himself at the disposal of his neighbours' most depraved fancies, panders to his needs, excites unhealthy appetites in him, and pounces on every weakness, so that he can then demand the money for his labour of love.'[42] Marx would appear to have identified the phenomenon known today as consumerism – the production of insatiable desires.

Second, it was Marx's view that the living conditions to which the working class were subjected were inimical to aesthetic enjoyment. While those with purchasing power became dependent on an ever-increasing mass of worthless and harmful products, the worker must learn to live without some of the most elementary goods needed for a decent life. 'Man reverts once more to living in a cave, but the cave is now polluted by the mephitic and pestilential breath of civilization . . . Light, air, etc. – the simplest *animal* cleanliness – ceases to be a need for man. *Dirt* . . . becomes an *element of life* for him . . . None of his senses exist any longer, either in their human form or in their *inhuman* form, i.e. not even in their animal form.'[43] Marx evidently had in mind here the slum urban living conditions that grew up in the first half of the nineteenth century. He thought these conditions worse than those of the most primitive cave-dwellers. He thought this for two reasons: first, because the worker was aware that his domicile belonged to another, the landlord. He could, thus, not look on his living quarters as his own. Second, the modern industrial worker suffered from his living quarters more than the primitive cave-dweller did from his because the modern worker is aware of the contrasting living conditions of the affluent.

The fate of the three human potentialities in communism could not be more different than their fate in capitalism. We shall now consider why Marx says this.

5. How Communism Overcomes Alienation

According to Marx, communism secures the full actualization of the distinctively human potentialities of the individual members of communist society. It is for this reason that Marx writes that 'Communism is . . . the true appropriation of the *human* essence through and for man, it is the complete restoration of man to himself as a *social*, i.e. human, being.'[44] In order to appreciate Marx's reasons for making this claim, we shall adopt the same procedure as before. We shall consider each of the potentialities in turn and see what Marx says becomes of it in communism.

It will be recalled that Marx identified two main ways in which capitalism prevented the actualization of the potentiality for autonomy. The first was to do with the impersonal forces of the market ruling productive activity. The second was to do with the uncongenial nature of work. Both these obstacles to autonomy are done away with in communism according to Marx. First, democratically regulated central planning enables members of a communist society to achieve overall control of their productive activity. Marx writes: 'With the communistic regulation of production (and, implicit in this, the abolition of the alien attitude of men to their own product), the power of the relation of supply and demand is dissolved into nothing, and men once again gain control of exchange, production and the way they behave to one another.'[45]

In *Capital*, Marx characterized production in communism as

being 'production by freely associated men,' and [something which] stands under their conscious and planned control'.[46]

As regards the nature of work in communism, Marx's views oscillate between two different reasons. In his earliest communist writings, the freedom and creativity of individuals were envisaged as being promoted in communism as a result of the abolition of the division of labour. The influence of Fourier's views on Marx was most prominent here. Individuals in communism were to be provided with the opportunity to move freely between different forms of productive activity as inclination moved them. Two consequences would result from such freedom. The first is that individuals would be able to develop and freely exercise a wide range of creative skills and talents. The second consequence of such freedom of occupation would be that, collectively, the members of society would be able to do all that needs to be done in order to provide society with means of subsistence without anyone being obliged to do anything they did not want to do for its own sake. The result would be that all productive activity would be freely undertaken for the sake of doing it. Marx writes: 'In communist society, where nobody has one exclusive sphere of activity but each can become accomplished in any branch he wishes, society regulates the general production and thus makes it possible for me to do one thing today and another tomorrow, to hunt in the morning, fish in the afternoon, rear cattle in the evening, criticize after dinner, just as I have a mind.'[47]

What allows this to happen is that, in communism, individuals become entitled to means of subsistence on the basis of their need for them. No one is forced to engage in productive activity in order to procure the remuneration necessary for the purchase of his or her means of subsistence. Productive activity is, thus, undertaken purely for its own sake. It is, therefore, freely chosen.

It is worth noting that later Marx envisaged this happy situation as coming about only when society has reached a very high state of technological development. Technology has to be such that all the work that needs to be done is of a predominantly intellectual rather than manual kind. '[L]abour becomes attractive work, the individual's self-realization, . . . only when it is of a scientific and at the same time general character, not merely human exertion as a specifically harnessed natural force, but exertion as subject, which appears in the production process . . . as an activity regulating all the forces of nature.'[48]

In his later years, Marx would appear to have become sceptical as to the possibility of work becoming an adequate forum for creative self-expression. He still believed that communism would maximize free, conscious, creative activity. But now his reason became that it provides its members with the maximum leisure or freedom from work. Thus he writes: 'The realm of freedom really begins only where labour determined by necessity and external expediency ends; it lies by its very nature beyond the sphere of material production proper. Just as the savage must wrestle with nature to satisfy his needs, to maintain and reproduce his life, so must civilized man, and he must do so in all forms of society and under all possible modes of production . . . Freedom, in this sphere, can consist only in this, that socialized man, the associated producers, govern the human metabolism with nature in a rational way, bringing it under their collective control instead of being dominated by it as a blind power; accomplishing it with the least expenditure of energy and in conditions most worthy and appropriate for their human nature. But this always remains a realm of necessity. The true realm of freedom, the development of human powers as an end in itself, begins beyond it, though it can only flourish with this realm of necessity as its basis. The reduction of the working day is the basic prerequisite.'[49]

The above passage comes from the third volume of *Capital*. It is difficult to reconcile it with his early communist writings when he spoke of labour in communism as 'the free expression and enjoyment of life'.[50] Even if, with time, Marx came to locate freedom in the sphere beyond work, it was still his opinion that communism maximized free activity. This was because, as Marx saw it, communism minimizes the length of the working day. It does so for three reasons, according to Marx. The first is that, since in communism private ownership of the means of production no longer exists, no one capable of work is able to live on the basis of the labour of others without also working themselves. The fact that all able-bodied persons will work in communism will cut down the time which each must spend in working.

Second, communism eliminates the need for wasteful forms of labour such as supervising workers to make sure they are working. Third, conscious control through planning is thought capable of eliminating waste and ensuring that the most efficient forms of production are adopted.

The potentiality for sociality is likewise thought by Marx to be granted maximum scope for actualization. Marx offers two reasons why this should be so. The first is that communism does away with class antagonisms and divisions, replacing them with harmony and an identity of interests. Fraternity is envisaged by Marx as springing up between communist workers even prior to the advent of communism. Marx writes: 'When communist *workmen* gather together, their immediate aim is instruction, propaganda, etc. But at the same time they acquire a new need – the need for society . . . The brotherhood of man is not a hollow phrase, it is a reality, and the nobility of man shines forth upon us from their work-worn figures.'[51]

The second reason Marx believes that sociality is promoted by communism is that, since the means of subsistence are distributed to individuals on the basis of their need or want for them, human beings will no longer be greedy or selfish. Instead, Marx says, each person will come to regard the well-being of others as the source of their own happiness. 'Let us suppose that we had produced as human beings [i.e. otherwise than on the basis of exchange] . . . In your use or enjoyment of my product I would have the *immediate* satisfaction and knowledge that in my labour I had gratified a *human* need . . . In the individual expression of my own life I would have brought about the immediate expression of your life, and so in my individual activity I would have directly *confirmed* and *realized* my authentic nature, my *human, communal,* nature.'[52]

The extinction of acquisitiveness and selfishness that follows the replacement of market relations by communist ones does more than simply promote altruism and cooperation. It also fosters that attitude of disinterestedness that makes for the appreciation of beauty in art and nature. Marx writes that 'the supersession of private property is the complete *emancipation* of all human senses and attributes'.[53] At the same time, the abolition of the division of labour (and, perhaps also, the maximization of leisure) will bring about a prodigious flowering of human artistic talent. Marx writes 'The exclusive concentration of artistic talent in particular individuals, and its suppression in the broad mass which is bound up with this, is a consequence of the division of labour . . . With a communist organization of society, there disappears the subordination . . . of the individual to some definite art, making him exclusively a painter, sculptor, etc.; the very name amply expresses the narrowness of his professional development . . . In a communist society there are no painters but only people who engage in painting among other activities.'[54]

6. Appraising Marx on Alienation

Marx's commitment to communism was initially and abidingly based on the conviction that communism could and would make people far more autonomous, other-regarding, and aesthetically sensitive than capitalism allows them to become. It is time now to submit this conviction of Marx's to critical scrutiny.

Let us begin with Marx's contentions concerning autonomy. It will be recalled that Marx offered two main reasons for his claim that human beings would necessarily enjoy far greater autonomy in communism than they can in capitalism. The first was that, as a result of replacing the market by central planning as the prime regulator of economic activity, communism is able to bring it under conscious human direction rather than allowing it to be governed by blind impersonal market forces. Marx's second reason was that the organization of work in communism would afford greater opportunity for individual self-direction and, hence, for self-expression. Two different, and seemingly incompatible reasons were offered by Marx in support of this latter contention. The first is that communism abolishes the division of labour, thereby enabling work to become a totally adequate forum for creative self-expression. The second is that communism reduces the length of the working day to less than that required of workers in capitalism, thereby increasing free time or leisure.

Let us consider Marx's contention that, where the economic

activity of society is centrally planned, the members can be said to enjoy more freedom than they do when that society's economic activity is regulated by the market. The first point that needs to be made is that it does not follow merely from the fact that the questions of what gets produced in a society, and how, are decided according to some overall plan rather than by market forces that the autonomy of the members of that society is necessarily enhanced. An autocratic dictator who determines what everyone does in a society might well so arrange matters that production is organized according to some plan. He does not thereby promote the autonomy of those whose activity is regulated by it. A planned society can promote the autonomy of its members only if those members have had a voice in the formulation of the plan. This means that a centrally planned society promotes the autonomy of its members by virtue of its being centrally planned only if the plan was the result of democratic decision. Marx, doubtless, would be happy to go along with these claims, since he always conceived communism as being a fully democratic society. But to anyone who thinks about it for a moment, it should be obvious that in a large, complex industrial society, only the most general matters of policy, at best, are going to be susceptible to democratic decision by all members. Even if the individual members were to elect revocable full-time representatives, these representatives in turn are only going to be able to make very general decisions about social priorities. Of necessity, any detailed determination of what society produces and how it is to be organized to produce it will of necessity have to be the work of a *specialist minority*. A complex economy simply cannot be planned without an enormous bureaucracy of planners. As far as the average member of society goes, there is at best likely to be little to choose, as regards the degree to which he can influence either what society as a whole does or what he finds himself personally able to do, between a centrally planned soicalist society and a capitalist one. At worst, the average individual is in danger of finding himself with considerably less autonomy should there be central direction of labour and if he is deprived of being able to choose what to consume.

At this point, some defenders of Marx might say that the reason why central planning provides members of a communist society with greater autonomy than they are capable of attaining in capitalism is that communism spares them from the vagaries of the business cycle which they will allege is an endemic feature of capitalism. What makes capitalism provide less autonomy is that the business cycle subjects individuals to being thrown out of work periodically and thereby creates a perennial sense of economic insecurity. The validity of this charge, however, depends upon its being true that business cycles are endemic to capitalism. The truth of this contention will be contested in Chapter 4.

On balance, it has to be said that Marx does not offer any compelling reason for supposing that the mere fact that a communist society would be centrally planned thereby shows that members of such a society would enjoy more autonomy than their counterparts do in capitalism.

What of the idea that communism promotes greater autonomy for its members by providing much greater scope for creative self-expression both during and after the working day? Let us first consider the claim advanced by Marx that communism permits each individual to do what he likes, as he likes, when he likes during the period of work. This, surely, must be rejected as purest fantasy. Apart from anything else it seems totally incompatible with having a centrally planned economy. How could planners ensure that there would be enough people in each branch of industry at each moment of the working day should each individual have complete freedom to decide what he does during it?

If the thesis is that the work which communist man does would be more fulfilling than work is in capitalism, this could only be maintained upon the grounds that communism is able to reduce the degree of division of labour to the point of offering each individual member of society the chance to participate for at least part of his working day or life in some form of mentally stimulating labour. By way of defence of capitalism, it has to be said that the fact that capitalism permits intrinsically unfulfilling forms of employment to exist does not in itself show that, in capitalism, anyone's autonomy is thereby reduced. If capitalism divides up the way work is distributed amongst members of society in a way that makes work unfulfilling for many, it does so because such a division of labour has been found to be more *productive* than a distribution that offers more fulfilling work. Capitalist employers in search of profits would be quick to introduce job rotation should output not be impaired thereby. If output were increased with job rotation, then they would be able to make larger profits. Even if output did not rise but only remained static should job rotation be introduced, an employer seeking loyal workers and good industrial relations would have an economic incentive to introduce it. The fact that more meaningful work is not created in capitalism means that it could only be introduced at the cost of reducing the productivity of the workers who engage in it.

Assuming the real income of workers is proportionate to their productivity, it follows that more meaningful work than naturally gets established in capitalism could be introduced only at the cost of reducing the income of workers. Where workers choose intrinsically unfulfilling work because they prefer the greater income it brings them to a more fulfilling but less well-paid job, their autonomy has not been impaired. Such workers perform the intrinsically unfulfilling work they do because they have chosen it (plus the higher income it brings) rather than more fulfilling work accompanied by a lower income. Capitalism does not and cannot prevent workers from bargaining for more fulfilling work in return for an acceptance of lower wages than they could earn by accepting less intrinsically fulfilling jobs. If workers elect to opt for unfulfilling work plus higher wages, then this is *their* decision. Indeed, capitalism can be claimed to augment the autonomy of workers by offering them the choice between meaningful work or higher income.[55]

This takes us to the claim that communism will provide workers with more leisure than capitalism can. Marx's main grounds for this contention were that there will be no unearned incomes arising from mere ownership of capital. By not being obliged to maintain capitalist 'parasites', workers are relieved of hours of work per day. The scope for reducing the working day that would arise as a result of eliminating the capitalist class by taking from them effective control of the means of production is apt to be much exaggerated. 'About 80 per cent of the total national income of the United States currently goes to pay the wages, salaries, and fringe benefits of workers . . . Corporate profits . . . total less than 10 per cent of national income. And that is before taxes. After taxes, corporate profits are something like 6 per cent of national income.'[56] Assuming the USA is representative, it would seem from such figures that the working day could be reduced at present by no more than 15 per cent were socialism introduced overnight. Admittedly that is not a figure to be sneezed at. But against the immediate increase in leisure that the working class could gain by 'expropriating' the capitalists is to be set the following consideration. Capitalists increase their profits by increasing the productivity of their labour-force. This is the motive for the incessant search in capitalism to improve productivity: to reduce the amount of man-hours it takes for goods to be produced. If capitalism were destroyed and replaced by socialism, the profit motive would be destroyed. Without profit motive, it is doubtful if there would be the same degree of incentive in society for people to search for new ways of increasing the productivity of labour. It might well be, therefore, that in the long run, capitalism does more to increase the scope for leisure than communism could. Of course, it would be up to the workers in capitalism to avail themselves of the opportunity for leisure that capitalism creates by seeking shorter working hours rather than higher wages. If they opt for consumer goods rather than leisure, it is not obvious that their autonomy has been reduced by capitalism. It may well be the case that workers prefer consumer goods to free time, especially if those consumer goods are themselves labour-saving devices which enable workers to make more fulfilling use of the leisure hours they have. Were workers today content to enjoy the material standard of living that workers had in Marx's day, they could have massive amounts of leisure. The idea is unthinkable. Why? Because the material aspirations of workers are vastly higher today.

At this point in the discussion, it is customary for Marxists and other socialists to point to the advertising that occurs in capitalism as the source of workers' desires for consumer goods. It is customary for Marxists to say that workers have the desires for consumer goods that they do because they have been 'conditioned' to have them by advertising. In the absence of an advertising industry, workers would not have the wants that make them choose higher incomes over free time when their productivity is caused to rise by the introduction of new technology.

This claim about the source of acquisitiveness in workers is best considered in conjunction with Marx's view of the relative capacities of capitalism and communism to promote altruism and aesthetic sensitivity in members of society. In connection with this latter pair of potentialities, we have seen it to be Marx's view that capitalism promotes selfishness and acquisitiveness. As well as advertising being alleged to be a source of these traits, there is the fact that capitalism is a market society in which economically active participants are self-interested in their economic transactions with each other. Through fostering self-interestedness, capitalism was said by Marx to promote selfishness and indifference to others. There seems to be one absolutely crushing objection to these contentions of Marx. It is the simple fact that acquisitiveness and selfishness antedated capitalism by thousands of years. If one considers the teachings of Buddha or Plato's political philosophy as propounded in the *Republic*, one finds acquisitiveness and craving singled out as the greatest source of evil in the world. There was no advertising in those days. Nor was there capitalism. It makes far more sense to view acquisitiveness and limited sympathy as inherent human traits. On this view, advertising is not so much a source of people's desires as a means of providing information of what is available to satisfy generalized wants for gratification that were already present. Once altruism and egoism are viewed in this way, the relative capacities of capitalism and communism to promote altruism and fellow-feeling are liable to appear very different. If one accepts that people on the whole are self-seeking, and that their sympathies are relatively confined to a small sub-set of people, then a communist economic structure will not necessarily call forth more altruism in people. Capitalism has the great virtue of allowing people to pursue their self-interest in ways that at the same time promote the interests of others. For the essence of exchange is that, where uncoerced, both parties are better off for having engaged in it. Capitalism, thus, provides a way in which predominantly self-seeking individuals can harmoniously cooperate together to their mutual advantage. By contrast, a communist society provides no mechanism whereby the pursuit of self-interest positively benefits others. The consequence is that, in such circumstances, people are liable to be self-seeking in ways that damage the well-being of others. It may be no accident that societies which have attempted to establish socialism have succumbed to dictatorship by power élites who have been unable to resist exploiting their positions of authority for their own ends.

The sad conclusion of this review of Marx's philosophical anthropology must be that Marx has not succeeded in demonstrating communism to be more conducive to human flourishing than capitalism. Of course, where scarcity has been abolished, then individuals can be free to spend their time in creative self-expression, and can afford to be altruistic and other-regarding. But what grounds are there for supposing scarcity can be abolished? As man becomes capable of producing more, so his desires and expectations increase. In the presence of scarcity, people will be obliged to expend effort in activity which is not undertaken as an end in itself if they want to be able to get what they want. That is what it means for scarcity to exist. Work cannot be turned into activity that people will want to do for its own sake. Nor in the presence of scarcity will the predominantly self-regarding beings we are be capable of displaying the other-regardingness Marx claims communism will bring into being.

3 The Materialist Conception of History

1. Outline of the Theory

In 1845, Marx formulated a view of history which has come to be called *the materialist conception of history* or *historical materialism* for short. It undoubtedly constitutes Marx's most important and influential contribution to ideas.[1]

At bottom, the materialist conception of history comprises two things. The first is a synoptical overview of human history from its dawn up to the present and beyond into the future. The second is an explanation as to why history has taken this course.

At the core of the synoptical overview of history is the contention that human history has been, is, and will be, marked by the growth of human productive capacity. What this contention amounts to is the thesis that history has witnessed (and will continue to witness) the improvement in the capacity of human beings to produce the various things which they need in order to be able to satisfy the various wants and needs they have. The various forms of society that have succeeded one another through history are linked to this growth of productive capacity. The materialist conception of history maintains that the different forms which human societies have assumed at different times have been precisely such forms as were necessary for the productive capacity that existed at those times to be fully used or exercised. Different forms of society have come into being as they have initially promoted the use of productive capacity. And these forms have come to be replaced by new forms when, as a result of the growth of productive capacity, these initial forms of society have ceased to be able to make as full use of productive capacity as their successors can.

So much, at least for the moment, for the synoptical view of history provided by the materialist conception of history.

Let us now turn to what the theory offers by way of explanation of the course it claims history has taken and will continue to take. Marx offers little by way of explanation of the growth of human productive capacity through history. He would appear to have regarded it as the consequence of something the existence of which he simply assumed: namely, a perennial disposition on the part of human beings to improve their productive capacity.

What the materialist conception of history is primarily concerned to explain is the succession of forms of society that has occurred through history. The rise and fall of social forms is explained by reference to the growth of productive capacity. In order to see how it is made to do so, it will be necessary to introduce and briefly explain the meaning of a set of technical terms which Marx employed in writing about history and society.

The first of these terms is *forces of production* or *productive forces*. By this expression, Marx means the various things which human beings make use of in the process of producing the things that satisfy their wants and needs. Forces of production are of two main sorts. First, there are what economists speak of as the means of production. These comprise natural resources (like natural deposits of coal and petroleum), raw materials (like raw cotton or iron ore that has been mined), and instruments of production (like tools and machines such as steam engines and industrial robots). Second, there is what Marx calls human *labour-power*. By this term Marx meant to refer to the various mental and physical capacities that human beings use in producing the various things they desire to satisfy their wants and needs. Included as a part of human labour-power is the technologically usable scientific knowledge that human beings possess as well as their physical strength.

The growth of human productive capacity which Marx claims has occurred through history is identical with what Marx often calls the development of the productive forces. Human beings become increasingly more adept at producing useful articles. They do so as they invent and perfect new tools and machines, draw upon new sources of energy, and, above all, increase their scientific understanding of the world. One given set or ensemble of productive forces is more highly developed than a second set when either the first set is capable of producing a greater quantity of useful articles than the second in the same number of man-hours, or the first set is capable of producing the same quantity of useful articles as the second in a smaller number of man-hours of labour. As Marx put it: 'Growing productive power of labour mean(s) . . . that less immediate labour is required to create a greater product.'[2] The historical growth of productive capacity that has taken place has meant that human societies have become ever more able to produce the means of subsistence needed to sustain each member with a smaller and smaller expenditure of human effort.

Marx calls those members of society who actually produce society's means of subsistence the *immediate producers*. Immediate producers always produce (collectively) at the bare minimum what they themselves collectively consume. Very often – indeed, typically – the immediate producers produce more than they themselves consume. Marx calls the useful articles which a set of immediate producers produce that are in excess of what they themselves consume the *surplus product*. Marx thus distinguishes between two different sorts of labour performed by immediate producers. The first sort of labour is that which goes towards the production of the immediate producers' means of subsistence. The second sort goes towards the production of the surplus product. The first sort of labour is called by Marx *necessary labour*. The second sort of labour is called *surplus labour*. As the forces of production in a society develop, so the magnitude of the surplus product which that society is capable of producing increases. Since, according to the theory, the productive capacity of human beings tends to be fully utilized, the growth of productive capacity results in the growth of the size of the surplus product. It follows that, for Marx, as human history has unfolded, the surplus product which human beings have produced has increased. Why it should have done so if it is not consumed by those who have produced it is something that will become apparent after the next expression of Marx's has been introduced and explained.

The next expression of Marx's that needs to be explained is *relations of production*. Marx used this term to refer to the relations of effective control or power that obtain between persons and productive forces. Human beings can and do enjoy different degrees of individual and collective effective control over forces of production. Each of these relations of control enjoyed by some person(s) over some productive force(s) is a relation of production. Thus, for example, one relation of production is that which obtains between a peasant farmer and the plough which he uses and which belongs to him. Another is the relation which obtains between you, the reader, and your own labour-power. Assuming that you enjoy the power to decide whether you exercise it or not, you enjoy effective control of your labour-power. You have it if you enjoy the real power to withdraw that labour-power in an industrial dispute, for instance. Relations of production are most conveniently conceived of as relations of ownership of forces of production by persons. Assuming you, the reader, are a free person and not a slave or serf, you own your own labour-power. This means you enjoy the right to employ or to withhold your labour-power from use. In short, you enjoy the right to decide whether to work or not.

A person may enjoy total, partial, or no degree of effective control of some productive force. Different forms of society may be distinguished from one another according to the sort of relations of production that obtain between the immediate producers and the forces of production. Thus, the immediate producers may individually enjoy total, partial, or no degree of effective control of the means of production with which they work. And the same goes for the relation they stand in to their own labour-power.

Individuals in a given society who stand in similar relations of production to the forces of production make up what Marx calls *a class*. Those members of a society who collectively or jointly enjoy effective control of the means of production in that society Marx calls the *ruling class*. Societies in which some members do and others do not enjoy control of the means of production are *class-divided societies*. In all class-divided societies, the ruling class is composed of people other than the immediate producers. In such societies, the immediate producers form the main other class besides the ruling class. Thus, in class-divided societies, there are two main classes: the ruling class and the immediate producers. In ancient Greece and Rome, these two classes were respectively those of slave-masters and slaves. Slaves enjoyed no degree of effective control over either their own individual labour-power or the means of production with which they worked. Both these things – that is, the slaves' labour-power and the means of production – were subject to the effective control of the class of masters. In medieval, feudal society, the two main classes were those of lords and their serfs. The serfs enjoyed a partial degree of control of the means of production. This was because serfs had strips of land of their own and their own rudimentary instruments of production. Equally, serfs enjoyed a degree of partial control of their own labour-power. This was because for part of the year at least they were free to work for themselves on their own plots of land. For the remaining part of the year, serfs were obliged to work for their lords on the lords' lands or demesnes. Thus, the lords enjoyed partial control of the serfs' labour-power as well as total control of some of the means of production. In capitalist societies, the main class division is between capitalists and wage-labourers. The capitalists jointly control the totality of means of production but enjoy no degree of effective control of the labour-power of the wage-labourers, who are, in theory and to some extent in practice, free to withdraw it. Wage-labourers enjoy total control of their individual labour-power, but no degree of control of the means of production. Socialism and communism will be classless societies. There will only be the associated producers who collectively control the means of production and individually control their own labour-power.

The members of a ruling class are able to reap considerable economic and social advantage from enjoying control of the means of production. They are able to set the terms under which the immediate producers are able to produce their means of subsistence. By virtue of the control of the means of production which members of a ruling class enjoy, the members of this class can ensure that a surplus product is produced by the immediate producers and that this surplus product, or at least the greater part of it, goes to the ruling class. In class–divided societies, therefore, the ruling class is able to obtain its means of subsistence without having to engage in any productive activity in order to do so. Marx writes: 'Wherever a part of society possesses the monopoly of the means of production, the worker, free or unfree, must add to the labour–time necessary for his own maintenance an extra quantity of labour–time in order to produce the means of subsistence for the owner of the means of production, whether this proprietor be an Athenian aristocrat, an Etruscan theocrat, a *civis romanus*, a Norman baron, an American slave–owner, a Wallachian boyar, a modern landlord or a capitalist.'[3]

Class–divided societies differ from one another according to the manner in which surplus labour is extracted from the immediate producers. In ancient and feudal societies, surplus labour was extracted by means of coercion: the slave and serf were physically punished if they failed to perform labour for their master or lord. In capitalism, surplus labour is extracted by means of the wage contract between worker and employer. The control of the surplus product which members of a ruling class are able to acquire by virtue of their control of the means of production confers two benefits upon members of the ruling class. First, it confers upon them considerable relative economic advantage *vis-à-vis* the class of immediate producers. Ruling–class members are able to obtain their means of subsistence without having to labour in its production. Their time is free for other pursuits besides labour: they can engage in cultural and political pursuits. They can also be idle. Second, control of the surplus product confers upon members of the ruling class considerable social power. They have available to them, in the form of the surplus product, resources which enable them to preserve their control of the means of production.

Marx conceives the political, legal, intellectual and cultural institutions of a society to be established by its ruling class, or by agents of that class, in order to preserve those relations which make that class rule. The form of government and laws of a society Marx calls the society's legal and political *superstructure*.

The legal and political superstructure of a society is regarded by Marx as being constructed and maintained for the purpose of rendering the economic structure or existent production relations stable. Accordingly, Marx calls the latter *the base*. The following quotations reveal Marx's view of the state and law: 'The state is the form in which the individuals of a ruling class assert their common interests.'⁴ 'Political power . . . is merely the organized power of one class for oppressing another.'⁵ '[It is always] in the interest of the dominant section of society to sanctify the existing situation as a law and to fix the limits given by custom and tradition as legal ones . . . [T]his regulation and order is itself an indispensable moment of any mode of production that is to become solidly established and free from mere accident and caprice . . . [T]he production process and the social relations corresponding to it . . . [are] reinforced as usage and tradition and finally sanctioned as an explicit law.'⁶

As well as being responsible for creating and maintaining the legal and political superstructure, ruling classes are also responsible, either directly themselves or, more typically, through their agents, for creating one other very important constituent of society. This is the ideas and ideals which generally prevail in a society. Marx calls the philosophies, religions, moral codes, and other ideas and ideals which tend to prevail in a society at any time the society's *ideological forms of consciousness* or *ideology* for short. Marx conceives the ideology of a society to be created by the ruling class, or its agents, through their devising and disseminating bodies of belief and moral standards which confer legitimacy upon the relations of production which make that class the ruling class. Marx writes: 'The ideas of the ruling class are in every epoch the ruling ideas: i.e. the class which is the ruling *material* force of society is at the same time its ruling *intellectual* force. The class which has the means of material production at its disposal, consequently also controls the means of mental production, so that the ideas of those who lack the means of mental production are on the whole subject to it. The ruling ideas are nothing more than the ideal expression of the dominant material relations . . . , the relations which make the one class the ruling one . . . The individuals composing the ruling class . . . among other things rule also as thinkers, as producers of ideas, and regulate the production and distribution of the ideas of their age . . . their ideas are the ruling ideas of the epoch.'[7]

Again, 'Morality, religion, metaphysics, and all the rest of ideology as well as the forms of consciousness corresponding to these . . . no longer retain the semblance of independence. They have no [autonomous] history, no development; but men, developing their material production, and their material intercourse, alter, along with their actual world, also their thinking and the products of their thinking.'[8]

In a stable society, therefore, there will be a set of relations of production which confer control of the society's productive forces upon some class. This class will then establish laws and form of state, which institutions jointly support those relations of production. At the same time, this ruling class will see to it that there prevails in the society a body of ideas and set of ideals which justify and in other ways legitimate the prevailing relations of production. This is how Marx pictures the structure of a stable society. In the light of it, we may now proceed to consider how he explains major social or epochal change: the change of one major form of society to another.

For Marx, major social change involves the change of a society's relations of production. This will involve a change in a society of its ruling class. When such change takes place, the legal and political superstructure and ideology will also undergo change. Those legal and political institutions and bodies of belief which have previously prevailed will have to give way to new institutions and ideas which offer support to the new relations of production which have replaced the ones previously prevailing. Such wholesale change of a society's relations of production, legal and political superstructure, and ideology amounts to what Marx called a *social revolution*.

Why should one set of relations of production ever have to give way to another set? Why should there ever be social revolutions or epochal change? As may be expected, the answer which the materialist conception of history gives involves reference to the growth of productive capacity. First of all, as already noted, the theory maintains that productive capacity tends to grow. Second, the theory claims that there is a tendency for human beings to make as full use as they can of such productive capacity as exists in society at any given time. Third, the theory holds that relations of production differ in their ability to promote or facilitate the use of each different amount of productive capacity. For any given quantity of productive capacity, not all different relations of production are equally well able to promote the use of that quantity of productive capacity. Relations of production which have been able to promote the maximum use of society's productive capacity for a certain period may cease to be able to do so should that productive capacity grow beyond some critical point. Relations of production which have begun to prevent productive capacity from being fully used are said by Marx to have become *fetters* upon the forces of production. Assume that there is a tendency for productive capacity to grow and a tendency for it to be utilized as fully as possible. It follows from the aforementioned considerations that there will be a periodic tendency for relations of production to undergo major change of type. Marx writes about this as follows: 'The mode of production, the relations in which productive forces are developed, are anything but eternal laws . . . They correspond to a definite development of men and their productive forces . . . and . . . a change in men's productive forces necessarily brings about a change in their relations of production. As the main thing is not to be deprived of the fruits of civilization, of the acquired productive forces, the traditional forms in which they are produced must be smashed. From this moment the revolutionary class becomes conservative.'[9]

It is the view of the materialist conception of history that legal and political superstructures and ideologies are established in order to provide support and legitimation for certain sorts of relations of production. It follows from the thesis that relations of production undergo periodic changes, that there is a corresponding periodic tendency for superstructures and ideologies to change. These changes will be roughly concurrent with the changes in the relations of production. Now, it has already been noted that the prevalence of relations of production of some type confers upon some class control of the means of production, and, with this, control of society's surplus product. Members of a ruling class are highly resistant to the replacement of those relations of production that make them the ruling class. This is because if these relations of production are replaced by others they will lose their position as ruling class and all its attendant benefits. Thus, relations of production that have ceased to promote the optimum use of productive capacity cannot be replaced by use-promoting relations without engendering considerable social conflict. There will be the members of one class seeking to establish new relations of production that will make possible greater use of productive capacity. Leading the movement for the establishment of the new relations of production will be those upon whom the new relations of production will confer control of the forces of production. They will have to be able to obtain the support of the mass of society in order to dislodge the old ruling class. This is so in those cases where the ascendant class is not the class of immediate producers. An example is the transition from feudalism to capitalism. The ascendant class will have to develop and disseminate a body of new ideas and new moral ideals which justify the new relations of production and associated forms of state and law. In short, whenever relations of production undergo a major change of type, a new ideology will be needed. Epochal change is thus marked by ideological change and conflict. Equally, epochal change is marked by political conflict as the ascendant class seeks to challenge the political and legal institutions which help to preserve the ruling class in power. Whenever relations of production undergo major change in type, therefore, there will be major legal and political changes in process also. Indeed, Marx, in fact, interprets all large-scale political and intellectual conflict in society as the manifestation of clashes between a ruling class that has hitherto ruled and some new ascendant class seeking to establish new relations of production that will make it rule in place of the existing ruling class. Marx writes: 'The contradiction between the productive forces and the form of intercourse [relations of production] . . . necessarily on each occasion bursts out in a revolution, taking on at the same time various subsidiary forms such as all-embracing collisions,

various classes, contradictions of consciousness,
ιs, political struggle, etc . . . Thus all collisions in
their origin, according to our view, in the contradic-
the productive forces and the form of intercourse
production].'¹⁰

Marx, thus, offers an economic interpretation of history. The
social, intellectual and political history of society is to be understood in terms of its economic history. This theory of society and
history is used by Marx to explain the sequence of forms that
Western society has assumed, as well as to shed light on such
events as the English Revolution of the seventeenth century and
the French Revolution. It was equally this view of history that
led Marx, after 1845, to abandon his attempt to address a middle-
class audience on the desirability of communism. Instead, he saw
it to be his prime task to address the industrial working class and
to explain to them that it was their historical mission to overthrow the capitalist order and replace it with communism. To do
this he would demonstrate how capitalism was inevitably destined to become a fetter on the forces of production, and how the
foundations of the new order were in process of emerging from
capitalism. By providing such a demonstration, Marx hoped to
awaken the working class to a consciousness of its own class
interests and historical role. In so doing, he hoped to bring forward in time what he believed to be the inevitable victory of
communism.

This is how Marx summed up his view of history in 1859 in
his most famous and important formulation of it: 'In the social
production of their existence, men inevitably enter into definite
relations, which are independent of their will, namely relations
of production appropriate to a given stage in the development of
their material forces of production. The totality of these relations
of production constitutes the economic structure of society, the
real foundation, on which arises a legal and political superstructure and to which correspond definite forms of social consciousness. The mode of production of material life conditions the
general process of social, political and intellectual life. It is not the
consciousness of men that determines their existence, but their
social existence that determines their consciousness. At a certain

stage of development, the material productive forces of society come into conflict with the existing relations of production or – this merely expresses the same thing in legal terms – with the property relations within the framework of which they have hitherto operated. From forms of development of the productive forces these relations turn into their fetters. Then begins an era of social revolution. The changes in the economic foundation lead sooner or later to the transformation of the whole immense superstructure . . . In broad outline, the Asiatic, ancient, feudal, and modern bourgeois modes of production may be designated as epochs marking progress in the economic development of society. The bourgeois mode of production is the last antagonistic form of the social process of production – antagonistic not in the sense of individual antagonism but of an antagonism that emanates from the individual's social conditions of existence – but the productive forces developing within bourgeois society create also the material conditions for a solution of this antagonism.''[11]

2. Historical Materialism and the Russian Revolution

One *prima facie* difficulty for the materialist conception of history concerns the fact that socialist revolution first occurred not in the economically advanced capitalist societies of Western Europe and America but in economically backward Russia. Historical materialism asserts that socialism follows capitalism. In the case of Russia we find a society that acquires socialism without going through capitalism. Does the Russian Revolution falsify any of the central tenets of historical materialism? I shall now argue that it does not.

The first thing to note is that, since the 1840s, many Russian communists, most notably Alexander Herzen, had maintained that agrarian, feudal Russia could proceed directly to communism without having to pass through a capitalist phase. Their grounds for this belief were that the institution of communal property already existed in Russia in the form of the communal village (the *mir* or *obschina*). Such a view was called *populism*.

Initially, Marx was opposed to populism. He maintained that

communism could only be established in countries with advanced productive forces where class consciousness had been produced in an industrial labour force living in capitalist conditions. Marx changed his mind, however, in the mid 1870s after he had developed contacts with Russian populists. Marx was much influenced by a Russian book entitled *The Situation of the Working Class in Russia*, written by the populist N. Flerovsky. This book argued that the condition of the peasants had worsened since their emancipation in 1861. Marx predicted on the basis of this book that 'a fearful social revolution' would take place in Russia. In a letter to Laura and Paul Lafargue in March 1870, Marx wrote of Flerovsky's book that 'after studying his work one is firmly convinced that an extremely frightful social revolution . . . is inevitable and imminent in Russia'.[12]

In November 1877, Marx was to write about the possibility of socialist revolution in Russia. This was in response to an article that had been published in a Russian journal. The article was entitled 'Karl Marx before the Tribunal of Mr Zhukovsky'. Its author was a Russian populist. On the basis of the Russian edition of *Capital* (Volume 1) published in 1872, this article had attributed to Marx the view that, before socialism was possible in Russia, it was necessary for her to pass through a capitalist phase, a byproduct of which would be the break-up of the *obschina*. Marx drafted a reply to this article which he did not publish. In the reply, Marx denied that he had ever espoused the view that had been attributed to him. He wrote of *Capital* as follows: 'The chapter on primitive accumulation does not pretend to do more than trace the path by which, in Western Europe, the capitalist order of economy emerged from the womb of the feudal order of economy.'[13]

Marx continued: 'Now what application to Russia could my critic make of this historical sketch. Only this: if Russia is tending to become a capitalist nation after the example of the Western European countries – and during the last few years she has been taking a lot of trouble in this direction – she will not succeed without having first transformed a good part of her peasants into proletarians . . . That is all. But that is too little for my critic. He feels he absolutely must metamorphose my historical sketch of the genesis of capitalism in Western Europe into a historico-philosophic theory of the general path every people is fated to tread, whatever the historical circumstances in which it finds itself, in order that it may ultimately arrive at the form of economy which ensures, together with the greatest expansion of the productive powers of social labour, the most complete development of man. But I beg his pardon.'[14]

Marx then cites the example of what happened to the plebs in ancient Rome. They were originally free peasants, each cultivating his own plot of land. In the course of Roman history, they were expropriated from their land. The same historical tendency which separated these erstwhile peasants from their plots of land involved the formation not only of big landed property but also of big money capital. The social conditions for capitalism had thus been created. But instead of these Roman proletarians becoming wage-labourers, they became 'a mob of do-nothings' and alongside them developed a mode of production which was not capitalist but based on slavery. Marx concludes from this case as follows: 'Thus events strikingly analogous but taking place in different historical surroundings led to totally different results. By studying each of these forms of evolution separately and then comparing them one can easily find the clue to this phenomenon, but one will never arrive there by using as one's master key a general historico-philosophical theory, the supreme virtue of which consists in being super-historical.'[15]

Marx wrote in this letter that the conclusion he had reached about Russia was that 'if Russia continues to pursue the path she has followed since 1861, she will lose the finest chance ever offered by history to a people and undergo all the fatal vicissitudes of the capitalist regime'.[16]

It is clear from this last quotation that Marx thought it possible for Russia to achieve socialism without needing to pass through a capitalist phase. He also made no mention of the need for a socialist revolution in Western Europe as a condition of successful socialist revolution in Russia, which was Engels' view.

In February 1881, a young Russian revolutionary by the name of Vera Ivanovna Zasulich wrote to Marx from Geneva asking him to clarify whether he thought it possible for Russia to have a socialist revolution without first going through a capitalist phase. The reply that Marx actually sent was short and highly non-committal. He pointed out that his account in *Capital* was only intended to apply to Western Europe. He concluded: 'The analysis presented in *Capital* thus gives reasons neither for nor against the vitality of the village community, but the special study which I have made of it . . . has convinced me that this community is the strategic point of social regeneration in Russia. But before it can function as such, it is necessary to eliminate first the pernicious influences which attack it from all sides, and then assure it of normal conditions for a spontaneous development.'[17]

This statement of Marx's reveals very little as to his views on the issue. However, Marx had previously drafted three lengthy responses in which he had been less non-committal. In these drafts, Marx observed that contemporary Russia appeared to be moving in the direction of capitalism and the attendant break-up of the *obschina*. However, the *obschina* retained collectivist features which 'permit an alternative development'.[18] Marx then wrote the following highly significant statement: 'If Russia were isolated in the world, then it would have to work out by its own forces the economic advances which Western Europe has achieved only by passing through a long series of evolutions from its primitive communities to its present state. There would be, at least in my opinion, no doubt that its communities would be condemned to inevitable disappearance with the development of Russian society. But the situation of the Russian community is fundamentally different from that of the communities of the West. Russia is the only European country in which communal property has been preserved on a vast nation-wide scale. But, at the same time, Russia finds itself in a modern historical environment. It is contemporaneous with a superior civilization, it is tied to a world market in which capitalist production predominates. By appropriating the positive results of this mode of production, it is in a position to develop and transform the yet archaic form of its village community, instead of destroying it . . . If the patrons of the capitalist system in Russia deny the possibility of such a combination, let them prove that in order to use machinery, Russia was forced to pass through the early stages of production by mechanical means! Let them explain how they succeeded in introducing in Russia in a few days, so to speak, the mechanism of exchange (banks, credit institutions, etc.), the elaboration of which has taken centuries in the West.'[19]

Thus, Russia in Marx's view could make the transition to socialism without first needing to go through a capitalist stage of development. Her collectivist institution, the *obschina*, plus the fact that she was able to borrow advanced technology from Western Europe, meant that Russia did not have to pass through capitalism before becoming socialist as was necessary for Europe. Given this view of Marx, therefore, it would seem that the fact that socialist revolution first occurred in economically backward Russia poses no serious problem for historical materialism and is not inconsistent with any of its central tenets.

It is important to note, however, that although he thought socialist revolution possible in economically backward Russia, Marx never abandoned the view that the viability of socialism in a country depended upon that country possessing advanced productive forces. Marx's confidence that socialism could be established in an unindustrialized Russia on the basis of the *obschina* was founded upon the belief that, very soon after socialist revolution occurred there, Russia would acquire the advanced agricultural technology of the capitalist West. So, for Marx, socialism always requires advanced productive forces. It was just that in the case of Russia such productive forces were capable of being acquired after socialist revolution had occurred.

It is also worth bearing in mind that, when socialist revolution did occur in Russia in 1917, it bore a different character from the one Marx had conceived were it to occur in advance of the industrialization of Russia. First, the *obschina* had by then disappeared. The collectivization of agriculture was, thus, imposed upon an unwilling peasantry rather than having been the product of their surviving collectivist traditions as Marx had surmised. Second, Marx had foreseen such revolution to be the outcome of the discontent of the peasant masses. In actuality, the socialist nature of the Russian revolution was the achievement of a vanguard party of a type which Marx deplored. We shall have to wait until Chapter 5 before examining Marx's attitude towards vanguard parties of the Leninist kind.

3. Objections to Economic Determinism

Marx's initial formulations of historical materialism suggest that he subscribed to the following two theses. First, the level of development of the forces of production in a society determines the society's economic structure. Second, the economic structure of a society determines that society's legal and political superstructure and ideology. It is difficult to read the following quotations in any other way: 'Are men free to choose this or that form of society? By no means. Assume a particular level of development of men's productive forces and you will get a particular form of commerce and consumption. Assume particular stages of development in production, commerce and consumption and you will have a corresponding social system, a corresponding organization of the family, of social estates or of classes, in a word a corresponding civil society. Assume such a civil society and you will get a political system appropriate to it, a system which is only the official expression of civil society.'[20]

'Social relations are closely bound up with productive forces. In acquiring new productive forces men change their mode of production; and in changing their mode of production, in changing the way of earning their living, they change all their social relations. The hand-mill gives you society with the feudal lord; the steam-mill, society with the industrial capitalist. The same men who establish their social relations in conformity with their material productivity, produce also principles, ideas and categories, in conformity with their social relations.'[21]

'This conception of history . . . relies on expounding the real process of production . . . and comprehending the form of intercourse connected with and created by this mode of production . . . as the basis of all history; describing it in its action as the state, and also explaining how all the theoretical products and forms of consciousness, religion, philosophy, morality, etc., etc. arise from it, and tracing the process of their formation from that basis . . . It explains the formation of ideas from material practice.'[22]

To say that one thing, A, *determines* another thing, B, is to say that the character of B is fixed or decided by the character of A. Suppose that it had been Marx's intention to say that forces of production determine economic structures and that economic structures determine political superstructure and ideology. Had it been Marx's intention to make such assertions, then he would have to have been making the following pair of assumptions. First, for each level of development of productive forces, there is no more than one sort of economic structure that can coexist with forces at that level. Second, for each sort of economic structure, there is not more than one sort of political superstructure and one sort of ideology that can coexist with that sort of economic structure. Both these assumptions are contradicted by historical fact. Consider first economic structures. Different sorts of economic structure have coexisted stably alongside forces of production at comparable levels of development. For example, consider the present-day USSR and the USA. Their forces of production are today at comparable levels of development. Yet, the economic structure of the USA is predominantly capitalist, whilst the USSR, if arguably not socialist, is certainly not capitalist. Some say that the economic structure of the USSR is capitalist: namely, a form of capitalism known as state capitalism in which the state occupies the place assumed by capitalists in ordinary capitalism. Such a classification of the economy of the USSR seems to me a mistake. There is at least one vitally important respect in which the economic structure of the USSR fails to be capitalist. Labour in the USSR is not free. Workers do not have the right to strike. The freedom of labour to withdraw its labour was always regarded by Marx as a distinguishing characteristic of capitalism.

Consider next political superstructure and ideologies. Different sorts of legal and political institutions and ideologies have coexisted alongside economic structures of the same type. Consider, first, political institutions. The economic structures of ancient Greece and Rome were similar. Both were dominated by the master-slave relations of production. Yet, these societies assumed a great variety of political forms. Ancient Greek societies experienced aristocracy, tyranny, oligarchy, democracy, despotism, to name but a few of the political forms found in ancient Greece. Classical Rome experienced elective monarchy, aristocracy, democratic republic, and the absolute monarchy of the Caesars.

Consider next religion. Societies have undergone major changes in religious belief without undergoing changes in their economic structures. Europe became Christianized without undergoing a change of its economic structure. Similarly, the Arabian world became Muslim without a change of its economic structure. Marx and Engels tried to explain religious belief by reference to economic factors. Thus, the rise of Protestantism in Europe roughly coincided in time with the rise of capitalism. Marx held that the former was determined by the latter. He would not have disagreed with Engels's statement that 'when the burghers began to thrive, there developed in opposition to feudal Catholicism, the Protestant heresy . . . Calvinism justified itself as the true religious disguise of the interests of the bourgeoisie.'[23]

The actual historical facts do not support the thesis that the rise of capitalism determined the rise of Protestantism. First, both Luther and Calvin opposed ordinary commercial practices. Money-lending was never portrayed by Protestantism as something pleasing to God. Second, capitalism first developed in the Catholic areas of Italy where the leading capitalists were Catholics. Protestantism developed in sixteenth-century Germany which was comparatively feudal and economically backward. Holland was commercialized prior to its becoming Calvinist. Catholic Belgium was industrialized well before countries that were more Protestant. As the historian G. R. Elton has written: 'There is no good reason for linking Protestantism and capitalism in significant relationship . . . Looked at with an open mind, the whole idea of a meaningful correlation – even geographical coincidence – of these historical phenomena simply disappears.'[24]

It seems that there simply are not the appropriate correlations between forces of production, economic structures, political institutions and systems of ideas to entitle Marx to the thesis that forces determine relations and relations determine political superstructures and ideologies. Instead of the relations being one-one, they are one-many. Even supposing there to have been such one-one correlations between these entities, Marx's theory would still be open to insuperable objections, as the following two sections make clear.

4. The Problem of Explanatory Primacy

The materialist conception of history maintains that a society's forces of production explain that society's relations of production more than society's relations of production explain its forces of production. It also maintains that a society's relations of production explain that society's legal and political superstructure and ideology more than the superstructure and ideology explain the relations of production. Thus, forces of production are claimed to have explanatory primacy with respect to relations of production. And, likewise, relations of production are claimed to have explanatory primacy with respect to superstructure and ideology.

These foregoing assertions concerning explanatory primacy seem contradicted by fundamental facts which Marx himself was fully prepared to acknowledge. Specifically, the assertion that productive forces have explanatory primacy with respect to relations of production seems contradicted by the fact that it is the relations of production in a society that explain the degree of use that is made of a society's productive forces as well as their rate of development. Similarly, the assertion that relations of production have explanatory primacy with respect to superstructure and ideology seems contradicted by the fact that it is the superstructure and ideology that explain the degree of stability enjoyed by the relations of production. From the first of these facts, it would seem that relations (of production) have too great an influence upon forces for the forces to have explanatory primacy with respect to the relations. Likewise, the second fact seems to suggest that superstructures and ideologies have too great an influence upon relations for relations to have explanatory primacy with respect to them. Can the primacy of the forces with respect to the relations be maintained in face of the fact that relations have such a great influence upon forces? And, can the explanatory primacy of relations with respect to superstructure and ideology be maintained in face of the fact that these latter have such a great influence upon relations?

G. A. Cohen has sought to defend affirmative answers to these questions.[25] He has attempted to do so by maintaining that the materialist conception of history makes use of a special form of explanation which he calls *functional explanation*. A functional explanation, according to Cohen, is an explanation of something in terms of the effects which that thing has. According to Cohen, functional explanations are commonplace in biology. Paradigm cases of a functional explanation are the following propositions: *Birds have hollow bones because hollow bones facilitate birds' flight. Human beings perspire because perspiration reduces body temperature.* What the proposition about birds' bones says is that the fact that hollow bones help birds fly explains why birds have hollow bones. Similarly, the proposition about human beings says that the fact that perspiration reduces body temperature explains why human beings perspire. Cohen maintains that the central explanatory claims made by the materialist conception of history are these:

(1) The relations of production in a society are as they are (at any time) because they bring about the full use of the society's productive forces.

(2) The legal and political superstructure and ideology in a society (at any time) are as they are because being so they confer stability upon the society's relations of production.

Cohen argues that, when historical materialism's explanatory claims are construed in this fashion, it is possible to hold both that forces explain relations *and* that relations greatly affect forces. A corresponding claim is made with respect to the relation between relations and superstructures and ideologies. Relations explain, and have explanatory primacy with respect to, superstructures and ideologies whilst being rendered stable by them. Cohen takes (1) to entail the explanatory primacy of forces with respect to relations, and (2) to entail the explanatory primacy of relations with respect to superstructures and ideologies.

If propositions (1) and (2) were genuine cases of explanation, then Cohen would have succeeded in showing how Marx's claims about explanatory primacy could be reconciled with the fact that relations affect forces and with the fact that superstructures and ideology affect relations. Cohen maintains that propositions (1) and (2) are genuine cases of explanation. Ted Honderich has convincingly argued that they are not.[26] He has also shown how the fact that they are not has devastating consequences for historical materialism as we, following Cohen, have interpreted it.

In order to see what the problem is, let us concentrate on proposition (1). Cohen recognizes that their promoting the full use of forces is not something which, as it stands, can literally explain a set of relations of production. This is because a thing cannot be explained by its effects. Before it can have any effects, a thing must first be. The effects a thing has, therefore, cannot account for that thing. In order to get around this problem, Cohen contends that propositions such as (1) must be understood in a different way. Cohen advances no less than three different alternative understandings of proposition (1). Honderich has shown that none of these understandings works.

The first understanding of proposition (1) that Cohen offers interprets the proposition as asserting that relations of production are explained by the fact that such relations would promote the full use of forces of production. On this understanding, the item that supposedly explains (the coming to be and persistence of) a set of relations is a certain fact: namely, the fact that such relations would promote the full use of forces. As Honderich points out, however, the only items that can explain (the coming to be and persistence of) things such as relations are other things, properties, events, or systems of such items. What is being alleged by the first understanding of proposition (1) to explain relations is not any such item as these. Rather, what is being alleged to explain relations is the fact that, if these relations existed, then forces of production would be fully used. This fact, however, is a purely abstract item. Abstract objects such as this simply cannot explain a particular thing or set of things such as a set of relations of production. Consequently, this first suggested way of understanding proposition (1) does not provide us with an explanation of relations.

The second way of understanding proposition (1) suggested by Cohen has the coming to be of certain relations of production explained by the propensity of those relations to promote full use of productive forces. As Honderich points out, however, the propensity of relations to promote the full use of forces can never explain the coming of those relations. The reason is that this propensity of relations is a property of those relations. A property of a thing, however, can never explain the coming to be of that thing. Nothing can explain itself.

There is a further objection to this second understanding of proposition (2). Suppose, *per impossibile*, the propensity of certain relations to promote full use of forces did explain the coming to be of those relations. It would then be the case that these relations would not be explained by forces of production. But should relations not be explained by forces of production, the explanatory primacy of forces *vis-à-vis* relations would no longer hold true. The second proposed way of understanding proposition (1), therefore, is incompatible with the explanatory primacy of the forces of production.

The third way of understanding proposition (1) has relations of production explained by the propensity of the forces which these relations embrace to be fully used when embraced by these relations. This way of understanding proposition (1) makes the propensity of forces to be fully used within certain relations explanatory of those relations. Now, the propensity of forces to be fully used within certain relations is a property of forces. When this property is conjoined with certain relations, there thereby obtains a state of affairs which is sufficient to bring about the full use of those forces which have this property. The crucial question is whether relations can be explained by the fact that a certain property of forces, conjoined with those relations, is sufficient to bring about full use of those forces. Honderich maintains that relations cannot be so explained. The reason is that, in this putative explanation of relations, the relations are entering into an explanation of themselves. But since nothing explains itself, relations cannot enter into their own explanation.

There is an additional difficulty with this third way of understanding proposition (1). Suppose, *per impossibile*, this explanation were allowed. It would then follow that forces would no longer have explanatory primacy with respect to relations. For the relations would have just as prominent a role in their own explanation as forces did.

It seems, then, that there is simply no way of understanding proposition (1) which makes that proposition amount to an explanation of relations of production. However, propositions of this form are both meaningful and, on occasion, true. Honderich calls propositions with the same logical form as proposition (1) *explanation-claims*. An explanation-claim is an assertion that there exists a standard causal explanation of a thing in which the fact that this thing has certain effects plays an essential part. Thus, consider the proposition: *Birds have hollow bones because hollow bones facilitate birds' flight*. This proposition is to be understood as an assertion to the effect that there exists an explanation of the hollowness of the bones of birds in which the fact that hollow bones facilitate birds' flight plays an essential part.

It follows from this analysis of explanation-claims that they are not themselves genuine instances of explanation. Rather, they are only assertions that certain explanations exist. It is possible to make such assertions and to confirm the truth of these assertions without knowing what the relevant explanation of the thing in question is. Thus, prior to Darwin's theory of evolution by natural selection, people knew that there was an explanation of why birds had hollow bones. And, they also knew that in this explanation, the fact that hollow bones facilitate birds' flight plays an essential role. However, they did not know what that role was. Some thought God had created birds that way in order that they could fly. Darwin's theory of evolution supplied the missing general explanation of why animals have the biologically useful equipment they do. According to Darwin, certain reptilian forebears of birds developed hollow bones by so-called 'chance variation'. The creatures with such bones were thereby helped to fly. This ability to fly enhanced their ability to survive and reproduce. Reptilian creatures similar to birds but lacking hollow bones were not so well able to survive and reproduce successfully. The result was that the hollow-boned creatures and their offspring survived, while their solid-boned cousins eventually became extinct.

To return to proposition (1), on Honderich's analysis of explanation-claims, all that proposition (1) does is to assert that there exists an explanation of relations of production in which the fact that relations promote full use of forces plays an essential part. Likewise, all proposition (2) does is to assert that there exists an explanation of superstructures and ideologies in which the fact that these things stabilize relations of production plays an essential part. Now, this way of construing propositions (1) and (2) creates a major difficulty for historical materialism. Suppose we concern ourselves with the questions: *How* does the fact that relations promote full use of forces explain relations? *How* does the fact that superstructures and ideologies stabilize relations explain superstructures and ideologies? The most plausible answer to these questions is that these facts have these effects by way of the effect which apprehension of these facts has upon the *beliefs* of human beings. Consider, for example, the rise of capitalist relations of production. The suggestion is that, at some time near the dawn of capitalism, apprehension of the fact that capitalist relations of production would promote fuller use of forces of production caused certain people to believe that capitalist relations of production would promote fuller use of forces. Now, assume that such people wanted to make fuller use of forces. Then, their belief served to motivate them to establish such relations.

A similar causal chain can be posited between apprehension of the fact that superstructures and ideologies would stabilize relations and the coming to be of those superstructures and ideologies. That is, something like the following may be presumed to have occurred. There were certain people who benefited from relations of production of a certain sort. They therefore desired such relations to be stable. By apprehending the fact that certain political institutions and systems of belief would stabilize those relations, those people came to believe that those political institutions and systems of belief would stabilize those relations. This belief, together with their desire for these relations to be stable, motivated these people to establish such political institutions and to propagate such systems of ideas. As a result, those political institutions and ideologies which stabilized the prevailing relations came into being.

These explanations of relations, superstructures and ideologies sketched above are instances of purposive explanation. Should relations, political superstructures and ideologies have such purposive explanations, then historical materialism is open to a fatal objection. According to historical materialism, relations of production are supposedly explicable by forces of production in a way that makes relations of production independent of facts about human consciousness and will. Likewise, historical materialism maintains that social existence determines consciousness and is not determined by it. If relations, superstructures and ideologies have purposive explanations of the kind sketched above, then social existence *is* determined by consciousness, and relations of production are not independent of consciousness and will. It would seem, then, that Cohen's functional interpretation of historical materialism saves the theory from one objection only by exposing it to another that is no less damaging.

5. The Development of Productive Forces

There is one final claim advanced by historical materialism that must be examined. This is the claim that there is a tendency for productive forces to develop. It is this tendency which underlies Marx's account of changes of social form. Such change is necessary, according to Marx, to accommodate the development of productive forces. Were there to be no such tendency, Marx would have failed to explain epochal change.

As remarked, Marx does not supply any argument for the existence of this tendency. G. A. Cohen has attempted to remedy this deficiency. He argues for the existence of this tendency by appeal to facts about human rationality and intelligence in the face of the human condition of material scarcity. According to Cohen, men's condition to date has been one of scarcity (at least in societies which have displayed productive growth). What this comes to is that 'given men's wants and the character of external nature, they cannot satisfy their wants unless they spend the better part of their time and energy doing what they would rather not do, engaged in labour which is not experienced as an end in itself.'[27] But, argues Cohen, men are intelligent and somewhat rational. Their intelligence disposes them to devise ever more efficient ways of satisfying their wants. And their rationality disposes them to introduce these more efficient ways. The net result is that human beings are disposed to introduce more efficient ways of satisfying their material wants. So, they are disposed to develop their forces of production. Accordingly, there is a tendency for the productive forces to develop.

There are a number of objections that can be raised against this argument. The first is quite simply that members of a society may have other priorities besides improving their material situation.[28] Human beings will be disposed to improve their capacity to satisfy their material wants in a condition of scarcity only if they attach greater value to the satisfaction of their material wants than to any other objectives which might clash with that end. One example of such another objective is the preservation of a traditional way of life. There is no value-free notion of human rationality which dictates that it is more rational to give priority to improving productivity than preserving the traditional way of life. It would seem that Cohen has erred in imputing as a general trait of humanity a disposition that is peculiar only to capitalist man.

In the second place, even if the members of a society *do* attach priority to improving their material situation, it does not follow that they will be disposed to do so by developing productive forces. As has been pointed out by Joshua Cohen, only within certain economic structures does an interest in improving one's material situation issue in a tendency to improve productive forces. 'The formation of extractive empires, the extension of cultivation, and an increased extraction of surplus from dependent producers are each ways in which individuals and groups can pursue their material interests without promoting productive development, and even (as, for example, in the case of Athens and Rome) in the face of knowledge capable *in principle* of being applied to improve productive forces.'[29]

Thirdly, even where relations of production are fettering production and even when there is some class of members of society who wish to unblock the productive forces by establishing new relations, this class may lack the power to do so because of the power-structure created by the existent system of relations of production. Andrew Levine and Erik Olin Wright have pointed out that Cohen's argument that productive forces tend to develop neglects the question of *class capacities*. Class capacities are 'those organizational, ideological and material resources available to classes in class struggle'. Cohen suggests that class interest in social change is enough to give rise to the requisite capacity to effect such change. He writes: '[H]ow does the fact that production would prosper under a certain class ensure its dominion? Part of the answer is that there is a general stake in stable and thriving production, so that the class best placed to deliver it attracts others from other strata in society. Prospective ruling classes are often able to raise support among the classes subjected to the ruling class they would displace. Contrariwise, classes unsuited to the task of governing society tend to lack the confidence political hegemony requires, and if they do seize power, they tend not to hold it for long.'[30]

Levine and Wright object to this reasoning. They maintain that 'there are systematic processes at work in capitalist society that disorganize the working class, block its capacities and thwart its ability to destroy capitalist relations of production. These processes range from labour-market segmentation and the operation of the effects of racial and ethnic divisions on occupational cleavages within the working class, to the effects of the bourgeois legal system and privatized consumerism in advertising. All of these processes contribute to reproducing the disorganization of the working class rather than the progressive enhancement of its class capacity.'[31]

Finally, even if members of a class have an interest in overthrowing a ruling class in order to unfetter productive forces, and even if they have the collective capacity to do so, nothing may happen because, as Allen Buchanan has pointed out, concerted revolutionary action is a public good. A public good is any 'object or state of affairs such that if it is available to anyone in a group it is available to every other member of the group including those who have not shared the cost of producing it'.[32] Marx portrays the working class as being driven to overthrow capitalism out of self-interest. If revolutionary action is a public good, then they will desist from embarking upon such action even if they have the capacity to accomplish it successfully and their interests would be better served by such action. The reason why revolution will not take place if the workers are rationally self-interested (which is how Marx depicts them) is that each will reason as follows: 'Either enough others without me will engage in revolutionary action to overthrow capitalism or not. If they do, then socialism will be available to me without the cost of my contribution (the dangers of revolutionary action). It follows that if enough others engage in revolutionary action to overthrow capitalism, I am better off not participating in such action. Alternatively, if not enough others participate, then, even if I do, the action will be unsuccessful, and my participation will be a net loss. Therefore, I am better off not participating in revolutionary action irrespective of whether enough others do to make such action successful.' Each rational, self-interested worker thinks this way. Consequently, no revolutionary action takes place. This argument does not prove that socialist revolution is impossible. But it does show that it will be impossible if the workers are motivated in the manner Marx takes them to be.

The conclusion from our survey of historical materialism must be that it fails to provide a satisfactory theory of society and social change. It is often useful and constructive to consider the economic life of society if one wishes to understand its politics and culture. However, understanding of history is prevented when it is taken to be a foregone conclusion that everything that happens in a society that is of any importance must have an economic explanation.

Given that there is so little to be said for historical materialism, what is it that accounts for its appeal? Part of the reason is undoubtedly that the theory gives one the feeling that history has an overall purpose. It is not simply a tale told by an idiot without rhyme or reason. Another part of the reason is surely a simple confusion of thought to which many people are subject. It is undoubtedly true that the mode of production is the foundation of the political and intellectual life of a society in the sense of being a causally indispensable condition of it. But it does not follow that economic life is the foundation in the sense of being the explanation of the political and intellectual life. Such a simple confusion of thought was expressed by Engels in Marx's funeral oration when he declared: 'Just as Darwin discovered the law of evolution in organic nature, so Marx discovered the law of evolution in human history; he discovered the simple fact . . . that mankind must first of all eat and drink, have shelter and clothing, before it can pursue politics, science, religion, art, etc.; and that, therefore, the production of the immediate material means of life and consequently the degree of economic development attained by a given people during a given epoch, form the foundation upon which the forms of government, the legal conceptions, the art and even the religious ideas of the people have been evolved, and in the light of which these things must therefore be explained.'[33]

This argument of Engels's is patently invalid. Human beings cannot engage in politics and cultural pursuits without eating and sleeping. It does not follow that eating and sleeping explain the form politics and intellectual activity take. The same goes for their economic activity. The materialist conception of history must be rejected.

4 Economic Theory

1. The Labour Theory of Value

The self-declared aim of Marx's *Capital* is to reveal 'the economic law of motion' of the capitalist mode of production. In other words, the aim of the work is to provide a rigorous demonstration of how capitalism must inexorably evolve. Marx's attempted demonstration of this law of motion is founded upon a particular theory of his concerning the source and nature of capitalist profit. This theory of profit formed the basis of Marx's charge that capitalism rests upon the exploitation of the wage-labourer by the capitalist. Marx's theory of profit rests in turn upon a still more fundamental doctrine of Marx's. This is his 'Labour Theory of Value', the subject of the present section.

Marx's Labour Theory of Value is designed to explain what accounts for the exchange-values which commodities possess in commodity-producing societies such as the capitalist. A *commodity* is a useful artefact that has been produced, not for the purpose of use or consumption by its producer, but for the purpose of exchange in return for other useful artefacts. The *exchange-value* of a commodity is that quantity of other commodities for which a given commodity can be exchanged. The exchange-value of a commodity is customarily represented by means of its money price. If one knows the money price of any two commodities, one can deduce what quantity of one commodity the other is worth. Marx conceives money to be a commodity which by virtue of the properties of indestructibility, divisibility, and marketability has come to serve as a useful medium of exchange in a society. Instead of different commodities being exchanged directly for each other, which might be difficult if not impossible, every commodity exchanges for a quantity of money. The quantity of this money for which a commodity exchanges is its money price. Through comparing the money prices of different commodities it becomes possible to determine their relative economic values. Marx equates money with quantities of the precious metal gold.

What Marx is after is some theoretical explanation of what it is that determines the exchange-values of different commodities. It does not matter whether one thinks of the value of a commodity in terms of the quantities of other commodities that are of equal worth as it or in terms of the amount of money it is worth. The general problem is the same. Thus, suppose, for example, that the price of a shirt is £10 and that the price of a long-playing record is £5. In these circumstances, a shirt will be worth twice as much as an LP record. That is, one shirt is worth two LP records. The problem is to explain what accounts for these relative magnitudes.

There must be something that determines the exchange-values of commodities. What is it? Marx's Theory of Value is designed to answer that question.

Marx's Theory of Value may be stated in the form of three propositions. The first is that the amount of exchange-value which any commodity has at any time is determined by the amount of value which that commodity possesses at that time. The second is that the amount of value which a commodity possesses at any time is determined by the amount of socially necessary labour that is required at that time to produce a sample of that commodity. The third proposition is that, in its normal state, the exchange of commodities is the exchange of commodities of equal value.

In order to understand Marx's Theory of Value, it is necessary to understand what he means by *socially necessary labour-time*. Marx defines it so: 'Socially necessary labour-time is the labour-time required to produce any use-value [useful object] under the conditions of production normal for a given society and with the average degree of skill and intensity of labour prevalent in that society.' The amount of socially necessary labour-time required to produce a commodity is, thus, the number of man-hours of averagely skilled and intense labour needed to produce a sample of that commodity using the standard tools and technology exist-ent at that time. Marx illustrates the difference between the num-ber of man-hours that were actually spent producing a commodity and the number of hours of labour that are socially necessary to produce that commodity by reference to the textile industry. He writes: 'The introduction of power-looms into England, for example, probably reduced by one half the labour required to convert a given quantity of yarn into woven fabric. In order to do this, the English hand-loom weaver in fact needed the same amount of labour-time as before; but the product of his individual hour of labour now only represented half an hour of social labour, and consequently fell to one half its former value.'[2]

Marx calls the actual number of man-hours that were spent producing a commodity its *individual value*. The number of man-hours of labour that are socially necessary to produce a com-modity Marx calls its *social value*. It is the social value of a com-modity not its individual value that Marx believes determines its exchange-value.

Marx's Theory of Value makes two simplifying assumptions. The first is that average skilled labour in capitalism is unskilled labour. 'It is the expenditure of simple labour-power, i.e. of the labour-power possessed in his bodily organism by every ordinary man, on the average, without being developed in any special way.'[3] The second assumption is that skilled labour is equivalent to concentrated unskilled labour: so that one hour of skilled lab-our is one hour plus of unskilled labour. 'More complex labour [more complex than simple labour] counts only as *intensified* or rather *multiplied* simple labour, so that a smaller quantity of com-plex labour is considered equal to a larger quantity of simple labour.'[4] This conception of the relation between skilled and unskilled labour allows Marx to refer throughout only to unskilled labour. Thus, Marx proceeds as if all labour that is more skilled than average has been reduced to the greater quantity of unskilled labour to which Marx thinks it is equivalent.

It cannot be denied that Marx's Labour Theory of Value is not without a good deal of initial plausibility. At first glance, it is not implausible to suppose that motor cars are more expensive than bicycles because more labour is required to produce a car than is required to produce a bicycle. And, supposing a custom-built bicycle is more expensive than a car, it is plausible to suppose that this is explained by the fact that construction of such a bicycle requires an enormously greater than normal amount of labour. However, there are alternative theories of value. Indeed, it is fair to say that modern non-Marxist economics is founded upon an entirely different theory of price, one which does not assume that exchange-values of commodities are determined by underlying objective properties of them such as Marx supposed value to be. This alternative theory is the Subjective Theory of Value.[5] This theory explains exchange-value purely in terms of the degree of *utility* of commodities: that is, their capacity to satisfy human wants and needs. Now the utility of commodities is a property which Marx's Theory of Value finds indispensable. On Marx's view, commodities only have value if they have some degree of utility. Without utility, an artefact lacks value no matter how many hours of labour has gone into its manufacture. Nevertheless, Marx does not seek to explain exchange-value in terms of utility. Instead, he explains it in terms of the concept of socially necessary labour. Since such a concept is highly abstract and artificial, there is a clear *prima facie* reason to prefer a theory of value that explains exchange-value in terms of utility to Marx's theory, provided it is capable of explaining the phenomena as well as Marx's theory. Marx thought that no theory of value that did not explain it in terms of labour was possible. He attempted to prove his theory to be the only correct one by an *a priori* argument. We shall first examine this proof. We shall find that it is invalid. We shall then go on to see that Marx's theory offers an inadequate explanation of exchange-value. Finally, we shall sketch the rudiments of the Subjective Theory of Value, which provides an alternative and more satisfactory account of exchange-value than Marx's theory does. The rejection of Marx's Labour Theory of Value removes the foundation of his entire economic theory.

This is Marx's 'proof' of his Labour Theory of Value: 'Let us now take two commodities, for example, corn and iron. Whatever their exchange-relation may be, it can always be represented by an equation in which a given quantity of corn is equated to some quantity of iron, for instance one quarter of corn $=$ x cwt of iron. What does this equation signify? It signifies that a common element of identical magnitude exists in two different things, in one quarter of corn and similarly in x cwt of iron.

'This common element cannot be a geometrical, physical, chemical or other natural property of commodities. Such properties come into consideration only to the extent that they make the commodity useful, i.e. turn them into use-values. But clearly, the exchange-relation of commodities is characterized precisely by its abstraction from their use-values. Within the exchange-relation, one use-value is worth just as much as another, provided only that it is present in the appropriate quantity . . .

'As use-values, commodities differ above all in quality, while as exchange-values they can only differ in quantity, and therefore do not contain an atom of use-value.

'If then we disregard the use-value of commodities, only one property remains, that of being products of labour.'[6]

We may represent this argument as follows:

(1) The ratios in which two different commodities can be exchanged for one another can always be represented in the form of an equation: 'So much of one commodity = so much of the other commodity.'

(2) An equation of the form 'So much of one commodity = so much of another commodity' signifies that each quantity of each commodity possesses some common property in equal values.

(3) The only property that is common to all the different quantities of commodities that are capable of being exchanged for one another is the property of being producible by means of labour.

Therefore, (4), when different commodities can be exchanged for one another, this is because each is producible with the same amount of labour.

This argument is remarkably weak. Both premise (2) and premise (3) are open to question. Premise (2) completely begs the question. Suppose that one quarter of corn has the exchange-value of x cwt of iron. Let us grant that this fact may be represented by means of the equation 'one quarter of corn = x cwt of iron'. Why should it be accepted that, if this equation is true, the two different amounts of those different commodities possess the same magnitude of some common property? This is to assume that exchange-value is a property like weight. There is, however, no reason to suppose that this is how the equation must be interpreted. The equation can just as well be interpreted by simply stating that these two different commodities can be exchanged for one another in the specified ratio. There is simply no reason why we must assume that all commodities that are capable of being exchanged possess some common property in equal magnitude in order for them to have the same exchange-value.

It may be asked *how* it is possible for specific exchange ratios to hold between different commodities unless they all possess some common property in specific magnitude. The answer to this question is provided by the Subjective Theory of Value. This theory succeeds in explaining prices and exchange-value in terms of the fundamental fact that different people have opposing preferences for the different things they hold. For example, A holds x but would prefer to have object y, which is held by person B who would prefer to hold x. Such facts as these are sufficient to account for an act of exchange between A and B of x for y. In this situation, we can say, if we like, $x = y$. But there is no equality here. Rather, there is a double inequality: A prefers y to x, and B prefers x to y. It is not necessary that x and y have any property in common in order to be preferred in this different manner by different persons. It is, ultimately, such elementary facts as those concerning people's preferences that explain the exchange-values of commodities. There is simply no reason to assume an underlying common property possessed by all objects capable of entering into exchange-relations with each other.

Even if premise (2) is granted, however, the argument would not be free from difficulty. This is because of premise (3). This premise is simply false. There are other properties common to all exchangeables besides being produced by labour. For example, there is the property of having some degree of utility or of being wanted in greater quantity than is available. Marx asserts, 'Clearly the exchange-relation [of commodities] is characterized precisely by its abstraction from their use-values.'[7] But *why* is that clear? Without a commodity having some utility or use-value, it would lack exchange-value – a fact that Marx himself acknowledges. How can commodities stand in exchange-relations unless they each have a use-value? Of course, if one says, '1 quarter corn = 1 cwt iron', one is not suggesting that each commodity has the same use-value as the other. But they could not stand in this relation unless each had some use-value. Contrary to what Marx says, there is not complete abstraction from use-value. Marx does not prove his conclusion therefore.

It is not simply that Marx offers no satisfactory reason for accepting his Labour Theory of Value. There are positive reasons for rejecting it.[8] First, there are what are called *rare goods*: goods which, because of factual or legal obstacles, cannot be reproduced at all, or not in unlimited quantity. Examples are works of art by particular dead artists, rare books and coins. Such commodities as these have exchange-values. But their values cannot be determined by how much labour it would take to reproduce them, since they are no longer capable of being reproduced. Second, there is the fact that one commodity, x, may have a greater value than commodity y, despite being producible with the same amount of average labour, if the production of x requires that the period of time between the expenditure of labour and the readiness of x is greater than that between the expenditure of labour to produce y and the readiness of y. Thus, a hundred-year-old oak tree has a higher value than a young oak sapling despite the fact that they have both been produced by an act of planting of equal duration.

We may also express scepticism about Marx's account of skilled and unskilled labour. What is produced by a sculptor in a day's labour typically has greater value than what is produced by an unskilled labourer in a day. Almost all goods fall into this category. As we have seen, Marx claims that skilled labour can be reduced to unskilled labour, simply being a case of more concentrated unskilled labour. He writes, 'Experience shows that this reduction is constantly being made.'[9] Experience shows nothing of the sort. All experience shows is by how much more we value the product of an hour's skilled labour than we value the product of an hour's unskilled labour. In saying that we make such a reduction of skilled to unskilled labour, Marx is using the exchange-ratios of the products of skilled and unskilled labour to determine the magnitude of socially necessary labour required to produce what is produced by skilled labour. Exchange-ratios are thus being used by Marx to *determine* value; whereas Marx's theory is designed to explain exchange-ratios in terms of value.

How, then, is it that different commodities have different and similar exchange-values? What is it that determines the exchange-value of a commodity if it is not value understood as quantum of socially necessary labour? The answer to these questions is provided by the Subjective Theory of Value. This theory offers an entirely different approach to the understanding of exchange-value, an understanding which accounts for exchange-value purely in terms of utility. I shall now present the rudiments of this theory.[10]

To explain exchange and exchange-value, we start out from individuals' value scales. Different things are necessary to satisfy the various wants that different people have. People also value the satisfaction of one want more highly than they will value the satisfaction of other wants. The things that satisfy a more urgent want will be *preferred* by an individual to things that satisfy less urgent wants. The preferences of an individual for things may be set out in rank order. This list of preferences in rank order constitutes the individual's scale of values or value scale. Now, each individual's value scale determines for that individual a minimum selling price for each useful thing that individual can hold. The value scale also determines a maximum buying price for each thing that individual does not hold. If, for example, item m is immediately above item n on the individual's scale of preferences, then the individual's minimum selling price of n is m. The individual would be willing to exchange n in return for an m. Likewise, if item o is immediately below n in that individual's scale of preferences, then o will be that individual's maximum buying price of n. The individual is willing to exchange an o for an n.

Suppose that, for individual A, the minimum selling price of x is $2y$. That is, A is prepared to sell x only for at least $2y$. Suppose, also, that the maximum buying price of x for individual B is $1y$. That is, B is prepared to pay no more than $1y$ for an x. In these circumstances, no exchange will take place between A and B. A is willing to sell x to B only for more ys than B is willing to offer.

Suppose, however, that the maximum buying price of x for B were $4y$. That is, B is willing to pay up to $4y$ for an x. In these circumstances, exchange between A and B can take place. The price for an x that will be agreed on by A and B will be somewhere between $2y$ and $4y$. There is, in these particular circumstances, no *purely* economic factor which will determine where the price will be fixed between these two margins in this case.

Suppose, now, that we have, as before, A and B. But suppose that there is another potential buyer of x, namely C. Suppose that, as before, B's maximum buying price of x is $4y$, but that C's maximum buying price of x is $6y$. In these circumstances, A will sell x to C for a price somewhere between fractionally above $4y$ and $6y$. Again, no purely economic consideration will determine precisely what price will be agreed between these two margins.

Now, suppose that there is only one potential buyer of x, namely B, whose maximum buying price is, as before, $4y$. Suppose, now, there are two potential sellers of x: A, whose minimum selling price is $2y$ as before, and D, whose minimum selling price is $1y$. In these circumstances, B will be able to purchase x from D for $1y$.

We have now to imagine the case where there are multiple potential buyers and sellers. Suppose that, for a set of potential buyers of xs, the maximum buying price of an x is as follows:

$$B \ldots 4y$$
$$C \ldots 6y$$
$$E \ldots 7y$$
$$F \ldots 8y$$
$$G \ldots 10y$$
$$H \ldots 11y$$
$$I \ldots 13y$$

Suppose that the minimum selling price of 1 unit of x for a set of potential sellers of x is as follows:

$$D \ldots 1y$$
$$A \ldots 2y$$
$$J \ldots 3y$$

K . . . 4y
L . . . 5y
M . . . 8y
N . . . 10y

Potential buyers will seek to obtain the goods they want at the least expense to themselves. Likewise, sellers will seek to sell their goods for the highest prices they are able to get. Potential buyers, therefore, will begin with low offers and will outbid their competitors only as it becomes necessary to do so, dropping out of the bidding when the price being offered by buyers has started to exceed their maximum buying price. Likewise, sellers will at the outset offer their goods at high prices and will reduce their asking prices only as it becomes necessary to do so. They will stop reducing their asking price when the price being asked reaches their minimum selling price.

Suppose the potential buyers begin by offering 1y for an x. In these circumstances, D will be willing to accept. However, there will be only one x for sale at this price, and no fewer than seven people wishing to buy at that price. There will be a shortage of xs at that price. Two circumstances will tend to prevent the situation from freezing at this point. First, the other potential buyers will start to increase their offers and bid up the price. Second, as soon as they do, other potential sellers besides D will come forward to offer their goods at these prices. The potential buyers will start to raise the price of x. Suppose the buyers begin offering to pay 2y for an x. Then, we will have two potential sellers willing to sell an x at that price (namely D and A). But we will have no fewer than seven people willing to buy at that price. Again, at the price of 2y, there is still a shortage of xs on the market. Accordingly, potential buyers will again increase the offers, forcing the price up. To how much?

Let us continue to observe what happens as the price rises. At a price of 3y for an x, there will be three persons willing to sell and seven persons willing to buy. At 4y, four persons willing to sell and seven willing to buy. At 5y, there will be five willing sellers and six willing buyers; at 6y, five willing sellers and six willing buyers. At a price of 7y, there will be exactly five persons willing to sell an x and exactly five persons willing to buy one. At a price of $7y$ for an x, demand and supply will be brought exactly into balance. There will be no unsatisfied demand at that price and no one willing to sell at that price who will be unable to find a buyer. Accordingly, $7y$ is the price that will tend to be established. In economics, this price is called the *equilibrium price*. At any price lower than the equilibrium price, there will be more buyers than there will be sellers. These buyers will push the price up, since the maximum buying price of at least some of them will be higher than this lower price. At any price higher than $7y$, there will be more xs on offer than there will be buyers of xs. In these circumstances, there will be some sellers of xs who will be willing to reduce their asking prices and who will bring the price of an x back down to the point where demand and supply are in balance.

We have seen how an exchange ratio of $7y = 1x$ can be established purely by reference to the utility of xs and ys to individuals and without the need to invoke any underlying 'values'. All that is necessary to explain exchange-value is the fact that different people have different preferences for things. There is no need to postulate that, if $7y$ is the equilibrium price of an x, this is because $7y$ and $1x$ each possess equal magnitudes of some common property. There is absolutely no reason to accept a theory of value such as Marx's. With the rejection of Marx's Theory of Value, we have undercut the basis of his entire economic theory. We shall, however, suspend our disbelief in this theory in order to see to what use Marx puts it.

2. The Theory of Surplus Value

How are capitalists able to make profits? Marx's answer to this question is given by his Theory of Surplus Value. Before we can appreciate what this answer is, we must first define what capitalist profit is. A capitalist is a person with a given sum of money who seeks to turn that sum into a greater sum by means of a series of exchange transactions – that is, a series of acts of buying and selling. Profit is the monetary difference between the initial monetary investment (the initial purchase) and his receipts (from the final sale). Marx represents the process of formation of profit by a capitalist by means of a schema which he calls the *circuit of capital*. The circuit of capital goes as follows. A capitalist starts out with a given sum of money, M. His aim is to turn M into a larger sum through a series of exchange transactions. To this end, the capitalist uses M to purchase a stock of commodities, C. Marx distinguishes two different types of capitalist: merchant and industrial. The merchant capitalist simply sells C for a sum of money, M_1. Assuming that M_1 is greater than M, the merchant capitalist has made a profit. The circuit of merchant capital is, thus, $M–C–M_1$. Given the Labour Theory of Value, it will be evident that, if a merchant capitalist makes a profit, it cannot be the case that the merchant capitalist has bought and sold his commodities at their value. For in that case $M = C$ and $C = M_1$, so that M_1 would have to equal M. Marx wished to explain profit upon the assumption that commodities exchange at their values. It follows from such an assumption that the ultimate source of profit cannot be exchange. Profit, for Marx, is something that is made by production, not exchange.

To discover the origin of profit, we must look at the industrial capitalist and examine the circuit of industrial capital. In this circuit, the commodities (C) which the capitalist purchases consist of two sorts of thing: first, means of production and, second, labour-power. The amount of labour-power that the capitalist purchases will be that which is necessary and sufficient to turn the purchased means of production into a stock of new commodities. The capitalist sets the labour-power he has purchased to work upon the means of production which he has purchased. The result of the ensuing process of production is the formation of a stock of new commodities, C_1. The capitalist sells C_1 for a sum of money, M_1. The circuit of industrial capital is, thus, $M–C–C_1–M_1$. If all commodities are sold and purchased at their values, it will follow that $M = C$ and that $C_1 = M_1$. If profit is made, it will follow that M_1 is greater than M. It follows that C_1 is greater in value than C. By means of the circuit of capital, Marx has traced the source of profit to the production process itself: that is, to that phase of the circuit where means of production are transformed by labour-power into finished commodities. As previously remarked, the value of C_1 is greater than the value of C.

The difference between these two amounts Marx calls *surplus value*. The question 'How do capitalists make profits?' becomes the question 'How is surplus value created?'

Marx's Theory of Surplus Value is an answer to this question. According to it, surplus value is created because one of the commodities which the capitalist purchases with *M* is a source of value greater than the value which it possesses. The Theory of Surplus Value states that the commodity with this property of being a source of value greater than itself is labour–power. The means of production that are used up merely transfer the value they possess to the final product that is made with them. The case of labour–power is different. In being used up, labour–power generates a certain quantity of hours of labour. All these hours of labour add value to the final product. But the value that is *created* by a given quantity of labour–power can be greater than the value which that same labour–power *possesses*. This is because the number of hours of socially necessary labour that would be generated by using a certain quantity of labour–power can be greater than the number of hours of socially necessary labour that were needed to produce that quantity of labour–power.

Labour–power is not a commodity as such; that is, it is not something produced for exchange. But in the wage–contract, it is treated as a commodity. Accordingly, it is purchased at its value. The value of labour–power is the number of hours that are socially necessary to produce it. The number of hours of socially necessary labour that are required to produce a quantity of labour–power is the number of hours required to produce the means of subsistence that are necessary to keep the labourer alive and in a fit condition to work for that period. Let us suppose, as Marx did, that it takes six hours of socially necessary labour to produce the means of subsistence consumed daily by a worker. With those means of subsistence consumed, the labourer is able to work for a certain period. Let us suppose that the maximum period that a person is able to work daily is twelve hours. Suppose that that person does work for twelve hours. These twelve hours will become incorporated in the value of the commodities which the labourer produced during the working day. We thus find that labour–power is a source of value greater than it possesses. It possesses the value of six hours of labour. It is capable of producing value of twelve hours of labour. It is thus a source of surplus-value. Marx's account of profit is based upon the supposition that the number of hours which are required to produce the worker's means of subsistence is smaller than the number of hours that the worker works. The origin of profit, for Marx, is labour-power and labour-power alone.

This is a convenient point at which to introduce a set of technical terms which will be important later on in our examination of Marx's economic theory. Marx calls that portion of the capitalist's initial capital invested in means of production *constant capital*. He represents this amount of value by the letter c. The portion of the initial capital that is invested in labour-power – that is, the portion of the initial capital paid out as wages – is called *variable capital*. It is represented by the letter v. In value terms, $C = c + v$. Whenever profit is made, the value of C_1 (the commodities produced) is greater than the value of C. Marx calls the difference in values between the value of C and C_1 *surplus value*. He represents it by the letter s. We thus obtain the formula: $C_1 = c + v + s$. The capital expended upon means of production is called 'constant' by Marx because the value of the means of production is simply transferred to the final commodities without change. By contrast, the capital expended upon labour-power is called 'variable' because the amount of value transferred to the finished commodities by labour-power is an amount that is capable of variation. Labour-power is a source of value equal in sum to v plus s. The magnitude of s varies according to how many more hours are expended in labour by that labour-power than were used to produce it. Marx assumes that labour-power is bought and sold at its value. Thus v will equal the value of labour-power, which in turn will equal an amount of value equal to the value of the labourer's means of subsistence.

Marx makes a theoretical division of the working day into two portions. The first portion consists of a number of hours equal in amount to that number of hours of labour which are socially necessary to produce the labourer's daily means of subsistence. By engaging in labour for this portion of the working day, the labourer creates a sum of value equal in amount to that sum which he is paid in wages per day. The day's wage pays for the daily means of subsistence of the labourer, which in turn are what is needed to produce a day's labour-power. Marx calls the labour that is expended during this portion of the working day *necessary labour*. During the period of necessary labour, the labourer replenishes that quantity of value which he consumes per day in consuming his daily means of subsistence. Even were the labourer working for himself and not for the capitalist, he would still have to work for that period which it is necessary for him to work to produce (an equivalent in value to) what he consumes per day as means of subsistence. Marx calls the remaining portion of the working day the period of *surplus labour*. During this period, the labourer is creating value in excess of that amount which he is paid in wages. Surplus value is created as a result of the worker engaging in surplus labour. According to Marx, therefore, capitalists are able to make profits as a result of their labourers engaging in surplus labour.

The distinction between constant capital, variable capital, and surplus value, together with the distinction between necessary and surplus labour, enable us to understand a concept which plays an extremely important role in Marx's economic theory. This is the concept of the *rate of surplus value*. The rate of surplus value is the ratio between surplus value and variable capital. In other words, the rate of surplus value $= s : v$. This ratio corresponds exactly with the ratio between surplus and necessary labour. The reason for this correspondence should be obvious. A magnitude of value equal in amount to that of the variable capital is created by the labourer during the period of necessary labour upon the assumption (made by Marx) that labour-power is purchased at its value. A magnitude of value equal in amount to that of the surplus value is created during the period of surplus labour upon this same assumption. Thus, assume, for example, that the length of the working day is twelve hours. Assume, also, that it takes six hours' labour to produce the labourer's daily means of subsistence, and that the labourer is paid in wages per day a sum of value equal in amount to the value of his labour-power for a day. Since the value of a day's labour-power is equal to the amount of labour required to produce that day's labour-power, it follows that the value of a day's labour-power is equal to the amount of labour required to produce the labourer's means of subsistence consumed per day. Given that this is six hours, it follows: first, that the value of the labourer's daily labour-power is six hours; second, that the period of necessary labour is six hours; third, that the period of surplus labour is also six hours; and, finally, that the rate of surplus value is 6 : 6 or 100 per cent.

Before proceeding further it is important to note carefully two points. The first point is that, on Marx's account of profit, all that is needed for the creation of surplus value is that the worker be paid in wages a sum of value which is less than that created by him as a result of his activity of labour. For this to happen, it is not necessary that the labourer be paid in wages a sum of value no greater than the value of his labour-power. Surplus value can be created even where the worker is paid more than the value of his labour-power. All that is needed for the creation of surplus value is that the labourer expend more time in labour than is necessary to create a sum of value equal to the value of his wage. In other words, Marx's Theory of Surplus Value does not require that v be no greater in magnitude than the value of labour-power. All that is needed is that the labourer create by his labour a sum of value that exceeds v by some amount s. The significance of this point is that workers do not need to be paid only subsistence wages in order for profit to be possible. Profits are compatible with more-than-subsistence wage levels. When labour-power is purchased at more than the value of labour-power, the wage represents more than necessary labour.

The second point to note is that both the period of necessary labour and the length of the working day are capable of varying in magnitude over time, and varying in magnitude independently of each other. As previously remarked, Marx makes a number of assumptions about necessary labour and the length of the working day. He assumes, first, that six hours of labour are socially necessary to produce the labourer's daily means of subsistence; second, that the labourer labours for twelve hours; and, third, that the labourer is paid in wages per day a sum equal in amount to the value of his daily means of subsistence. It follows from these assumptions that the period of necessary labour is six hours and that the rate of surplus value is 100 per cent. As the forces of production develop within capitalism, the productivity of labour-power increases. As a result, it takes less and less time to produce the daily means of subsistence required by the worker. This is so notwithstanding the fact, acknowledged by Marx, that, as capitalism develops, the subsistence requirements of the worker increase. Suppose that, at present, it takes two hours of labour to produce the means of subsistence required daily by the labourer. Suppose also that, at present, workers receive in wages no more (and no less) than the value of their labour-power. Suppose, finally, that the length of the working day is six hours. In these circumstances, the period of necessary labour is two hours, and the period of surplus labour is four hours. A smaller quantity of surplus labour is now being performed per day than Marx supposed was being performed per day in his day: four hours as against six hours. Despite this, the current *rate* of surplus value is greater than the rate which Marx believed to have prevailed in his day: 4 : 2 or 200 per cent as against 6 : 6 or 100 per cent.

The importance of these two points will only become fully apparent when we come to consider Marx's account of capitalism's laws of motion.

Let us summarize the results of our examination of Marx's Theory of Surplus Value. According to Marx, capitalists are able to make profits because surplus value is created during the production processes which they finance. Surplus value is created during these production processes because during them labourers engage in surplus labour. Surplus labour is what labourers perform by engaging in labour for periods of time greater than what is necessary for the creation of a sum of value equal to the value of their wages.

In the next section, we consider an important implication which Marx took his Theory of Surplus Value to have. This is the implication that capitalists make profits by means of the exploitation of their workers.

3. Exploitation

According to Marx, capitalists are able to make profits only by exploiting their workers. Profits are made by the capitalist's appropriation of the surplus value created by the labour of his workers. In other words, profits are made by the workers producing for their capitalist employers sums of value greater than they are paid in wages. That sum of value which the workers receive in wages they pay back to the capitalist by working for the period of necessary labour. The sums of value that are created by workers during the period of surplus labour represent for the capitalist pure gain. It is a return for which they make no equivalent outlay. Marx called the rate of surplus value, therefore, 'an exact expression for the degree of exploitation of labour-power by capital, or of the worker by the capitalist'.[11]

What exactly did Marx mean by 'exploitation'? What did he think was wrong with it? Was Marx correct to regard capitalism as a system involving the systematic exploitation of the workers? These are the questions we shall now attempt to answer.

Broadly speaking, there are two schools of opinion on the question of what Marx meant by the term *exploitation*. Both schools agree that exploitation, for Marx, involves non-reciprocal benefit: that is, one person benefits another without the second benefiting the first in return. Further, both schools agree that non-reciprocal benefit is not a sufficient condition of exploitation for Marx. This is because both schools agree that Marx recognizes there to be cases of non-exploitative, non-reciprocal benefit of one party by another. The paradigm case of such non-exploitative non-reciprocal benefit is the deductions to earnings of the able-bodied that are to be made in socialism for provision of welfare for the disabled. As a result of these deductions, the disabled are benefited by the able-bodied without benefiting the able-bodied in return. Yet such welfare deductions to earnings are not regarded by Marx as instances of the disabled exploiting the able-bodied. Granted that such welfare provision will be present in socialism and that welfare provision involves the able-bodied benefiting the disabled, it follows that non-reciprocal benefit is not a sufficient condition of exploitation for Marx.

What more is needed for exploitation besides non-reciprocal benefit? It is in their answers to this question that the two schools part company. According to the interpretation of one school, which I will call the *justice interpretation*, as well as there being non-reciprocal benefit, it must be unjust that the benefited party gain their benefit without reciprocating the benefit.[12] In other words, proponents of the justice interpretation advance the following understanding of exploitation: A exploits B if and only if: (1) B benefits A in some way without A benefiting B in return, and (2) A's failure to benefit B in return for B's benefiting A is unjust.

According to proponents of the justice interpretation, Marx believed that capitalism involves exploitation because he believed it was unjust that the capitalist appropriates the surplus value created by the worker without making a reciprocal return to the worker. On this view, Marx believed that a person was morally entitled to the full product of his labour, minus certain deductions that are necessary for replenishing and expanding means of production and for providing public goods and welfare for the disabled. Workers in socialism will receive such a product of their labour. In capitalism, workers receive less than this. Some surplus value that the worker produces which rightly ought to go to the worker goes to the capitalist. On this view, the deductions made from the product of the labour of the able-bodied for provision of welfare for the disabled are not instances of exploitation because such deductions are not unjust. The disabled are morally entitled to them.

The other school denies that injustice is part of – or even implied by – exploitation as Marx understands it. According to this interpretation, which I will call the *coercion interpretation*, what makes non-reciprocal benefit exploitation is that the unreciprocated benefit is forced from the benefactors by the beneficiaries.[13]

The coercion interpretation of exploitation gives us the following understanding of it: A exploits B if and only if: (1) B benefits A in some way without A benefiting B in return, and (2) A *forces* B to benefit A.

According to the coercion interpretation, the provision of welfare for the disabled by deductions from the product of the labour of the able-bodied is not exploitation because it is not the case that the disabled force the able-bodied to make such provision. Such contributions are either made voluntarily or, if forced, are forced by the state. In the case of capitalism, the provision of surplus value for the capitalist is a non-reciprocal benefit forced from the worker by the capitalist. It is, therefore, a case of exploitation. The worker in capitalism is not forced to engage in surplus labour in the same way that slaves and serfs were. In the case of the latter it was threat of punishment if they refused. Rather, what forces the wage-labourer in capitalism to engage in surplus labour is the fact that the capitalist owns the means of production. Lacking means of production of their own, the wage-labourers are forced to accept the wage offers of the capitalists to procure their means of subsistence, and the wage contracts to which they are forced to agree bind them to perform surplus labour.

According to the coercion interpretation of exploitation, not only is injustice not part of the notion of exploitation, it is not implied by it. The foremost proponent of this interpretation, Allen Wood, claims that Marx did not regard exploitation as unjust. Wood's coercion interpretation is based upon a number of remarks of Marx's which are *prima facie* difficult to reconcile with the view that he took exploitation to be unjust. The most notable of such remarks are the following:

(1) 'The use-value of labour-power, in other words labour, belongs just as little to its seller as the use-value of oil after it has been sold belongs to the dealer who sold it. The owner of the money has paid the value of a day's labour-power; he therefore has the use of it for a day, a day's labour belongs to him. On the one hand the daily sustenance of labour-power costs only half a day's labour, while on the other hand the very same labour-power can remain effective, can work, during a whole day, and consequently the value which its use during one day creates is double what the capitalist pays for that use; this circumstance is a piece of good luck for the buyer, but by no means an injustice towards the seller.'[14]

(2) 'The justice of transactions between agents of production consists in the fact that these transactions arise from the relations of production as their natural consequence. The legal forms in which these economic transactions appear as voluntary actions of the participants, as the expressions of their common will and as contracts that can be enforced on the parties concerned by the

power of the state, are mere forms that cannot themselves determine their content . . . The content is just so long as it corresponds to the mode of production and is adequate to it. It is unjust
as soon as it contradicts it. Slavery, on the basis of the capitalist
mode of production, is unjust.'[15]

(3) 'What is "just" distribution? Does not the bourgeoisie
claim that the present system of distribution is "just"? And given
the present mode of production is it not, in fact, the only "just"
system of distribution? Are economic relations regulated by legal
concepts of right or is the opposite not the case, that legal relations
spring from economic ones.'[16]

(4) 'The obscurantist foists on me the view that "surplus
value", which is produced by the workers alone, remains with
the capitalist entrepreneurs in a *wrongful* manner. But I say the
direct opposite: namely, that at a certain point, the production
of commodities necessarily becomes "capitalistic" production of
commodities, and that according to the *law of value* which rules
that production "surplus value" is due to the capitalist and not to
the worker. In my presentation, the earnings on capital are not
in fact "only a deduction or 'robbery' of the worker". On the
contrary, . . . I show in detail that even in commodity exchange
only equivalents are exchanged; the capitalist – as soon as he pays
the worker the actual value of his labour-power – earns *surplus
value* with full right, i.e. the right corresponding to this mode of
production.'[17]

Wood takes these remarks to establish conclusively that Marx
regards capitalist exploitation to be just. However, according to
Wood, the fact that exploitation is just, for Marx, does not constitute any defence of it. According to Wood, justice, for Marx, is
simply whatever conforms to and harmonizes with the prevailing
mode of production. That an act or institution is just, therefore,
does not justify or commend the act or institution in any way.
Wood writes: '[for Marx] it is not an analytic proposition or trivial
truth to say that the just, the virtuous or the morally right thing
is the thing which, all things considered, should be done. For
Marx, in fact, it is sometimes a pernicious falsehood.'[18]

Such an account of Marx's view of morality as Wood offers
squares with Marx's assertion that talk of 'fair distribution' by

socialists constitutes 'obsolete verbal rubbish'.[19] It also squares with the fact that Marx nowhere ever says that capitalist exploitation is unjust, nor ever says that socialism and communism will establish justice.

Despite the impressive *prima facie* case in support of the coercion interpretation of exploitation made out by Wood, the case is by no means conclusive. There is, in fact, considerable reason for preferring the justice interpretation to it. First, as G. A. Cohen has pointed out, coercion seems to be neither a necessary condition, nor – together with non-reciprocal benefit – a sufficient condition, of exploitation as Marx understands the term. That coercion is not a necessary condition of exploitation, for Marx, becomes evident from the following case. Imagine a rich capitalist B who has no need to work but who – for a bet or for amusement – finds employment as a wage-labourer with capitalist A. In this case, A would obtain surplus value through B's labour and B would accordingly be exploited by A. Yet, in the case as presented, B is not forced to work and therefore is not forced to provide surplus value for A. Accordingly, since he is exploited but not coerced, it follows that coercion is not a necessary condition of exploitation. As Cohen has pointed out, coercion seems also not to be, together with non-reciprocal benefit, a sufficient condition of exploitation.[20] Cohen asks us to imagine involuntarily unemployed adults with many dependants who threaten violence in the streets unless welfare payments are made to them by those able to provide them. On Wood's definition, these people would be exploiters. Yet it is difficult to believe that would have been Marx's view of them. Accordingly, coercion and non-reciprocal benefit are not jointly a sufficient condition of exploitation. The role that coercion plays in capitalist exploitation is that the workers' lack of means of production forces them to suffer exploitation. So, coercion is a cause of exploitation but is not itself part of what exploitation consists in.

A second reason for preferring the justice interpretation of exploitation to the coercion interpretation is that Marx makes many assertions which are otherwise difficult to understand if he did not think exploitation to be a form of injustice. Thus, for instance, Marx talks of 'the theft of alien labour-time on which the present wealth is based'.[21] He also speaks of 'the learned dispute between the industrial capitalist and the wealthy landowning idler as to how the booty pumped out of the workers may most advantageously be divided for the purposes of accumulation'.[22] Why did Marx talk of 'theft' and 'booty' if he regarded exploitation as just?

A third reason for preferring the justice interpretation is that the remarks of Marx which are taken to support the coercion interpretation admit of alternative readings to that given them by Wood. When Marx calls capitalist transactions 'just' he may be taken to be engaged in the sociology of morals – that is, reporting on how capitalist transactions are normally viewed in capitalism. He would not then be endorsing the transactions as just. Indeed, one commentator has argued that, while Marx may have regarded all exchanges in capitalism to be just, he does not regard the transaction between wage-labourer and capitalist to be a genuine instance of an exchange. (This is argued for by Young. See note 12 for reference.) Although it is presented as an exchange within capitalist ideology, Marx, by considering capitalist-worker transactions in their totality, displayed the total transaction between capitalist and worker to be nothing but an instance of taking by the capitalist for nothing in return. In support of this interpretation, a passage from *Capital* may be cited where Marx says of the entire capitalist-worker transaction that 'the whole thing still remains the age-old activity of the conqueror who buys commodities from the conquered with the money he has stolen from them'.[23] The suggestion is therefore that, even if Marx did regard any genuine exchanges that go on within capitalism as just, he did not regard the extraction of surplus value as just because he did not regard it as arising from a genuine exchange. The appearance of there being one is ideological illusion.

Finally, it is possible to reconcile the justice interpretation of exploitation with Marx's assertion that talk of 'just distribution' is obsolete verbal rubbish. Allen Buchanan has argued that Marx thought capitalism unjust but did not wish to emphasize its injustice because he thought that the very need for justice was a shortcoming in society. A virtue of communism would be that it would dispense with the need for justice. Justice is necessary only where there is scarcity and an opposition of interests between members of society. In full communism, scarcity will have been abolished on Marx's view and there will be complete identification between people. The circumstances giving rise to the need for justice will thus no longer obtain. This view leads to a very interesting interpretation of Marx. A famous passage of Marx's is the following one from the *Critique of the Gotha Programme*: 'In a more advanced phase of communist society, when the enslaving subjugation of the individual to the division of labour, and thereby the antithesis between intellectual and physical labour, have disappeared; when labour is no longer just a means of keeping alive but has itself become a vital need; when the all-round development of individuals has also increased their productive powers, and all the springs of cooperative wealth flow more abundantly – only then can society wholly cross the narrow horizon of bourgeois right and inscribe on its banners: From each according to his abilities, to each according to his needs.'[24]

It is Buchanan's view that Marx refrained from calling capitalism unjust (despite his speaking of the appropriation of surplus value as theft) because he believed that communism would be a society 'beyond justice'. The principle 'From each according to his abilities, to each according to his needs' is not, says Buchanan, a communist principle of distributive justice. Rather it is a description of how things will in fact be in communism. Thus, Marx refrained from calling the capitalist's exploitation unjust, even though Marx thought it to be unjust, because this would have obscured the fact that what Marx thought special about communism was not that it would be a just society, but that it would dispense with the need for justice by abolishing the circumstances that give rise to it.[25]

I have argued in favour of the justice interpretation of exploitation. But it does not really matter which of the two interpretations one accepts when it comes to the validity of the charge against capitalism. For I aim now to argue that what the two different interpretations hold in common to be the case about capitalism is mistaken. That is, I wish to argue that it is false that, through wage-labour, workers benefit their capitalist employers without capitalist employers benefiting their workers in return.

Accordingly, I aim to deny that workers are exploited by capitalists no matter whether one accepts the justice or the coercion
interpretation of exploitation.

4. Why Capitalism Need Involve No Exploitation

It may be conceded that capitalists exploit their workers, if capitalists make no contribution to production that benefits the
workers. We may grant, therefore, that if capitalists make no
contribution to the production that benefits the workers, workers
would be morally entitled to the full product of their labour minus
such deductions as may legitimately be made for the provision of
welfare for the indigent and other just social causes. Capitalists
would exploit workers, if capitalists made no contribution to
production that benefits the workers, because two conditions
would hold true: First, the workers would benefit the capitalists
whilst receiving no benefit from them in return. Second, the non-
reciprocal benefit gained by capitalists from workers would be
unjust. It would be unjust because workers would be entitled to
the full product of their labour minus such deductions as may
justly be made for provision of welfare and other just causes.
The crucial question, therefore, is whether capitalists make any
contribution to production which benefits workers in some way.

Traditionally, defenders of capitalism have wished to ascribe
to capitalists two positive functions which, so they say, constitute
genuine contributions to production that benefit workers and
which accordingly entitle them to some part of the product of the
workers' labour. The first function is to make available means
of production and to advance the workers (the wherewithal to
purchase) means of subsistence in advance of the completion of
the product. This provisioning of capital by capitalists is said to
require abstinence on the part of the capitalists. They abstain
from consuming the wealth they make available as capital. This
abstinence involves a sacrifice on the part of capitalists and entitles
them to some of the final product in addition to the return to
them of what they made available. This extra return is interest on
loaned or invested capital. John Stuart Mill endorsed the legitimacy of such non-wage income when he wrote: 'The institution

of property, when limited to its essential elements, consists in the recognition, in each person, of a right to the exclusive disposal of what he or she have produced by their own exertions, or received either by gift or by fair agreement, without force or fraud, from those who produced it. The foundation of the whole is, the right of producers to what they themselves have produced. It may be objected, therefore, to the institution as it now exists, that it recognizes rights of property in individuals over things which they have not produced. For example (it may be said) the operatives in a manufactory create, by their labour and skill, the whole produce; yet, instead of its belonging to them, the law gives them only their stipulated hire, and transfers the produce to someone who has merely supplied the funds, without perhaps contributing anything to the work itself, even in the form of superintendence. The answer to this is, that the labour of manufacture is only one of the conditions which must combine for the production of the commodity. The labour cannot be carried on without materials and machinery, nor without a stock of necessaries provided in advance to maintain the labourers during the production. All these things are the fruits of previous labour. If the labourers were possessed of them, they would not need to divide the produce with anyone; but while they have them not, an equivalent must be given to those who have, both for the antecedent labour, and for the abstinence by which the produce of that labour, instead of being expended on indulgences, has been reserved for this use. The capital may not have been, and in most cases was not, created by the labour and abstinence of the present possessor; but it was created by the labour and abstinence of some former person, who . . . transferred his claims to the present capitalist by gift or voluntary contract: and the abstinence at least must have been continued by each successive owner down to the present.'[26]

The second alleged function of capitalists is to bear the burden of risk that is an inevitable feature of all commodity production. When goods are produced for sale, there is always a risk that there will not be a sufficient demand for the product at a price which covers the costs of production. By paying wages to workers in advance of the sale of their product, the capitalist guarantees a return to the worker for his labour irrespective of whether his labour will turn out to have been worthwhile from an economic point of view when the commodities come to be sold. The capitalist spares the worker this risk by shouldering it all himself. The capitalist, therefore, deserves some return for having borne this risk in the event the productive enterprise should prove to have been economically unworthwhile. The return for bearing this risk is entrepreneurial profit. Even Marx himself with his Labour Theory of Value was obliged to recognize that it is the market, i.e. demand, that determines how many hours of socially necessary labour have been expended in the production of a commodity. However many hours the labourer has actually worked and no matter with what degree of intensity or technical efficiency, the worker cannot know how many hours of socially necessary labour have been incorporated in his product and therefore what it is worth economically until he sees how many people are willing to buy his product and at what price. Marx admits this when he writes: 'Suppose . . . . that every piece of linen on the market contains nothing but socially necessary labour-time. In spite of all this, all these pieces taken as a whole may contain superfluously expended labour-time. If the market cannot stomach the whole quantity at the normal price of two shillings a yard, this proves that too great a portion of the total social labour-time has been expended in the form of weaving. The effect is the same as if each individual weaver had expended more labour-time on his particular product than was socially necessary.'[27]

Marx is effectively saying here that it is only when the products come to be sold that it is possible to tell whether it has been economically worthwhile to produce them. Were workers to produce commodities for the market as self-employed associated producers, they would not know until the point of sale whether their labour had been worthwhile. They would have to bear the risk that their labour had been misdirected into a line of products that could not be sold at a price that justified their labour input. Capitalists spare workers these risks through advancing wages to their workers irrespective of whether there is final effective demand for their products. In return for accepting the risk of loss themselves, the capitalists become entitled to the profits.

Capitalists are entitled to profits for having spared the workers the risk of loss.

Now, as Allen Wood has observed, 'Marx is aware of all these apologetic claims and regards them as obscene falsehoods.'[28] We shall now examine Marx's objections to these claims of capital. It shall be argued that Marx's objections are invalid, and that the conclusion must be that capitalists perform useful functions in connection with production which entitle them to the non-wage incomes of interest and profit.

Let us begin by considering the claim that capitalists contribute to production through abstinence. Marx challenges the claim that the advance of capital by capitalists involves abstinence on their part. He contests this claim, first, in connection with the historical origin of the capitalist mode of production, and, second, in connection with capitalism after its inception. Marx's views about the origin of the capital which funded the first capitalist industrial ventures are contained in his Theory of Primitive Accumulation, expounded in Part VIII of *Capital* Volume I. Marx denies that the sums of capital which financed the first capitalist ventures were formed as a result of the frugality of the initial capitalists. Marx writes: 'In actual history, it is a notorious fact that conquest, enslavement, robbery, murder, in short, force, play the greatest part [in the formation of capital].'[29] In writing of the genesis of the industrial capitalist, Marx spells out in more detail what he takes to be the true source of the original fund of capital that financed the first capitalist ventures. 'The discovery of gold and silver in America, the extirpation, enslavement and entombment in mines of the indigenous population of that continent, the beginnings of the conquest and plunder of India, and the conversion of Africa into a preserve for the commercial hunting of black-skins, are all things which characterize the dawn of the era of capitalist production. These idyllic proceedings are the chief moments of primitive accumulation.'[30]

As to the subsequent provisioning of capital, Marx denies that capitalists genuinely abstain from consumption when they make capital available for production. He advances two arguments in support of this denial. The first argument is to the effect that every action involves abstention – the abstention from contrary actions. Therefore, the non-consumption of capital is not any special act of abstinence that warrants any special return. Marx writes: 'Every human action may be conceived as an "abstinence" from its opposite. Eating is abstinence from fasting, walking is abstinence from standing still, working is abstinence from idling, idling is abstinence from working.'[31]

Marx's second argument is that capitalists do not abstain from consumption when they make capital available, since they *could* not consume this capital. He characterizes the abstinence theory in the following ironic terms: 'All the conditions necessary for the labour-process are now converted into acts of abstinence on the part of the capitalist. If the corn is not all eaten, but in part also sown – abstinence of the capitalist. If the wine gets time to mature – abstinence of the capitalist. The capitalist robs himself whenever he "lends (!) the instruments of production to the worker", instead of eating them up, steam-engines, cotton, railways, manure, horses and all; or, as the vulgar economist childishly conceives, instead of dissipating "their value" in luxuries and other articles of consumption.'[32]

Let us now assess the validity of these arguments. Twentieth-century historical research into the sources of the capital that funded capitalist production at the start of the Industrial Revolution has not borne out Marx's contentions as to its origin. It has shown that the capital employed by the first industrial capitalists was obtained from nothing else besides their own extreme and prolonged frugality. It is enough to cite the following four facts. First, the first industrial capitalists of the Industrial Revolution in England were of lower middle-class and working-class origin.[33] To take just one notable but not unrepresentative example, consider the case of Richard Arkwright. He has a claim to be regarded as the founder of the modern factory system having been the first industrial capitalist to introduce water-power machinery into the cotton industry. He was, as Marx himself knew, the son of a wig-maker.

Second, the amounts of capital that were needed at the start of the Industrial Revolution to set up as a capitalist producer were comparatively very small. £100 was more than ample. These sums of money were invariably obtained out of the accumulated savings of the relatively modestly well-off families of the original industrial capitalists. Reference to the Yorkshire woollen industry in the last half of the eighteenth and first half of the nineteenth centuries will provide a good illustration. It has been found that 'external supplies of capital . . . were less important than the personal or family sums which the industrialists scraped together and ventured in the new productive equipment . . . Yet rarely was the amount adequate, and if the family firm eventually survived, it did so after many years of grim abstinence, of pared family budgets, and of frantic efforts to find supplementary funds outside.'[34]

Third, the further capital that was needed was invariably obtained by ploughing back virtually all the profits, having subtracted very little for personal subsistence by the capitalists. 'Once a new firm was established its growth took place predominantly by means of the reinvestment of profits. The usual practice among English industrialists, especially in the early days of the industrial revolution, was to allow themselves 5 per cent on their invested capital for their living expenses. Only the net income in excess of that amount was called profit, and it was usually invested in the business.'[35]

Fourth, landed and colonial wealth played virtually no part in financing the first capitalist industrial ventures. Contrary to what Marx asserts, 'the fortunes amassed by West India planters and merchants, or by East India nabobs, were used to buy landed estates in Britain, or government stocks, and to make mortgage loans to planters, but not for investment in industry. As for "landed capital", i.e. that of the great landowners, it seems to have played an altogether minor part in financing the industrial revolution, with the exception of the coal industry.'[36]

We may conclude that capitalist production arose from genuine abstinence on the part of the original capitalists. What of today? Here we face Marx's two arguments against the abstinence theory. Neither argument is very convincing. Against the first argument which invokes the thesis that all acts involve some abstinence, it may be observed that the argument rests upon a crude conflation of two different senses of the word 'abstain'. In the first sense, to abstain is to refrain from or omit doing. This sense of the word does not carry the implication of sacrifice or the forgoing of some satisfaction on the part of the abstainer. The second sense of the word 'abstain' does convey the idea of sacrifice and the forgoing of satisfaction. Now, all action involves some abstinence in the first sense of the word. But not all action involves abstinence in the second sense. It is in the second sense of the word that defenders of capitalism maintain that provision of capital involves abstinence on the part of the capitalist. The fact that all action involves abstinence in the first sense of the term is irrelevant to the truth of this thesis.

Marx's second argument against the abstinence theory was that capitalists do not abstain because they are not able to consume the capital that they make available. Again, this argument seems to involve a fallacy. Of course, capitalists cannot consume the machinery and raw materials they provide their workers. But were it not for the prospect of a return in the future on their investment, the capitalists would have been unwilling to invest their money in these non-consumables. Moreover, it is arguable that these very means of production would not themselves have been produced had it not been for the expected demand arising from capitalists wishing to invest their wealth for a return. By investing in means of production and advancing wages, the capitalist ties up money he would otherwise have had available for personal consumption. Thus, provision of capital does involve abstinence even though the capitalist cannot literally consume what he invests his capital in. As David Friedman has observed, 'Paying for tools today and waiting for years to get the money back is itself a productive activity . . . and the interest earned by capital is the corresponding payment.'[37] It is sometimes said that capitalists do not abstain when they invest because they do not actually consume fewer consumer goods than they previously did. The reply to this claim is that the sacrifice made does not require a reduction in consumption levels. It only requires a deliberate refraining from possible consumption. In this case as well as in reducing consumption levels, some possible present enjoyment is deliberately forgone for the sake of providing means of production.

We have seen that capital accumulation did not arise originally from capitalists forcibly stealing wealth from others. Rather, it arose from their prolonged abstinence. We have also seen that the provision of capital does involve a genuine forgoing of possible consumption, and, therefore, involves a genuine sacrifice upon the part of the capitalist. Accordingly, it may legitimately be maintained, contrary to Marx, that the provision of capital by capitalists is a genuine contribution to production involving a genuine sacrifice that entitles the capitalist to some return. Accordingly, we may deny that the subtraction from the product of labour for interest payments involves exploitation of the worker.

We must now consider what Marx had to say about the function that capitalists perform by shouldering the burden of risk. Marx denies that capitalists spare workers risk. They are spared, according to Marx, neither the risk of unemployment from the industrial cycle, nor unemployment arising from technological innovation and mechanization. The reply to the claim about the workers not being spared the ill effects of trade cycles is that its validity depends upon the validity of Marx's thesis that trade cycles are endemic to capitalism. The truth of this thesis will be contested below. As to Marx's claim that wages are not independent of the risks of technological unemployment, it may be replied that this misconstrues the sense in which capitalists may be said to spare workers risks. The point is that workers are guaranteed a return on their labour by the wage contract irrespective of whether the demand for the product will cover that wage. The wage contract no more guarantees the workers' employment for life than the worker guarantees the capitalist that he will always work for him rather than for another capitalist who might offer more money, or for himself. We may conclude that the assumption of entrepreneurial risk by the capitalist is a genuine contribution to production that entitles the capitalist to profit. The legitimacy of the claims of capital has been upheld.

The argument cannot be allowed to stop here. For some will be inclined to argue as follows: 'Rewards for risk-taking and for abstinence are legitimate if private ownership of means of production is legitimate. But they are illegitimate if private ownership of the means of production is illegitimate. What makes capitalism exploitative is that it is based upon this institution of private ownership of means of production. No private individual is morally entitled to own means of production. Consequently, capitalists are not entitled to the non-wage income they derive from such ownership.' We will not have successfully refuted the charge of capitalist exploitation unless we can successfully defend the legitimacy of private ownership of means of production. Can this be done? The next section addresses itself to this question.

5. The Moral Status of Private Property

The conclusion of the previous section has been that there is no exploitation of workers by capitalists if the capital that is made available to workers by capitalists is the morally legitimate property of the capitalists. This is because the provisioning of capital is a genuine contribution to production and one that benefits the workers. It, therefore, entitles the provider to some benefit in return from the workers, provided the capital is something to which those who provide it are morally entitled in the first place. If no capitalist is morally entitled to such capital as he possesses, then his making it available to workers would not be a contribution to production that entitled him to any part of the product of labour. It would no more be a contribution to production that entitled him to some return than would my giving you a good entitle me to some favour in return from you if I had previously unjustly deprived you of the good in the first place. The question of whether exploitation of the worker goes on in capitalism turns on the question, therefore, of whether private individuals are morally entitled to own capital.

Now, we have seen in the previous section that Marx attempted to portray capital as having had a blatantly unjust origin. Marx claimed that the original industrial capitalists came by their capital by naked extortion and force. We contested this claim, arguing instead that the original capital arose by way of abstinence from the consumption of wealth that had been created by the labour of the initial capitalist producers who abstained from consuming it to make it available as capital. We have also noted previously that Marx condones in socialism a principle of distributive justice that treats an individual as entitled to the product of his labour after certain deductions have been made for the provision of welfare for the disabled and the provision of certain public goods. It would seem to follow from this that Marx, to be consistent, must grant the moral legitimacy of ownership by a person of such capital as he has created by his abstaining from consuming what he has produced by his labour. One need only add that such capital can become the legitimate property of a non-producer of it by means of his being given it by a legitimate owner of it as a gift or in exchange in order for capital to become capable of becoming the legitimate property of non-producers of it. Now, if a person is the legitimate owner of something, it does seem arbitrary to deny that he may transfer legitimate ownership of that thing to whomsoever he wishes by gift or in exchange. It would, thus, seem that there need be nothing in principle unjust about the institution of private ownership of capital, provided all owners of it either had produced that capital by their labour and abstinence, or had been given it as a gift or in exchange by someone who had produced it by his labour and abstinence, or had been given it by someone who had been given it by someone who produced it by his labour and abstinence . . . and so on. It would seem, therefore, that there need be nothing inherently unjust about the private ownership of capital, provided, in the case of each owner of capital, his coming into possession of it had been morally innocuous: that is, he had produced it by his labour and abstinence or had been given it by a legitimate owner. The question of whether capitalism involves the exploitation of the workers becomes an empirical question as to the ancestry of the capital which capitalists own. Provided capital was originally created by the labour and abstinence of its first owners, and was subsequently subject to voluntary transfer, each owner of it would be morally legitimate. Making it available to others to work on would be a contribution to production that merited some return. This means its owner would be entitled to some non-wage income for making it available for production. This return could be saved and added to the original capital, and passed on in gift or exchange to others. We thus see how large agglomerations of capital can legitimately arise.

This defence of the moral legitimacy of private ownership of capital can be challenged by pointing out that, when Marx said that individuals are morally entitled to the product of their labour (minus the deductions for provision of welfare to the disabled), he restricted himself to *means of consumption* only. The charge that capitalism involves the exploitation of the worker has a chance of being upheld, then, if a case can be made out for the thesis that private appropriation of useful objects other than for purposes of their consumption by the appropriators is morally illegitimate. By *private appropriation* I mean the act of taking into personal possession as one's property previously unheld and unused resources such as areas of virgin land or natural resources and produce extractable from the land by means of labour. Capital is precisely wealth (useful objects) that has been set aside for a purpose other than consumption by its owner. It is wealth saved for the purpose of its being transformed into a larger amount by means of the performance of additional labour. (The person who performs the additional labour need not be identical with the person who did the saving.) Capital can only come into existence by useful artefacts being deliberately withheld from consumption for use in further production. Consequently, if no resources, including land, may be privately appropriated save for purposes of consumption, then no capital may ever be legitimately formed. Alternatively, if natural resources may be legitimately appropriated by private individuals for purposes other than consumption by the appropriator, then capital may legitimately be formed. The question whether workers suffer exploitation by capitalists, thus, turns on the question whether private individuals are morally entitled to make their own private property previously unheld and unused resources, including tracts of land, for purposes other than their personal consumption. By virtue of its nature, land is not something that persons can be said to consume save, perhaps, in the case where a person erects a dwelling upon a piece of land thereby excluding others from the use of that land. Such use of land can be regarded as a form of consumption of it in a way in which the clearing and farming of land only constitutes the use and not consumption of land, though it may involve consuming the land's fertility.

Let us at this point lay down as a general principle that a person is morally entitled to do any act he wishes provided it violates no one's rights. It follows from this general principle that the private appropriation by an individual of natural resources including land for a purpose other than his own personal consumption is morally legitimate, provided no one else's rights are violated thereby. The question of whether capitalism involves the exploitation of workers has, thus, been found to turn upon the question whether a person always or ever violates the rights of another person or persons by appropriating unheld natural resources including land for a purpose other than his own personal consumption. If such appropriation always involves the violation of the rights of another or others, then no such appropriation is ever morally legitimate. Hence, if such appropriation always involves violation of the rights of others, the private ownership of capital is morally illegitimate, and capitalism always involves the exploitation of the workers. If such appropriation only sometimes violates the rights of persons, then, in order to determine whether capitalism involves exploitation, it would be necessary to do two things: first, we would have to identify the conditions in which the private appropriation of natural resources, including land, for purposes other than consumption constitutes the violation of some person's or persons' rights. Second, we would have to determine whether such private appropriation of land and natural resources as has taken place for purposes other than consumption satisfies these conditions.

In order to discover whether the appropriation of land and resources for purposes other than consumption always or ever involves the violation of the rights of persons, we must first identify what (natural) rights people have. The question of what natural rights people have is a notoriously difficult question. The best way of approaching the issue seems to be by way of reflection upon what natural rights are for. The things to which people are said to have natural rights are invariably things which are regarded as of special importance and value for those who are said to have them. Following the very instructive suggestion of Samuel Scheffler,[38] we shall construe every person as having a natural right to a sufficient share of every good capable of distribution whose enjoyment is a necessary condition of a person's having a reasonable chance of living a decent and fulfilling life, subject only to one qualification. This qualification is that no one has a natural right to any good which can only be obtained by preventing someone else from having a reasonable chance of living a decent and fulfilling life. A sufficient share of a necessary good is the minimum amount large enough to enable a person to have a reasonable chance of living a decent and fulfilling life.

What things must people have in order to have reasonable chances of leading decent and fulfilling lives? About some things, there can be little doubt that they are needed by a person to have a reasonable chance of having a decent and fulfilling life. Consider life itself. It is impossible for a person to have a reasonable chance for a decent and fulfilling life without having life itself. So, all persons may be said to have a natural right to life. Again, in order to have a reasonable chance to lead a decent and fulfilling life, it is clear that a person needs means of subsistence. We can, thus, say that individuals have natural rights to means of subsistence. It need not follow from a recognition that people have a natural right to their means of subsistence that a person has a right to be supplied by others with means of subsistence even if he should refuse to work to obtain them. Provided a person is able to work to obtain his means of subsistence, he is not denied what is necessary for a reasonable chance for a decent and fulfilling life if his receipt of means of subsistence is made conditional upon his performing a certain amount of labour to obtain them. (Of course, if a man's receipt of means of subsistence were to be made conditional upon his performing an amount of work so large as to preclude his being able to lead a decent and fulfilling life, then his natural rights would be being violated, provided others were capable of supplying him with these means of subsistence without thereby forfeiting their own chance for a decent and fulfilling life.) If a person is unable to work, then our view of what people have natural rights to commits us to saying that he has a natural right to be provided with means of subsistence by those who are capable of providing it without thereby forfeiting a reasonable chance for a decent and fulfilling life for themselves.

Another necessary condition of having a reasonable chance for a decent and fulfilling life is having a certain amount of personal liberty. How much liberty a person needs to have in order to have a reasonable chance of being able to enjoy a decent and fulfilling life is a very difficult question. I do not propose to attempt to answer it here beyond observing that a person normally needs for a reasonable chance of a decent and fulfilling life at least sufficient freedom to be able to improve his individual condition indefinitely by his own effort. Without such a degree of personal liberty, a man cannot strive to improve his condition. Such an existence is bound to lead to frustration and indolence, neither condition being compatible with a fulfilling life.

Let us not try to determine further at this point what natural rights we may recognize people as having. Instead, let us turn to the question: Does a person always or ever violate the natural rights of others by appropriating unheld unused land and/or natural resources and produce for a purpose other than personal consumption? Let us first consider whether such private appropriation always involves violating the rights of others. When a person appropriates some resource, he thereby excludes other people from being able to use freely and to appropriate for themselves the resource. Our first question is, then, whether it is *always* the case that, when persons are excluded from being able to freely use or appropriate some natural resource, they are thereby denied a reasonable chance of being able to lead a decent and fulfilling life. The answer to this question is surely negative. In order for a person to have a reasonable chance of leading a decent and fulfilling life, it is not necessary that that person be able to use freely or appropriate every piece of land and natural resource there is. Persons can appropriate pieces of land and other natural resources without thereby denying those who are thereby excluded from the use and appropriation of what is appropriated a reasonable chance of leading decent and fulfilling lives. Provided there remains enough and as good of whatever is appropriated for the use and appropriation of others, no one's chances of leading decent and fulfilling lives are at all adversely affected by any number of private appropriations. Consider, however, the question: Can a person *ever* be denied a reasonable chance of leading a decent and fulfilling life by being excluded by another or others from freely using and appropriating land and other natural resources? Here the answer is surely affirmative. A person's chance of leading a decent and fulfilling life would be rendered unreasonably slender by being excluded from the free use and appropriation of land and other resources when that person's very survival was conditional upon his being able to use that land and appropriate those resources. Such cases are certainly conceivable. Suppose, for example, a ship-wrecked sailor is prevented from being able to land on an island, when the only alternative to his doing so is his drowning; the person preventing the sailor landing being someone who has claimed the island for himself. Or suppose the sailor manages to land on the island but the person who has got there first and claimed it for himself has gathered the total supply of food on the island and refuses to let the sailor have any (there being enough for the two). Or, finally, suppose the proprietor of the island allows the sailor to land and have food provided the sailor agrees to become the proprietor's slave, thereby giving up the liberty to improve his condition indefinitely by his effort. In these cases, the private appropriation by one person of land and resources would have denied another a reasonable chance of leading a decent and fulfilling life.

The difficult thing is to specify the conditions in which a person's exclusion from being able to freely use and appropriate land and natural resources and produce denies that person a reasonable chance for a decent and fulfilling life. One such condition, we have seen, is when such exclusion prevents the excluded person from being able to avoid death. Another, we have also seen, is when such exclusion denies the excluded person the liberty to improve his condition indefinitely by his own effort. Perhaps at the cost of some over-simplification, I shall assume there are no more such conditions.

The relevance of these considerations to the moral propriety of private ownership of capital is this. Private ownership of capital is morally illegitimate if and only if the private appropriation by persons of land and natural resources for purposes other than consumption has thereby prevented those excluded from being able to obtain means of subsistence and being able to enjoy sufficient liberty to improve their condition indefinitely by their effort. Once the issue is put like this, it becomes far from clear that private ownership of capital is morally illegitimate. For it is far from clear that those who have appropriated unused land and resources for purposes other than consumption have thereby prevented those who have been excluded from being able to obtain means of subsistence and from being able to improve their condition indefinitely by their effort. Being able to freely use land and to appropriate natural resources and produce obtainable from land by labour is not a necessary condition of being able to acquire means of subsistence or to improve one's condition indefinitely by one's effort. Provided there are employment opportunities, opportunities for accumulating savings by abstinence, and opportunities for entrepreneurship, it is possible for people to procure their means of subsistence and to improve their condition indefinitely by means of their effort without themselves needing to appropriate any natural resources or land. Even where a person is only able to labour upon land and with resources owned by others and subject to their terms, it is still possible for a person to have all that is necessary for a reasonable chance of living a decent and fulfilling life. To say otherwise one would have to maintain that being an employee was itself as such incompatible with leading a decent and fulfilling life. Now, Marx himself tried to give reasons for thinking this to be so in his account of the alienation of wage-labour. But we examined those reasons in Chapter 2 and found them not to be convincing. It is perfectly possible to lead a decent and fulfilling life as a wage-labourer, provided there are such things as employment opportunities, opportunities for saving, and opportunities for leisure. People only have their rights violated by private appropriation by others of land and natural resources where such exclusion from the free use of the land and appropriation of the resources denies those excluded a reasonable chance for a decent and fulfilling life. It is anything but obvious that such private appropriation of land and resources as has taken place has lowered rather than raised people's chances of leading decent and fulfilled lives. Without private appropriation of land for purposes other than consumption, there would have been little incentive for agricultural improvement, as Marx himself admitted.[39] Likewise, if people had been prevented from appropriating natural resources, there would not have been the incentives for developing the extractive industries.

In his account of the origins of the capitalist mode of production, Marx claims that the enclosures of the common land that took place in Britain from the fifteenth century but were particularly prevalent in the eighteenth deprived vast numbers who had previously farmed the commons as independent peasants of their traditional means of livelihood.[40] Marx says that it was these expropriated peasants and their descendants who drifted to towns to become the industrial proletariat, having been reduced to destitution in the interim. The flavour of Marx's account of the matter may be discerned from the following passage which is not unrepresentative of Marx's tone.

'The spoliation of the Church's property, the fraudulent alienation of the state domains, the theft of the common lands, the usurpation of feudal and clan property and its transformation into modern private property under circumstances of ruthless terrorism, all these things were just so many idyllic methods of primitive accumulation. They conquered the field for capitalist agriculture, incorporated the soil into capital, and created for the urban industries the necessary supplies of free and rightless proletarians.'[41]

If this account of the formation of capitalist farms and of the industrial proletariat were correct, then it would seem that the natural rights of the expropriated peasants and their descendants had been violated by those who effected these enclosures. The reason why this would seem to be the case is that the chance of leading a decent and fulfilling life would almost certainly have been significantly higher as an independent peasant than as a vagabond or as an industrial worker in the early stages of the Industrial Revolution. However, the accuracy of Marx's historical scholarship in this matter is open to question. Twentieth-century research has revealed, for instance, that 'from the later eighteenth century up to probably about 1815 small owners were actually increasing in number and acreage, even in some heavily enclosed counties . . . Enclosure was not a very important factor in the survival of owner occupiers.'[42] Although the less affluent cottagers and squatters may have lost, as a result of the enclosure movement, use-rights in common land previously enjoyed, they were compensated by more work and greater regularity of employment after enclosure. The improved farming methods of the eighteenth century were the opposite of labour-saving. 'In consequence there was in fact no general exodus of unemployed rural labour, pauperized by enclosure, to seek work in the industrial centres.'[43] What accounted for the marked rise in urban population in Britain in the eighteenth century was not expropriations from the land as a result of enclosure but the fact that in the eighteenth century, there was an enormous increase in population in town and country alike. The labour force increased at a rate that was higher than could be absorbed in agriculture. Without enclosure and the increased agricultural productivity it brought, and without the employment opportunities provided by capitalist manufacture, those increased numbers too large for maintenance on the land would not have survived. As F. A. Hayek has observed: 'The proletariat which capitalism can be said to have "created" was not a proportion of the population which would have existed without it and which it had degraded to a lower level; it was an additional population which was enabled to grow up by the new opportunities for employment which capitalism provided. In so far as it is true that the growth of capital made the appearance of the proletariat possible, it was in the sense that it raised the productivity of labour so that much larger numbers of those who had not been equipped by their parents with the necessary tools were enabled to maintain themselves by their labour alone . . . Although it was certainly not from charitable motives, it still was the first time in history that one group of people found it in their interest to use their earnings on a large scale to provide new instruments of production to be operated by those who without them could not have produced their own sustenance.'[44]

When viewed in this perspective, the emergence of private ownership of land and capital seems to have done anything but reduce the life chances of those who became the industrial proletariat. Provided workers have not subsequently had their life-chances impaired by the institution of private ownership of capital, the institution does not appear to be unjust. Now, as remarked, we have rejected Marx's grounds for the thesis that workers' life-chances are impaired by private property because of the alienation endemic to wage-labour. This, however, is not the only source of damage that Marx claimed capitalism did to workers. Marx also held that capitalism was injurious to workers because of the material poverty and insecurity it brought as a corollary of the industrial cycle. If Marx's claims about this are correct, then the claim that capitalism violates the rights of workers may well still stand. The exploitation charge, therefore, cannot be fully dealt with until we have examined the validity of Marx's claim that capitalism is responsible for impoverishing workers and exposing them to the vagaries of the industrial cycle. This is the subject of the next section.

6. Capitalism's Laws of Motion

Marx's prime purpose in *Capital* is to explain how capitalism must evolve. He does this by attempting to deduce from the nature of capitalist production a number of economic tendencies. These are the so-called 'laws of motion' of the capitalist mode of production. The deduction of these laws is intended to demonstrate that capitalism must inevitably become a fetter on the forces of production.

The laws of motion that Marx sought to demonstrate all derive in one way or another from a fundamental tendency which Marx took to be inherent within capitalism. This is the tendency towards technical progress – towards development of the forces of production. Marx regarded the tendency towards technological progress to be the most striking feature of capitalism. As he observed in the *Communist Manifesto*: 'The bourgeoisie, during its rule of scarce one hundred years, has created more massive and more colossal productive forces than have all the preceding generations together. Subjection of nature's forces to man, machinery, application of chemistry to industry and agriculture, steam-navigation, railways, electric telegraphs, clearing of whole continents for cultivation, canalization of rivers, whole populations conjured out of the ground – what earlier century had even the presentiment that such productive forces slumbered in the lap of social labour.'[45]

Marx did not consider it to be sheer coincidence that capitalism had been accompanied by technological progress. He wrote: 'The bourgeoisie cannot exist without constantly revolutionizing the instruments of production.'[46] 'Modern industry never views or treats the existing form of a production process as the definitive one. Its technical basis is therefore revolutionary, whereas all earlier modes of production were essentially conservative.'[47]

According to Marx, what gives rise to this tendency for techno-logical progress is the incessant search by capitalists for profits in conditions of competition between them. Technological progress increases the productivity of labour. When labour becomes more productive, then more commodities are producible per man-hour than previously. This means that, with technological progress, a labourer can turn out a greater number of commodities per day than previously. This means that unit labour costs of each com-modity are reduced by technological innovation. Should the innovating capitalist be able to sell his commodities for the same price that they previously commanded, he will have increased his profit margin. Now, according to Marx's Theory of Value, the market price of a commodity is determined by its social and not by its individual value. That is, the price of a commodity is deter-mined by the amount of time it takes to produce the commodity using the standard prevailing technology. The price is not deter-mined by the amount of time it has actually taken to produce the commodity. An innovating capitalist, therefore, is able to sell his commodities at or at least near their old price and, therefore, above their individual values. As a result, he is able to make what Marx calls *surplus profit*. The capitalist who is first to introduce some labour-saving technological innovation is able to make these surplus profits until his competitors have adopted the inno-vation themselves. Once this happens, the innovation becomes the standard method of production. The individual value of the commodities using this new method becomes the new social value of the commodity. The price of the commodity falls to this new lower level and surplus profits are eliminated.

The competitors of a capitalist who introduces a labour-saving technological innovation have a strong incentive for adopting the new method of production. The innovating capitalist, by improving the productivity of labour, will have increased the supply of the commodity. In order to sell this increased supply, he will have needed to extend the demand for the commodity (assuming previously the market had been in equilibrium). This will necessitate his reducing their price below their previous level. That is, he must offer them below their social value. (He still makes a surplus profit by selling them above their individual value.) His competitors will start to lose their customers to the innovating capitalist unless they are able to reduce their prices to the same level. In order for them to do this without squeezing their own profit margins, it is necessary for them to introduce the new technology into their own production processes. So, in order to stay in business, the competitors of an innovating capitalist must adopt the innovation as well. The result is that, in capitalism, there is an incentive both for the introduction of new labour-saving technology and for its widespread diffusion.

Marx is undoubtedly correct in imputing to capitalism a tendency towards technological progress. He is also correct in making competition between capitalists responsible for this tendency. However, it is not necessary to accept Marx's Theory of Value in order to believe that competition between capitalists generates a tendency for technological progress.

Marx believed that the tendency towards technological progress directly gives rise to two other tendencies. The first of these tendencies is towards what he called the *concentration of capital* by which he meant the growth in the size of firms. The second is towards what he called the *centralization of capital*, meaning by this the reduction in the number of independent firms in each sector of industry. The growth in the size of firms follows directly from the tendency for firms to increase in productivity as a result of technological innovation. Technological innovation typically increases the scale of production: that is, it encourages greater and greater mass production. As a result, we find Marx writing that 'It is a law, springing from the technical character of manufacture, that the minimum amount of capital which the capitalist must possess has to go on increasing'[48] and, 'The development of capitalist production makes it necessary constantly to increase the amount of capital laid out in a given industrial undertaking, and competition . . . compels [each industrial capitalist] to keep extending his capital, so as to preserve it, and he can only extend it by means of progressive accumulation.'[49]

The tendency towards technological progress as a result of competition imposes on capitalist firms the imperative that they grow in size. This imposes on capitalists an imperative to accumulate capital. Accumulation of capital consists in the capitalist investing (at least some portion of) the profits which he makes. The requirement that firms grow in size entails that accumulation takes the form of the profits being invested in the same production processes (the same firms) as the original capital was invested in. In short, accumulation of capital takes the form of concentration of capital.

The centralization of capital is, in Marx's words, 'Concentration of capitals already formed, destruction of their individual independence, expropriation of capitalist by capitalist, transformation of many small into few large capitals.'[50] Whereas the concentration of capital is the process by which profits are invested in the firms in order to increase their size and competitiveness, centralization is the process by which pre-existent, independent firms fuse together to form larger entities. Marx identifies two factors as responsible for centralization of capital. The first is competition between capitalists. Competition leads to the demise of the smaller, less competitive firms whose assets are bought up by their larger, more successful competitors. 'Competition . . . always ends in the ruin of many small capitalists, whose capitals partly pass into the hands of their conquerors, and partly vanish completely.'[51] The second factor making for the centralization of capital is the formation of joint-stock companies. This process enables many individual possessors of capital to pool their capitals together into very large masses. This enables large masses of capital to be built up far more quickly than would be possible by straightforward reinvestments of profits by firms. 'The world would still be without railways if it had had to wait until accumulation had got a few individual capitals far enough to be adequate for the construction of a railway. Centralization, however, accomplished this in the twinkling of an eye by means of joint-stock companies.'[52]

Marx must be judged entirely correct in imputing to capitalism tendencies towards the concentration and centralization of capital. Firm size has shown a constant tendency to grow, and branches of industry have tended to become dominated by giant firms. However, the reduction in the number of firms per branch of industry does not mean a reduction in the number of capitalists. Centralization of capital does not entail that there are increasingly fewer owners of capital. This should be borne in mind in view of the extent to which capitalist firms are these days funded by pension funds and other such large undertakings which control the savings of vast numbers of small investors.

Yet another tendency which Marx believed to be inherent in capitalism was for the number of wage-labourers for whose labour-power there is periodically no demand to increase. He writes: 'Capitalist accumulation . . . constantly produces, and produces indeed in the direct relation of its own energy and extent, a relatively redundant working population, i.e. a population which is superfluous to capital's average requirements . . . and is therefore a surplus population.'[53] This surplus labouring population Marx calls 'a disposable reserve army'.[54] He describes it as 'a mass of human material always ready for exploitation by capital'.[55]

According to Marx, the formation of a surplus labour population is the inevitable reaction to an equally inevitable periodic tendency for there to be shortages of labour-power. Shortages of labour-power arise whenever capitalists accumulate capital without making technological innovations that improve the productivity of labour. Marx writes that 'Growth of capital implies the growth of its variable constituent, in other words, the part invested in labour-power . . . [S]ooner or later a point must be reached at which the requirements of accumulation begin to outgrow the customary supply of labour.'[56] When the requirements of accumulation outgrow the supply of labour, capitalists start to bid up wages. Rising wage-levels cut into the profit margins of capitalists. This squeeze on profits causes capitalists to react in various ways that result in the creation of a surplus labour population. Marx identifies three such ways in which capitalists, reacting to labour shortages, create surplus labour. The first of these ways is for them to introduce labour-saving technology which reduces the demand for labour-power. Marx writes in illustration that 'between 1849 and 1859 a rise of wages . . . took place in the English agricultural districts . . . What did the farmers do now? . . . They introduced more machinery, and in a moment the labourers were redundant.'[57]

The second way in which capitalists can react to a labour shortage in a way that creates a surplus labour population is by temporarily refraining from accumulation. That is, they can refrain from investing their profits. 'A smaller part of revenue is capitalized, accumulation slows down, and the rising movement of wages comes up against an obstacle.'[58] This halt in investment precipitates an industrial crisis. Firms which have produced capital goods are unable to market their commodities. This leads to insolvencies, firms' closures and unemployment. This reduces demand for consumer goods, and so the crisis spreads to the consumer goods industries. The resultant competition between workers for jobs leads to falling wage-levels. Profit margins are restored and capitalists begin to accumulate once more. The industrial reserve army grows from the start of the crisis through the period of recession and begins to decline in size as employment picks up with the restoration of prosperity. 'Taking them as a whole, the general movements of wages are exclusively regulated by the expansion and contraction of the industrial reserve army, and this in turn corresponds to the periodic alternations of the industrial cycle.'[59]

The third way in which capitalists can contribute to the formation of a surplus labouring population is by increasing what Marx calls the degree of exploitation of their labour force. Capitalists extend the working day or demand more intensive exertion from their labour force during it. The competition between workers for jobs as a result of technological innovation forces workers to accept the more exacting terms of employment. In accepting them, the demand for labour is reduced. 'As the productivity of labour increases, capital increases its supply of labour more quickly than its demand for workers. The overwork of the employed part of the working class swells the ranks of its reserve, while, conversely, the greater pressure that the reserve by its competition exerts on the employed workers forces them to submit to overwork and subjects them to the dictates of capital. The condemnation of one part of the working class to enforced idleness by the overwork of the other part . . . accelerates . . . the production of the industrial reserve army on a scale corresponding with the progress of social accumulation.'[60]

Marx's case for the increasing surplus labour population is not very convincing. In the first place, the first and second ways in which a surplus labour population is supposed to be created appear to be incompatible with each other. If workers are made redundant by technological innovation, then capitalists will not be faced with the labour shortages which lead them to suspend investment. Secondly, technological innovation does not necessarily produce any overall increase in unemployment unless there is insufficient demand for labour-power from new industries. Marx says nothing to show that new industries cannot absorb those workers who are made redundant through technological innovation. Thirdly, as we shall see when we come to examine Marx's views on cyclical crises, contrary to what Marx says, periods of industrial prosperity and growth do not terminate as a result of shortages of labour producing wage levels that erode profit margins. Finally, capitalists are able to make their workers work harder and for longer only when there is substantial unemployment. But Marx has so far failed to show why there must be a sizeable pool of unemployed. Consequently, there is no reason to accept that unemployment is produced in the manner in which Marx says it is – namely, by way of being an inevitable reaction to an equally inevitable tendency for there to be periodic shortages of labour-power.

One of Marx's most famous predictions about capitalism is that, as it develops, the condition of the worker deteriorates. Marx says: 'In proportion as capital accumulates, the situation of the labourer, be his payment high or low, must grow worse.'[61] 'Accumulation of wealth at one pole is . . . at the same time accumulation of misery, the torment of labour, slavery, ignorance, brutalization and moral degradation . . . on the side of the class that produces its own product as capital.'[62]

Marx offers three reasons in support of his contention that the condition of the workers deteriorates in capitalism. The first is that the workers suffer increasing impoverishment measured in absolute real terms. The second is that workers suffer increasing impoverishment relative to capitalists. The third is that work in capitalism becomes increasingly dehumanizing as a result of mechanization and the increasing intensity of labour. Let us examine each of these reasons in turn.

In support of this assertion that workers suffer increasing absolute impoverishment in capitalism, Marx offered three reasons. The first is that the increasing size of the industrial reserve army results in an increasingly large number of the destitute. 'The greater the social wealth, the functioning capital, the extent and energy of its growth, and therefore also the greater the absolute mass of the proletariat and the productivity of its labour, the greater is the industrial reserve army . . . The more extensive . . . the pauperized sections of the working class and the industrial reserve army, the greater is official pauperism. *This is the absolute general law of capitalist accumulation.*'[63]

The second reason Marx offers in support of the thesis that workers become increasingly impoverished in capitalism is that the increasing mechanization of industry leads to a surplus supply of labour which allows wages to be forced down to their minimum possible levels. '[T]he general tendency of capitalist production is not to raise but to sink the average standard of wages, or to push the *value of labour* more or less to its *minimum limit*.'[64]

Marx's third reason for postulating increasing absolute impoverishment is that the increasing mechanization of industry leads to the increasing 'de-skilling' of labour. The subsistence requirements of unskilled labour are more modest than those of skilled labour. Consequently, as industry becomes more mechanized, the wage levels of the workers fall. Marx writes in the *Communist Manifesto*: 'Owing to the extensive use of machinery and to division of labour, the work of the proletarians . . . is only the most simple, most monotonous, and the most easily acquired knack, that is required of him. Hence, the cost of production of a workman is restricted, almost entirely, to the means of subsistence that he requires for his maintenance, and for the propagation of his race. But the price . . . of labour is equal to its cost of production. In proportion, therefore, as the repulsiveness of the work increases, the wage decreases.'[65]

Marx's thesis that workers become increasingly impoverished in absolute terms is based upon his claim that the reserve army of unemployed increases with the development of capitalism. For it is from the ranks of the reserve army that the destitute are recruited, and it is the reserve army that forces workers to accept lower wages due to pressure of competition for jobs. We have rejected Marx's claim that, as capitalism develops, the reserve army grows in size. Consequently, we have no reason to accept the thesis about the increasing absolute impoverishment. Not merely does Marx fail to provide any reason for accepting his thesis that workers become increasingly impoverished as capitalism develops: the course which capitalism has taken since his day would appear to constitute overwhelming grounds for rejecting the thesis. For the average member of the working class has enjoyed an enormous rise in living standards since Marx's day. Many followers of Marx faced with rising living standards among workers in capitalist societies have attempted to defend Marx's thesis about increasing impoverishment by arguing that rising living standards in advanced capitalist societies have been obtained by means of imperialist exploitation of the Third World. A view has become popular in both the West and the Third World to the effect that colonialism and capitalism have produced Third World poverty. This view does not stand up to critical scrutiny. As the development economist, P. T. Bauer, has said, 'Far from the West having caused the poverty in the Third World, contact with the West has been the principal agent of material progress there.'[66]

Marx's second reason for claiming a steady deterioration in the condition of the working class in capitalism is that they suffer increasing poverty relative to the capitalists. Marx claims that, even if the real wages of the workers increase, they become increasingly impoverished if the incomes of the capitalists increase still more. Marx first advanced this claim in *Wage-Labour and Capital* composed in 1849. Marx observes in that work: 'A house may be large or small; as long as the surrounding houses are equally small it satisfies all the social demands for a dwelling. But let a palace arise beside the little house, and it shrinks from a little house to a hut. The little house shows now that its owner has only a very slight or no demands to make; and however high it may shoot up in the course of civilization, if the neighbouring palace grows to an equal or even greater extent, the occupant of the relatively small house will feel more and more uncomfortable, dissatisfied and cramped within its four walls.'[67] A similar thesis is reiterated in *Capital*.[68] There would seem to be a large element of truth in what Marx says here. Yet, surprisingly enough considering what he says elsewhere about human nature, Marx does appear to have exaggerated the extent to which man is an acquisitive animal. Provided their lot is improving relative to what it has been, people tend in general to be content with it, despite seeing the lot of others better off improve as fast or faster. People are not in general as envious as Marx seems to be supposing them to be.

This leaves Marx's third reason for postulating the increasing immiseration of the worker. This is the increasing alienation arising from the increasing mechanization of work. We have examined and rejected this thesis in Chapter 2.

Marx claimed that, as capitalism develops, there is a tendency for the rate of profit to fall. Capitalists, that is, tend to receive a smaller and smaller rate of return on their investments. The rate of profit, for Marx, is the ratio between the surplus value created by some given sum of capital and that sum of capital. Marx represented the rate of profit by the letter p^1. In Marx's symbolism, $p^1 = s: C$. In other words, $p^1 = s: (c + v)$. (See p. 95.)

Marx deduced the existence of the tendency for the rate of profit to fall from another which he imputed to capitalism. This latter is a tendency for what Marx called the *organic composition of capital* to increase. The organic composition of capital is the ratio between the constant and variable capital employed in some production process. In other words, the organic composition of capital is equal to the ratio $c: v$. Marx deduced the existence of this tendency from another which we have seen he regarded as endemic to capitalism. This is the tendency for the productivity of labour to increase. As we have seen, according to Marx, as capitalism develops, capitalists strive to increase the productivity of labour in order to cheapen the costs of the commodities which they produce. Increasing productivity of labour means that the volume of means of production turned into finished commodities by each labourer increases. Marx called the ratio between the means of production and the labour-power involved in some production process the *technical composition of capital*. The tendency for technology to develop entails that there is a tendency in capital for the productivity of labour to increase. The tendency for the productivity of labour to increase entails that there is a tendency for the technical composition of capital to rise.

Marx claimed that there is a close correlation between the technical composition of capital and the organic composition. The former could not increase without the latter increasing too, although not necessarily by as large an amount. Given this correlation it follows that an increasing organic composition of capital may be inferred from an increasing technical composition of capital.

Marx derived the tendency for the rate of profit to fall from the tendency for the organic composition of capital to rise. He wrote: 'With the progressive decline in the variable capital in relation to the constant capital, this tendency leads to a rising organic composition of the total capital, and the direct result of this is that the rate of surplus value . . . is expressed in a steadily falling rate of profit . . . The progressive tendency for the general rate of profit to fall is thus simply *the expression, peculiar to the capitalist mode of production*, of the progressive development of the social productivity of labour . . . It is a self-evident necessity, deriving from the nature of the capitalist mode of production itself, that as it advances the general rate of surplus value must be expressed in a falling general rate of profit.'[69]

What Marx is claiming here may best be seen by referring to the example he offers to illustrate his thesis. This example envisages a total quantity of capital growing through a series of successive circuits. In each circuit, the organic composition rises, the quantity of variable capital remains unchanged, and the rate of surplus value remains unchanged at 100 per cent. With these assumptions, the rate of profit behaves as follows:

c	v	s	$s : (c + v) \ =$		p^1
					per cent
50	100	100	$100 : (\ 50 + 100) \ =$		66⅔
100	100	100	$100 : (100 + 100) \ =$		50
200	100	100	$100 : (200 + 100) \ =$		33⅓
300	100	100	$100 : (300 + 100) \ =$		25
400	100	100	$100 : (400 + 100) \ =$		20

Marx attached great importance to the law of the tendency for the rate of profit to fall. He described it as 'in every respect the most important law of modern political economy'.[70] His reason for doing so is this. Capitalists invest capital in order to make profits. If the rate of profit is too low, capitalists do not consider it worthwhile to invest. The law of the tendency for the rate of profit to fall suggested to Marx that capitalism generated its own barrier to production. In other words, Marx thought that the law established that capitalism must eventually become a fetter upon the forces of production. Marx had this law in mind when he wrote that: 'The development of the productive forces brought about by historical development of capital itself, when it reaches a certain point, suspends the self-realization of capital instead of positing it. Beyond a certain point, the development of the powers of production becomes a barrier for capital; hence the capital relation [becomes] a barrier for the development of the productive powers of labour.'[71]

Marx's deduction of the tendency of the rate of profit to fall is based upon two assumptions. The first is that, as capitalism develops, the organic composition of capital rises. The second is that, when the organic composition of capital rises, it rises faster than the rate of surplus value. Neither assumption is correct.

Marx derived his thesis that the organic composition of capital rises from two assumptions. The first is that, as capitalism develops, the technical composition of capital rises. The second is that there is a positive correlation between the technical composition of capital and the organic composition. A rise in the technical composition is always accompanied by a rise in the organic composition, although not always by as much.

That there exists in capitalism a tendency for the technical composition of capital to rise is something that may readily be granted to Marx. But Marx's other assumption is far more problematic. Nowhere does Marx provide any grounds in support of it. Yet it is anything but self-evident. It is perfectly possible for the technical composition of capital to rise without the organic composition rising with it. Indeed, it is possible for the technical composition to rise while the organic composition of capital falls. No less an authority than Marx himself said as much. For Marx identifies a number of tendencies that counteract the tendency for the rate of profit to fall. Among these is a tendency for the elements of constant capital to become cheaper. Marx wrote of this latter tendency: 'The same development that raises the mass constant capital in comparison with variable reduces the value of its elements, as a result of the higher productivity of labour, and hence prevents the value of the constant capital, even though this grows steadily, from growing in the same degree as its material volume, i.e. the material volume of the means of production that are set in motion by the same amount of labour-power. *In certain cases, the mass of the constant capital elements may increase while their total value remains the same or even falls.*' [72]

What this comes to is that the organic composition of capital need not always rise when the technical composition rises. The productivity of labour can be so much increased by the introduction of improved technology that the value of the new technology and the raw materials now used by labour decreases. The introduction of labour-saving technology can reduce the organic composition of capital while increasing the technical composition. Consequently, the tendency for the organic composition of capital to rise cannot be deduced from the tendency for the technical composition of capital to rise.

Suppose that the organic composition of capital does rise. Even then, Marx is still unable to infer a tendency for the rate of profit to fall. A tendency for the rate of profit to fall may only be derived from a rising organic composition of capital if the latter increases faster than the rate of surplus value. Marx offers no reason at all for supposing that, if the organic composition of capital rises, the rate of surplus value does not rise sufficiently fast to preserve the rate of profit unchanged or indeed to increase it. A rising technical composition of capital is equivalent to rising productivity of labour. If the productivity of labour increases, then it will take less time than previously to produce the workers' means of subsistence. Accordingly, provided that the working day does not diminish in length and that wages do not rise by a corresponding amount, a rising technical composition of capital will result in a rising rate of surplus value. Now, Marx rules out the possibility that, as capitalism develops, the length of the working day diminishes or that wage levels rise. Thus, that which produces a rising organic composition of capital – that is, the rising technical composition – also produces a rising rate of surplus value. The conclusion is clear. As Paul Sweezy has observed: 'There is no general presumption that changes in the organic composition of capital will be relatively so much greater than changes in the rate of surplus value that the former will dominate movements in the rate of profit. On the contrary, it would seem that we must regard the two variables as of roughly coordinate importance. For this reason Marx's formulation of the law of the falling tendency of the rate of profit is not very convincing.'[73]

Marx was convinced that the recurrence of business cycles was an inescapable feature of capitalism. He wrote: 'The path characteristically described by modern industry . . . takes the form of a decennial cycle . . . of periods of average activity, production at high pressure, crisis and stagnation.'[74] A crisis is that phase of the cycle that marks the turning point between prosperity (marked by low unemployment, rising price levels, rising wage levels, and full order books) and depression (marked by high unemployment, idle plant, reduced orders, and falling prices). Crises are characterized by a sudden outbreak of business failures, insolvencies and a sharp rise in unemployment.

Marx took the cyclical crises to be the clearest proof that capitalism is unable to make full use of productive forces. He wrote in the *Communist Manifesto*: 'For many a decade past, the history of industry and commerce is but the history of the revolt of modern productive forces . . . against the property relations that are the conditions for the existence of the bourgeoisie and of its rule. It is enough to mention the commercial crises that, by their periodic return, put on trial, each time more threateningly, the existence of the entire bourgeois society . . . The productive forces at the disposal of society no longer tend to further the development of the conditions of bourgeois property; on the contrary, they have become too powerful for these conditions by which they are fettered.'[75]

Because of the increasing size, complexity, and interdependence of the capitalist economy, Marx thought that crises were liable to become progressively more severe. He speaks of them recurring on a progressively 'higher scale'.[76]

At various places in his mature economic writings, Marx sought to provide an explanation of why cyclical crises are destined to occur in capitalism. It is possible to identify three different explanations of crises offered by Marx. We now consider each in turn.

Marx's first explanation of crises conceives them to be the effects of insufficient effective demand on the part of workers for the commodities they have produced. Marx writes: 'The ultimate reason for all real crises always remains the poverty and restricted consumption of the masses, in the face of the drive of capitalist production to develop the productive forces as if only the absolute consumption of society set a limit to them.'[77]

This explanation of crises in terms of underconsumption is open to the fatal objection that it is capital-goods industries not consumer-goods industries that are most affected through the phases of the cycle. Were the insufficiency of demand on the part of workers the cause of crises, one would expect fluctuations to be more extreme in the consumer-goods industries. This is not the case, and the explanation of crises in terms of underconsumption cannot explain why this is so.

Marx's second explanation of crises conceives them as the inevitable consequence of the falling rate of profit brought on by the rising organic composition of capital. The fall in the rate of profit is said to deter capitalists from investing. The drop in investment precipitates a slump in the capital-goods industries which widens into a general depression. Crises and depressions lead to the destruction of capital, which brings down the organic composition of capital allowing accumulation to continue at a restored rate of profit. Marx writes: 'The barriers of the capitalist mode of production show themselves . . . in the way that the development of labour productivity involves a law, in the form of the falling rate of profit, that at a certain point confronts this development itself in a most hostile way and has constantly to be overcome by way of crises.'[78]

This explanation of crises is open to three objections. First, Marx fails to establish the existence of the item in terms of which he explains crises – namely, the falling rate of profit. Second, he fails to identify any turning-point mechanism which explains why prosperity gives way at some point to crisis. Third, it is possible for the rate of profit to fall while the mass of profits made by capitalists continues to increase. Marx fails to provide any reason for supposing that capitalists will desist from investing at reduced rates of profit when they can nonetheless continue to make profits.

Marx's third explanation of crises conceives them as the inevitable consequences of reductions in the rate of profit attendant upon rising wage levels that occur during periods of growth. Marx writes: 'There would be an absolute overproduction of capital as soon as no further additional capital could be employed for the purpose of capitalist production. . . Thus as soon as capital has grown in such proportion to the working population that . . . the expanded capital produces only the same mass of surplus value as before . . . there would be . . . [a] sudden fall in the general rate of profit . . . on account of . . . a rise in the money value of the variable capital on account of higher wages . . . One portion of the capital would lie completely . . . idle . . . [This] leads to violent and acute crises.'[79]

Marx would appear to have been somewhat equivocal in his attitude towards this third explanation of crises. Elsewhere he wrote that, because the falling rate of profit is bound up with a tendency for the rate of surplus-value to rise, 'nothing is more absurd . . . than to explain the fall in the rate of profit in terms of a rise in the rate of wages'.[80]

Despite this disclaimer of Marx's, many commentators have

been inclined to regard this third explanation of crises as Marx's most considered opinion on the subject.[81]

This third explanation of crises appears vulnerable to the empirical objection that, in times of prosperity, although wage-levels rise, the rate of profit does not fall. 'The evidence appears to show that the wage share in net output . . . *diminishes*, rather than increases, in a boom.' [82] For example, it has been estimated that, between 1955 and 1970, a period of prosperity, the share of wages and salaries in the UK fell from 55·56 to 50·2 per cent after direct and indirect taxes have been taken into account.[83]

The verdict must be that Marx fails to provide any reason for supposing that business cycles are unavoidable features of capitalism. The possibility remains open that capitalism need not be subject to the business cycle. This would be so were business cycles due to wholly avoidable, externally produced interferences with the workings of the market. This is the contention of the Monetary or Circulation Credit Theory of the Trade Cycle first propounded by Ludwig von Mises in the twentieth century.[84] According to this theory, cyclical crises and the depressions that follow in their wake are the inevitable consequences of preceding booms. These booms, however, are not inevitable. They are produced by wholly avoidable periods of credit expansion. (Banks expand credit as a result of governments and their central banks purchasing assets and thereby increasing bank reserves.) Banks expand credit by lowering the rate of interest below what is called the natural rate of interest. This is the rate of interest that is determined by time-preferences of members of society. The time-preference of an individual is the degree to which the individual prefers a good in the present to the prospect of that good in the future. It is supposed that all individuals have some degree of time-preference in that they prefer present goods to the prospect of those goods in the future. The degree to which individuals prefer present to future goods determines the rate of interest which is charged for the use of money in society.

The expansion of bank credit artificially reduces the rate of interest below the natural rate. As a result, it sends misleading signals to business men. Business ventures appear to become profitable that would only actually be so were members of society to have genuinely reduced their degree of time-preference. As a result of the artificial reduction of interest rates, businessmen behave as if more had genuinely been saved and become available for investment. Production is expanded in the capital-goods industries. The money invested eventually finds its way through to consumers. Because there has been no reduction in time-preference on their part, they rush to spend this money in accordance with their unchanged consumption/savings ratios. There is an increase in demand for consumer goods. The capital goods industries find themselves without purchasers of their products. These firms are only able to stay in business by means of the supply of further credit. Banks may continue to extend credit and thereby prolong the boom. But eventually credit expansion must stop, as there are limits to the ability of banks to expand credit. When the credit expansion stops, interest rates go up and the over-extended capital-goods industries become insolvent. Bankruptcies follow and there are firm closures. This marks the period of depression during which the malinvestments are liquidated. After the structure of production has readjusted itself to the time-preferences of members of society, growth may begin again.

According to this theory, it is credit expansion by the banks that is responsible for the business cycle. By their nature, banks favour expansion of credit since they make profits by making loans. However, there are limits to their ability to extend credit since they must be able to meet all demands for withdrawals. The business cycle would be eliminated, so the theory says, if either fractional reserve banking were prohibited and there was a restoration of the gold standard or free-banking was established. This is a system of banking in which banks are free to make loans beyond their reserves but are not protected by a central bank from insolvency. To date, governments have been in favour of bank credit expansion since this is a politically expedient way of obtaining revenue other than by the unpopular method of taxation.

Marx was not unaware of the role which bank credit expansion plays in the aetiology of crises. He called banking and credit 'the most powerful means for driving capitalist production beyond its own barriers and one of the most effective vehicles for crises'.[85] However, for Marx to have acknowledged bank credit expansion as the sole cause of crises would be for him to have admitted the possibility that crises were not endemic to capitalism. His case for claiming that capitalism fetters the forces of production would have been imperilled. Thus, we find Marx saying that, 'The superficiality of political economy shows itself in the fact that it views the expansion and contraction of credit as the cause of the periodic alternations in the industrial cycle, whereas it is a mere symptom of them.'[86] Our verdict of his treatment of crises must be that he fails to show they cannot be explained simply by means of bank credit expansion. He thus fails to show that crises are endemic to capitalism and has therefore failed to show that capitalism necessarily fetters the forces of production.

5 Politics

1. Marx as Revolutionary

'Marx was before else a revolutionary. His real mission in life was to contribute in one way or another to the overthrow of capitalist society and of the forms of government which it had brought into being, to contribute to the liberation of the present-day proletariat, which he was the first to make conscious of its own position and its needs, of the conditions under which it could win its freedom. Fighting was his element.'[1]

This verdict was delivered at Marx's funeral in March 1883 by his lifelong friend and collaborator, Friedrich Engels. For many people, it expresses the single most important fact about Marx and provides sufficient information for being able to locate Marx in the political spectrum. This is because of the close association that exists in the public mind between revolution and political violence. For many people, and this includes supporters as well as opponents of Marx, a revolutionary is someone who is morally prepared to initiate, or at least is prepared to condone, political violence in pursuit of their favoured political objectives. Mao Tse-tung has, perhaps, given consummate expression to this conception of what is involved in being a revolutionary socialist. He wrote: 'Every Communist must grasp the truth, "Political power grows out of the barrel of a gun." Our principle is that the Party commands the gun . . . [H]aving guns, we can create Party organizations . . . We can also create cadres, create schools, create culture, create mass movements . . . All things grow out of the barrel of a gun.'[2]

A corollary of such a conception of the revolutionary socialist is that, in Western capitalist democracies at least, revolutionary socialists are necessarily in a minority so far as their ultimate objectives are concerned. For, if the majority of members of such societies were in favour of the same political objectives as those favoured by the revolutionaries, these objectives would be achieved by means of the ballot box. There would then be no need for recourse to political violence in furtherance of them. Associated in the public mind with the idea of revolutionary socialism, therefore, is the image of a small band of dedicated individuals ready to impose their will by force if necessary upon a majority that is unsympathetic to their goals. They are further thought to be prepared to maintain themselves in political power whilst still a minority until, by means of mass indoctrination, they have been able to engineer majority acquiescence and support for their policies.

Does this image of what is involved in being a revolutionary socialist offer a fair representation of Marx? Was he in favour of the promotion of socialism by means of political violence even in so-called bourgeois democracies? Was he in favour of coups by small bands of dedicated socialists who would establish communism by means of force, if necessary in defiance of the will of the majority?

Certainly there have been those who have thought so. (Most notably, Stanley Moore has contended that 'From the beginning of 1844, when Marx and Engels announced their conversion to communism, until the end of 1850, when they faced the fact that the crisis of 1848 was over, their revolutionary tactics were primarily influenced by the tradition of Babeuf, Buonarotti, and Blanqui.')[3]

Nor is there a lack of *prima facie* evidence in support of such a view. No fewer than five separate sets of considerations may be advanced in support of the contention that Marx favoured the promotion of socialism by means of a violent revolution to be carried out by a small number of dedicated revolutionaries, if necessary in defiance of the majority. First, there is Marx's membership of and activity within the Communist League between its creation in 1847 and its demise in 1852. The Communist League was a body of never more than between two and three hundred dedicated communist revolutionaries. It was born out of the merger between Marx's followers in the Brussels Communist

Corresponding Committee, established by Marx in 1846 as a propaganda group, and the older, conspiratorial League of the Just. This was a secret conspiratorial body, formed in 1836, whose leaders had taken part in Blanqui's abortive attempted insurrection in Paris in 1839. If there is such a thing as guilt by association, then Marx may, on one construction of the evidence, be deemed guilty of favouring minority revolution at least between 1847 and 1850, the period during which he was actively involved in the Communist League.

Second, during this same period Marx advocated for industrially and politically backward Germany a policy of what he called *permanent revolution*. This consisted in first supporting the bourgeoisie in their struggle for political rights against the reactionary, aristocratic powers, and then turning against the bourgeoisie, after they had gained them, to pursue the goal of socialism. Given that Germany was economically backward at the time, if the call for permanent revolution in that country is taken literally, this must mean that Marx favoured minority rule by the proletariat in the second stage of the revolution, since they would still have been a numerical minority.

Third, on a number of occasions during this period, Marx advocated the use of revolutionary violence against opponents of the revolution.

Fourth, in 1850, following his expulsion from Prussia in the wake of the successful counter-revolution, Marx entered into a formal alliance with the Blanquists, who favoured a forcible revolution to be carried out by a small minority. In April 1850, Marx became a founder member of the Universal Society of Revolutionary Communists. There were only six members of this secret society, two of whom were followers of Blanqui and another being Willich, who also favoured minority revolution.

Finally, there is the fact that, beginning in 1850, Marx called on a number of occasions for 'the dictatorship of the proletariat'. This phrase suggests that Marx favoured a form of rule that tolerated no opposition and that involved the imposition of the will of a minority. For, if the majority were in favour of socialism, why did they need dictatorship?

Together, these five sets of considerations do much to confirm the picture of Marx until 1850 as a communist who favoured forcible minority revolution. Closer examination of Marx's political activity during this period reveals, however, a very different picture of Marx the revolutionary, as we shall now see. The account that follows of Marx's politics during his period of association with the Communist League owes much to the first volume of Richard Hunt's monumental two-volume study, *Political Ideas of Marx and Engels*. The subsequent discussion of Marx's conception of the prospects for a peaceful transition to socialism and his conception of the post-revolutionary polity owes much to Hunt's second volume.

2. The Communist League

Marx became a member of the League of the Just in February or March 1847. In June of that year, the League of the Just held a congress in London (at which Marx was not present). This renamed the organization 'The Communist League', and reconstituted itself upon a more democratic basis. Shortly after, the Brussels Communist Corresponding Committee which Marx had established as a propaganda agency in 1846 transformed itself into the Brussels branch of the Communist League.

It is true that the League of the Just had been initially formed in 1836 as a conspiratorial society of German artisans. It is also true that its original leaders, William Weitling, Karl Schapper and Heinrich Bauer, had taken part in Blanqui's abortive coup of 1839. On the other hand, it is false that, by joining the League of the Just, Marx showed himself to have acquired conspiratorial leanings. It is equally false that the Communist League which grew out of the League of the Just was conspiratorial in nature. This is because, between 1836 and 1847, the League of the Just had abandoned its original conspiratorial character and assumed a purely propagandist function. Indeed, its having changed in this manner was a condition of Marx and Engels joining it. By the time of the Congress of June 1847, the leadership of the League had for some time been converted to Marx's view that the communist revolution, at least in Germany, lay in the future, and that it could only come about when the majority of the population had been led by economic circumstances to favour communism. The Communist League held another congress in London in November 1847 (at which Marx was present). At this second congress, Marx and Engels were mandated by the delegates to draft the programme of the League. The product of this request was the *Communist Manifesto*, which was almost entirely Marx's own work; he completed it at the end of January 1848.

Marx's motivation for joining the League of the Just when he did was not, therefore, that he wished to participate in a communist conspiracy along Blanquist lines. Rather, it was that, having formulated the essential tenets of historical materialism in 1845–6, Marx wished to propagate the doctrine as widely as possible in working-class circles – and particularly amongst German workers. The League of the Just was the most well-established working-class organization in Europe, for the Communist Corresponding Committee which Marx had founded in Brussels had failed to grow as Marx had hoped it would. If it is a misconception to think of the Communist League as having been a conspiratorial body preparing to carry out an insurrection, it is an equal mistake to think of it as having been a vanguard party of the type favoured for communist parties by Lenin. Although Lenin believed that a revolution was impossible without mass support for it, he believed that a party of dedicated full-time and highly disciplined members, whose numbers were deliberately kept small, was necessary in order for successful revolution to be possible. He thought this for two reasons: first, left to itself, so he argued, the working class could never develop beyond what he called 'trade union consciousness'. That is, they would never go beyond making demands for economic improvements within the capitalist framework. Second, a vanguard party was necessary in Lenin's eyes for carrying out the actual seizure of power at the precise historically correct moment: namely, when mass discontent was at its greatest. In these two vital respects, the Communist League was envisaged by Marx as something other than a vanguard party of the Leninist kind. First, Marx thought that communist class consciousness would spontaneously develop amongst the working class by force of economic circumstances. Second, Marx believed that the downfall of the government would be engineered by historical circumstance rather than by a deliberate plot by the Communist League.

Two facts bear out the thesis that Marx did not envisage the Communist League as a vanguard party of the Leninist type. First, after revolution broke out in Germany in March 1848, Marx sought to expand the membership and branches of the Communist League throughout Germany – without success as it turned out. Second, after Marx had acquired a mouthpiece for addressing German progressive opinion in 1848, in the form of editorship of the *Neue Rheinische Zeitung* which Marx started to edit in Cologne in June 1848, he formally dissolved the Communist League. He did not rejoin it, after it reformed in London in 1848 without Marx's approval, until March 1849. This was when he arrived in London following his expulsion from Prussia that had been ordered in the wake of the successful counter-revolution there. Further, had Marx envisaged the Communist League to have the indispensable role marked out for the vanguard party as conceived by Lenin, he would not have allowed it to dissolve so easily as he did in 1852 following the Cologne Conspiracy Trial of the Communist League.

3. Permanent Revolution

The *Communist Manifesto* predicted imminent revolution in Europe and declared that 'the Communists everywhere support every revolutionary movement against the existing social and political order of things'.[4] However, the revolutions that it envisaged as about to take place were not conceived in the *Communist Manifesto* as being everywhere the same. In industrially and politically advanced England, the forthcoming revolution predicted by the *Communist Manifesto* would be a proletarian revolution the immediate object of which was the establishing of communism. By contrast, the revolution that was predicted as about to take place in economically and politically backward Germany was to be a revolution against an autocracy in order to establish a bourgeois oligarchy such as already existed in England and France. In Germany, Marx declared that the communists were initially to fight together on the same side as the bourgeoisie against the absolute monarchy and feudal squirearchy. When the bourgeoisie had achieved the political dominance that would enable it to bring about the legal and economic conditions necessary for the unfettered development of capitalist industry in Germany, the communists must then turn against their former allies and press for their own more radical demands. In the *Communist Manifesto*, Marx says of Germany that it is 'on the eve of a bourgeois revolution' and that 'the bourgeois revolution in Germany will be but the prelude to an immediately following proletarian revolution'[5].

If Marx had literally meant that the proletarian revolution would begin the moment the bourgeoisie had successfully accomplished its political revolution, then Marx would necessarily have had in mind for the communists a minority revolution. This is because industrial capitalism was still undeveloped in Germany. The proletariat would only have been in a numerical minority as compared with other social classes, most notably, peasants and petty-bourgeoisie, that is, the self-employed tradesmen and craftsmen. Richard Hunt, however, persuasively argues[6] that Marx did not mean this phrase literally. Rather, what Marx had in mind for Germany was something altogether different. After the bourgeoisie had come to power, Marx envisages that the proletariat would enter into an alliance with the peasants and the petty-bourgeoisie. They would then campaign on behalf of a range of political and economic measures that would *gradually* move society in a socialist direction. Throughout this period, capitalist industry was envisaged as continuing. Capitalism thereby would bring about the development of the material conditions (large-scale industry) that alone could make communism possible in Germany. The political programme on which the proletariat would campaign in its alliance with the petty-bourgeoisie and peasantry was set out in the 'Demands of the Communist Party in Germany'. This document was composed by Marx and Engels in Paris in the last week of March 1848. Earlier that month there had taken place in Germany what Marx mistakenly believed had been a successful bourgeois revolution. These demands included universal suffrage, the abolition of feudal dues which had been a severe burden on the peasantry, and restrictions on the right of inheritance. It is notable that these demands did *not* include the socialization of the means of production. Further, the implementation of the Seventeen Demands could not but be expected to take a considerable amount of time. It was only after industry had developed to the point where the proletariat had become the majority that full communism would be possible. The 'immediately following proletarian revolution' predicted for Germany in the *Communist Manifesto* was intended by Marx to refer to a drawn-out period during which the proletariat would campaign on behalf of the Seventeen Demands. Marx was led to use deliberately ambiguous language in the *Communist Manifesto* when describing the revolution that was predicted for Germany in order to smooth over disagreements between his followers in the Communist League and the artisan former members of the League of the Just. These latter believed that Germany would undergo only one revolution – namely, a democratic one that would immediately introduce communism there regardless of the state of readiness of the productive forces. Each side in this dispute could interpret the expression 'immediately following proletarian revolution' according to its own predilections.

Marx's behaviour between 1847 and 1848 bears out the thesis that he never envisaged for Germany a literal proletarian revolution immediately following upon the heels of the bourgeois revolution.

Upon his return to Germany in 1848, Marx dissolved the Communist League, and joined instead the Cologne Democratic Society which was a petty-bourgeois organization. In June 1848, Marx also joined the Rhenish District Committee of Democrats which had been set up with the object of establishing an alliance between the proletariat members of the Cologne Workers' Party and the petty-bourgeois democrats of the Cologne Democratic Society. It is true that in April 1849, Marx and Engels resigned from these two associations and endeavoured to create independent proletarian organizations. However, they still sought to retain an alliance with the petty-bourgeois democrats.

The revolution in Germany of 1848 failed to achieve any significant gains for the bourgeoisie. Yet for at least the first part of 1850 Marx still continued to believe that a new revolution was imminent in Germany. He believed the new revolution would be precipitated either by a new rising of the proletariat in France or by an invasion of France by the Holy Alliance. In March 1850, Marx and Engels issued an 'Address of the Central Committee to the Communist League'. The 'March Address' as it has become known sets out what the policy should be of members of the reconstituted Communist League in the conditions of the anticipated new revolution. The Address states that in this new revolution the part that had been played by the bourgeoisie in the March Revolution would be played by the petty-bourgeoisie. Marx may be assumed to have included here the peasants whose interests he took to be similar to those of the petty-bourgeoisie. The policy of the communists should be cooperation with the petty-bourgeoisie in their fight against the autocracy, and opposition to the petty-bourgeoisie 'wherever they wish to secure their own position'.[7] The Address states: 'While the democratic petty-bourgeois want to bring the revolution to an end as quickly as possible . . . , it is our interest and our task to make the revolution permanent until all the more or less propertied classes have been driven from their ruling positions, until the proletariat has conquered state power and until the association of the proletarians has progressed sufficiently far – not only in one country but in all the leading countries of the world – that . . . at least the decisive forces of production are concentrated in the hands of the workers.'[8]

Tactics were spelled out for the members of the Communist League: They were to create their own separate workers' party. They were to make sure that the proletariat did not disarm. And they were to help maintain worker-controlled local councils or workers' clubs that would exert pressure on the bourgeois democratic governments.

The tactics that are prescribed by Marx in the March Address certainly sound as if Marx was condoning something approaching minority rule by the proletariat. However, the matter is not as straightforward as that. This is because the Address also says that '[t]he German workers cannot come to power and achieve the realization of their class interests without passing through a protracted revolutionary development'.[9] This suggests that Marx had in mind a lengthy period between the time the petty-bourgeoisie came to power and the time the proletariat did. That this was, indeed, what Marx envisaged is borne out by the testimony of P. G. Röser who in 1854 reported having received a letter from Marx in July 1850. In this letter, Röser said, Marx asserted that in Germany 'communism could be introduced only after a series of years, that it must pass through several phases, and that it could be introduced at all only by way of education and gradual development'.[10]

Röser's testimony goes on to relate that Marx wrote that he had been strongly opposed on this issue by his rival, Willich, and the latter's followers in the Communist League. They, by contrast, Marx said in the letter, had maintained that communism must be introduced in the next revolution even if it required the power of the guillotine and 'against the will of all Germany if need be'. As in the case of Marx's talk in the *Communist Manifesto* of an immediately following proletarian revolution, Marx's talk in the March Address of making the revolution permanent was intended to mask the rifts between the Willich faction in the League and Marx's own followers. In the event the gulf between Willich and his followers and Marx and his followers proved too great on this issue, and the League split in September 1850. The occasion of this split was a meeting of the Central Committee on 15 September 1850. The minutes of this meeting lend support to the view that Marx did not conceive of permanent revolution as an immediate proletarian uprising and minority rule. At this meeting, the minutes state, Marx said of the Willich position, which it will be recalled favoured immediate proletarian revolution, that it directly contradicted the March Address. Marx then went on to adumbrate his own position in these words: 'We [Marx and his followers] tell the workers: If you want to change conditions and make yourselves capable of government, you will have to undergo fifteen, twenty or fifty years of civil [class] war.'[11] This declaration by Marx suggests that when he had previously spoken of 'permanent revolution' he had a much lengthier process in mind than that which one might naturally associate with this phrase.

Further evidence that Marx was not in favour of an immediate proletarian revolution following a successful bourgeois revolution is provided by a letter from Marx to Engels written in February 1851. In this letter, Marx wrote that he was glad the split had occurred between himself and Willich, since both he and Engels were now free of 'the system of mutual concessions, the halfway positions tolerated for decency's sake'. This statement bears out the thesis that it was never Marx's real view that the proletariat should seek to establish minority rule in the revolution that the March Address was predicting.

4. Advocacy of Red Terror

On two separate occasions as editor of the *Neue Rheinische Zeitung*, Marx was to speak in approving tones of red terror. The first of these occasions was in November 1848 in an article entitled 'Victory of the Counter-Revolution in Vienna'. He wrote: 'The pointless massacres since the June and October days, the tedious sacrificial feast since February and March, the cannibalism of the counter-revolution itself, all these things will convince the peoples that there is only one way of *shortening*, simplifying and concentrating the murderous death-pangs of the old society, the bloody birth-pangs of the new, only *one way – revolutionary terrorism*.'[12]

The second occasion was in the final issue of the paper on 19 May 1849 after it had been ordered to close by the authorities. Marx wrote: 'We have no compassion and we ask no compassion from you. When our turn comes, we shall not make excuses for the terror.'[13]

There is no way in which these passages can be claimed to express anything other than Marx's own sentiments. However, it is to be noted that these passages predict red terror in the future. Neither amounts to direct incitement to immediate terroristic acts. Indeed, in the final issue of the *Neue Rheinische Zeitung*, Marx warned the workers against attempting an uprising in Cologne. Also, in the case of both these passages, Marx is invoking red terror in retaliation against counter-revolutionary force that had been exercised against workers. Marx never countenanced the use of revolutionary violence in conditions of bourgeois democracy, as we shall see below.

5. Alliance with the Blanquists

In April 1850, Marx and Engels became founder members of a secret society with four other people. These were Willich, Julian Henry, a Chartist leader, and two lieutenants of Blanqui's – Jules Vidil and Adam. The society was called the Universal Society of Revolutionary Communists. The statutes of this society begin: 'The aim of the association is the downfall of all the privileged classes, to subject these classes to the dictatorship of the proletarians by maintaining the revolution in permanence until the achievement of communism.' The society was in existence for six months until it was dissolved by Marx's dissociating himself from it. There is no record of any decisions having been taken by it.

Does it follow from his alliance with Blanquists in 1850 when he joined this society that Marx had come to subscribe to minority revolution as was favoured by Blanqui, or that Marx was now opposed to universal suffrage as Blanqui had been in 1848? The answer to these questions would appear to be negative. There is a perfectly convincing explanation of why Marx would have wished to establish contact with Blanquists in the first part of 1850 without having to suppose that he had suddenly come to favour Blanquist tactics. The explanation is that, owing to the prohibition of demonstrations in France that was in force at the time, the only revolutionary political organizations possible were secret societies. Such societies invariably happened to be Blanquist in character. Since, at the time, Marx believed that a fresh outbreak of revolution was imminent in France, and since he may be presumed to have wished to be able to play a part in this revolution, he had no option but to have dealings with the Blanquists.

That Marx was not in favour of Blanquist tactics during the short lifetime of the Universal Society of Revolutionary Communists is borne out by what Marx said about Blanquist-style revolutionaries at the time in a book review which Marx composed and published in May 1850. The review was of two books about the French Revolution of 1848 that had been published in 1850. The authors of these two books were former police-spies,

A. Chenu and Lucien de La Hodde. In the review, Marx made it clear that he absolutely abhorred the conspiratorial revolutionaries fashioned in the Blanquist mould. He wrote of such professional conspirators that 'these conspirators do not confine themselves to the general organizing of the revolutionary proletariat. It is precisely their business to anticipate the process of revolutionary development, to bring it artificially to crisis-point, to launch a revolution on the spur of the moment, without the conditions for a revolution . . . They are the alchemists of the revolution and are characterized by exactly the same chaotic thinking and blinkered obsessions as the alchemists of old. They leap at inventions which are supposed to work revolutionary miracles: incendiary bombs, destructive devices of magic effect, revolts which are expected to be all the more miraculous and astonishing in effect as their basis is less rational. Occupied with such scheming, they have no other purpose than the most immediate one of overthrowing the existing government and have the profoundest contempt for the more theoretical enlightenment of the proletariat about their class interests . . . To the extent that the Paris proletariat came to the fore itself as a party, these conspirators lost some of their dominant influence, they were dispersed and they encountered dangerous competition in proletarian secret societies, whose purpose was not immediate insurrection but the organization and development of the proletariat.'[14] This quotation shows clearly that Marx never embraced Blanquism in 1850 (assuming it represents Marx's sincere position).

Shortly after this review was published, Marx became convinced that the economic crisis had passed which alone made revolution a genuine possibility. As he wrote in Part Four of *Class Struggles in France: 1848–1850* composed at this time: 'While this general prosperity lasts, enabling the productive forces of bourgeois society to develop to the full extent possible within the bourgeois system, there can be no question of a real revolution. Such a revolution is only possible at a time when *two factors* come into conflict: *the modern productive forces and the bourgeois form of production . . . . A new revolution is only possible as a result of a new crisis; but it will come, just as surely as the crisis itself.*'[15]

This verdict of Marx's meant that continued association on the part of Marx with the Blanquists no longer had any point. Marx accordingly pulled out of the Universal Society of Revolutionary Communists, which led to the demise of the society.

6. Dictatorship of the Proletariat

Marx's view of why communism is historically inevitable in capitalism, at bottom, is that the logic of capitalism necessarily reduces the mass of workers to a state of dire poverty as proletariat. The economic plight of the masses would impel them to rise up to overthrow the political and economic institutions responsible for their destitution.

Communism, in Marx's view, was to be created by the majority of members of society. This was because, in an advanced capitalist society, the majority of members have become proletarians. As the *Communist Manifesto* puts it: 'The proletarian movement is the self-conscious, independent movement of the immense majority.'[16] The first step in the revolutionary process of the creation of communism was the establishment of universal suffrage. This is because it would bring about proletarian rule. (Marx was thinking here of advanced capitalist countries like England and not economically backward countries like Germany where the proletariat was still in a minority.) Thus, the *Communist Manifesto* states: 'The first step in the revolution by the working class is to raise the proletariat to the position of ruling class, to win the battle of democracy.'[17] Universal suffrage establishes proletarian rule. This is because the proletariat are envisaged as forming the vast majority of the population, and are, also, envisaged by this time as having acquired class consciousness, that is, consciousness that their interests lay in the establishment of communism.

The form of government with which Marx associated mature capitalism was not democracy but oligarchy, such as existed in England in the first half of the nineteenth century. Prior to the extension of the franchise to workers that occurred in England after the 1867 Reform Act, Marx envisaged that resort to force would be necessary, first, to establish universal suffrage, and then to defend the socialistic measures that would flow from it against the attempted minority bourgeois counter-revolution that Marx anticipated as being likely. The communist revolution, however, even though resorting to force, was democratic in character, since it was seeking to establish democracy.

It is *prima facie* puzzling, however, why, if Marx envisaged the proletarian revolution to be a majority undertaking, he should have chosen to call the form of rule that would immediately follow upon successful proletarian revolution a *dictatorship* of the proletariat. If, as Marx foresaw it, the revolution was to be carried out – or, at least, was to be supported – by the vast majority of members of society, why would the first form of post-revolution government be a dictatorship? Could it be that, in using the expression, Marx is betraying his conviction that communism was something that would have to be imposed on society by a minority of class-conscious proletarians without the active support of the majority?

In order to appreciate what Marx meant by the expression 'dictatorship of the proletariat', it is necessary to understand the history of the concept of dictatorship.

The term 'dictatorship' derives from the Latin word 'dictatura' which referred to a temporary form of one-man rule for which the Roman Republican Constitution made provision in times of emergency, such as war. The powers of the dictator were strictly limited by the constitution. Thus, for instance, the dictator could suspend laws but could neither enact nor repeal them. This was how the term 'dictatorship' was understood until the French Revolution of 1789. At this time, its meaning was to undergo a change. During the course of the French Revolution, dictatorship was to be called for a number of times by the Jacobins, Saint-Just and Marat, and by the extreme Jacobin, Babeuf. In the case of the former two, what they had in mind was an emergency temporary government with wide powers that would safeguard the gains of the revolution. Babeuf called for a 'dictatorship of the insurrection'. What he had in mind was strictly temporary rule by a small group of enlightened followers who were to establish a society of strict equality and who would maintain themselves in power until the masses had been educated to accept such a form of society.

Marx did not come to use the term 'dictatorship' to refer to rule by the proletariat until 1850. He was to use the expression 'dictatorship of the proletariat' only a comparatively few times thereafter. However, Marx had previously come to use the term 'dictatorship' frequently to refer to forms of rule in revolutionary situations. This usage occurs in his articles written in the *Neue Rheinische Zeitung* in 1848. However, Marx was not the first to do so at the time. The French National Assembly in 1848 had invested General Cavaignac with a 'commissioned dictatorship' to restore law and order in Paris as unrest built up prior to the June uprising of workers. Mostly in his writings in the *Neue Rheinische Zeitung*, Marx used the term to refer to counter-revolutionary military leaders such as Cavaignac. However, Marx also used the term 'dictatorship' in a purely descriptive sense which provides the clue to understanding his use of the term to apply to the rule of the proletariat after the revolution. In September 1848, Marx wrote an article about Germany entitled 'Crisis and the Counter-Revolution'. In it Marx called for more resolute action by the Prussian National Assembly in appointing officials. He wrote: 'Every state which finds itself in a provisional situation after a revolution requires a dictator, an energetic dictator at that. We attacked Camphausen [liberal Prime Minister of Prussia between March and July 1848] from the beginning for failing to act dictatorially, for failing to destroy and remove the remnants of the old institutions immediately.'[18] Such action as Marx was here calling for on the part of the Prussian National Assembly was conceived by Marx to be both democratic *and* dictatorial. It would be democratic, since the Prussian National Assembly had been democratically elected. It would be dictatorial, because it would be strictly temporary, extra-legal action by a government prior to the adoption of a new constitution and the establishment of a new legality. It was such a notion of democratic, extra-legal (that is, unconstitutional) temporary government that Marx had in mind in speaking of the dictatorship of the proletariat. There is no suggestion that Marx understood by the expression anything other than provisional government by a democratically elected assembly prior to the formal adoption of a new socialist constitution.

7. The Parliamentary Road to Socialism

Contrary to much popular opinion, Marx did not believe that violent revolution was the only way in which capitalism could be supplanted by communism. His view was that revolutionary violence was neither historically necessary nor desirable where parliamentary democracy had been established. Marx wrote in 1852: 'Universal suffrage is the equivalent of political power for the working class of England.'[19] This was an opinion which Marx was never to abandon. In 1871, Marx was interviewed by a reporter for the *New York World*. When asked where he stood on the issue of bloody revolutions, Marx replied: 'In England . . . the way to show political power lies open to the working class. Insurrection would be madness where peaceful agitation would more swiftly and surely do the work.'[20]

Again, in September 1872, at a speech on the Hague Congress of the International Workingman's Association which had just ended, Marx said: 'The workers will have to seize political power one day in order to construct the new organization of labour; they will have to overthrow the old politics which bolster up the old institutions . . . We do not claim, however, that the road leading to this goal is the same everywhere . . . We know that heed must be paid to the institutions, customs and traditions of the various countries, and we do not deny that there are countries, such as America and England, and if I was familiar with its institutions, I might include Holland, where the workers may attain their goal by peaceful means. That being the case, we must recognize that in most continental countries the lever of the revolution will have to be force; a resort to force will be necessary one day in order to set up the rule of labour.'[21]

The last quotation invites the question: why did Marx think peaceful revolution possible in the United States and England, and possibly Holland, but not in France and Germany?

Lenin maintained that the difference between these countries at the time of Marx's speech was that the United States and England both lacked, whereas France and Germany both possessed, large military-bureaucratic state apparatuses. It was the absence of such an apparatus that rendered peaceful revolution possible. Since both the United States and England subsequently came to acquire such apparatuses after the 1870s, peaceful revolution had become ruled out for these countries.

Richard Hunt in the second volume of the *Political Ideas of Marx and Engels* has provided a powerful refutation of Lenin's interpretation of Marx on this issue. Hunt argues that, if England had not yet acquired a developed military-bureaucratic apparatus by 1872, she would equally not have possessed one still earlier. Yet it was only after the 1867 Reform Act which gave the vote to workers that Marx began to take seriously the idea of a peaceful progression to socialism in Britain. Hunt's view, which makes far better sense than Lenin's of what Marx said, is that Marx associated the possibility of peaceful revolution with democratic institutions: universal suffrage *plus* a democratically controlled executive, and political freedoms such as freedom of the press and of assembly.

This is not to say that Marx was altogether optimistic about the prospects of a peaceful transition to socialism in countries like England. This was because he believed that a genuinely socialist government that had been democratically elected to office would be likely to spark off minority bourgeois rebellion if and when the government attempted to put through a genuine socialist programme.

As Marx was to say in his *New York World* interview: 'The English middle class has always shown itself willing enough to accept the verdict of the majority so long as it enjoyed the monopoly of the voting power. But mark me, as soon as it finds itself outvoted on what it considers vital questions we shall see here a new slave-owners' war.'[22]

Still, there was no clear reason to suppose that bourgeois rebellion against an elected socialist government is inevitable. So Marx must be considered to have endorsed the possibility and desirability of peaceful, parliamentary transitions to socialism.

Marx rather took for granted the view that the working class in an advanced capitalist society would be socialist in political persuasion. This was undoubtedly because he believed that they would inevitably suffer increasing immiseration as capitalism developed. Because this has not happened, Marx failed to foresee, apart from any other mistakes he may have made, that socialist class consciousness is not an inevitable development in capitalism. It is from an acceptance of this fact that Lenin and his followers were obliged to introduce the idea of a vanguard party who were supposed to introduce socialism to the masses from without.

8. The Post-Revolutionary Polity

In order to appreciate what Marx has to say about the form of political association in the post-capitalist society, it is necessary to consider his view of the state. The most famous statements of Marx about the state are those which occur in the *Communist Manifesto*. There, he writes: 'The executive of the modern state is but a committee for managing the common affairs of the whole bourgeoisie.'[23] And 'Political power, properly so called, is merely the organized power of one class for oppressing another.'[24] These and other statements like them portray the state as an instrument of class rule. The state is conceived of as a device for ensuring that the class whose members own the means of production continue to do so. This is how Marx conceived of the state in ancient Greece and Rome, in feudalism, and in the capitalist England of the first half of the nineteenth century.

With the state so conceived, it was also thought that, after the revolution, the proletariat would take control of the institutions of the state to effect and maintain their seizure of the means of production. With the socialization of the means of production and the consequent abolition of social classes, the state loses its *raison d'être*, and so eventually disappears as a coercive agency. After the revolution, the state would be needed to secure and enforce the workers' control of the means of production. When classes antagonistic to the workers were no longer in existence, the need for the state disappeared.

As both Ralph Miliband[25] and Richard Hunt have pointed out, Marx had a second conception of the state besides this instrumentalist conception of the state. Or, rather, Marx had a conception of a different sort of state. This second conception or theory of the state is what Hunt calls the *theory of the state as parasite*. The classic instances of such a form of state in Marx's view were Oriental despotism, absolutism and the Bonapartist State of the Second Empire. In his account of Louis Napoleon's rise to power as emperor of France, Marx provides a classic description of the modern parasite state as well as offering an account of its historical origin: 'The executive power possesses an immense bureaucratic and military organization, an ingenious and broadly based state machinery, and an army of half a million officials alongside the actual army, which numbers a further half million. This frightful parasitic body, which surrounds the body of French society like a caul and stops up all its pores, arose in the time of the absolute monarchy, with the decay of the feudal system, which it helped to accelerate. The seigneurial privileges of the landowners and towns were transformed into attributes of the state power, the feudal dignitaries became paid officials, and the variegated medieval pattern of conflicting plenary authorities became the regulated plan of a state authority characterized by a centralization and division of labour reminiscent of a factory. The task of the first French revolution was to destroy all separate local, territorial, urban and provincial powers in order to create the civil unity of the nation . . . Napoleon perfected this state machinery. The Legitimist and July monarchies only added a greater division of labour . . . Every *common* interest was immediately detached from society, opposed to it as a higher, *general* interest, torn away from the self-activity of the individual members of society and made a subject for governmental activity, whether it was a bridge, a schoolhouse, the communal property of a village community, or the railways, the national wealth and the national university of France. Finally, the parliamentary republic was compelled in its struggle against the revolution to strengthen by means of repressive measures the resources and centralization of governmental power. All political upheavals perfected this machine instead of smashing it . . .

'However, under the absolute monarchy, during the first French revolution, and under Napoleon, bureaucracy was only the means of preparing the class rule of the bourgeoisie . . . Only under the second Bonaparte does the state seem to have attained a completely autonomous position.'[26]

Thus, we find two conceptions of the state in Marx: first, the state as coercive force for the maintenance of the domination of a certain class against other classes. Second, the state as a parasitical body of professional bureaucrats and military. It is important to bear this twofold understanding of the state in mind in considering Marx's remarks about the political form society would assume after the revolution.

Marx's most extended discussion of the post-revolutionary political form of association is in his account of the Paris Commune in his *Civil War in France* (1871). This was an address which Marx was commissioned to compose in April 1871 by the General Council of the International Workingman's Association. This latter body was a loose federation of European and American workingmen's associations which was set up in London in 1864, and which lasted until 1876. Between the years 1864 and 1872, Marx was to play a leading role in this organization. It was the publication of the address in May 1871 which was finally to bring Marx international recognition and fame as 'the red terror doctor'.

The Paris Commune was the name given to the short-lived municipal council of Paris. It was named after its predecessor in the first French Revolution. The 1871 Paris Commune was set up by the Central Committee of the National Guard, the citizens' militia of Paris, which organized elections to the Commune. During its brief existence between 26 March and 29 May 1871, the Paris Commune was under military siege and then attack by the French national army. The rift between the central government and Paris originally arose as a result of a refusal on the part of the Parisian National Guard to surrender its arms to the central government following the French defeat by Prussia in the Franco-Prussian War. The Paris Commune was finally brutally crushed by the French army with 14,000 Parisian workers slaughtered by the French troops and another 10,000 deported or imprisoned.

Marx's account of the Paris Commune is particularly important as a source for understanding his conception of the form of political life after the revolution. This is because in the *Civil War in France*, Marx said of the Paris Commune that 'it was essentially a working-class government . . . the political form at last discovered under which to work out the economical emancipation of labour.'[27]

The essence of Marx's conception of the post-revolutionary polity is that the state as *parasite*, as separate bureaucratic-military apparatus manned by professionals, is smashed within a very short space of time: in the case of the Paris Commune, according to Marx, it was smashed within weeks. The basic mechanism for smashing the parasite state is by what Richard Hunt called the '*radical deprofessionalization of public life*'. The standing army is to be replaced by a part-time National Guard made up of ordinary citizens called up for strictly temporary duty. All governmental functions – legislative, executive and judicial – were to be carried out by democratically elected appointees responsible and revocable at short term, and paid no more than ordinary workmen's wages. 'The vested interests and the representation allowances of the high dignitaries of state disappeared along with the high dignitaries themselves. Public functions ceased to be the private property of the tools of the central government.'[28]

Marx envisaged that the radically deprofessionalized political institutions adopted by the Paris Commune would be copied elsewhere throughout France. A national legislature and executive were to be created on the same basis. Marx wrote: 'The Paris Commune was, of course, to serve as a model to all the great industrial centres of France . . . The commune was to be the political form of even the smallest country hamlet . . . The few but important functions which would still remain for a central government . . . were to be discharged by Communal, and therefore strictly responsible agents.'[29]

In contrast with what occurs in bourgeois democracies, in the proletarian democracy, all who engaged in public affairs, including judges, police and administrators, were to be elected. There is no scope for professional political careerism, since public officials receive no more than ordinary wages, and excutive tasks are to be discharged by committees rather than by single individuals. The membership of these committees was to be drawn from the legislative body. This is what Marx meant by the somewhat cryptic statement that 'The Commune was to be a working, not a parliamentary body, executive and legislative at the same time.'[30] He is here alluding to the fact that two thirds of the members of the Commune served on executive committees.

In the post-revolutionary polity, therefore, there is to be the maximum democratization of public life. So much for what Marx believed and hoped would become of the state as parasite.

As regards the state as organized coercive force, this, Marx believed, would gradually fade away as and when the need for a National Guard disappeared. The National Guard was needed to defend the workers' polity against the possibility of counter-revolution by the bourgeois opponents of the workers' state. Since, in time, bourgeois opposition to the workers' state would disappear, so would the need for a National Guard. Marx did not really envisage the need for a defence force to protect the workers' polity against hostile states. The reason why he failed to do so was because he judged that the advanced capitalist countries would all undergo the transition to communism at approximately the same time. Together, they would be too powerful to be threatened by external powers. It may even be supposed that Marx thought that eventually the need for a police force and judiciary would disappear. This is because individual citizens would eventually so internalize the rules and so strongly identify themselves with the collectivity that all anti-social and criminal acts would cease. People would abide by the decisions and rules of the legislative body of a communist polity for the same sort of reason as individuals are willing to abide by the decisions of the democratically elected leaders of any voluntary associations to which they belong. Thus, in Hegel's language, the state would eventually be *aufgehoben* or transcended both as parasite and as coercive body.

It is worth remembering that, in the initial phases of the workers' state, Marx acknowledges the right to peaceful opposition by the bourgeoisie. Talk of 'dictatorship of the proletariat' suggests that Marx would not have tolerated a political opposition in a workers' state. But this is wrong for the following reasons. First, Marx was willing to call the Paris Commune a workers' state despite the election to the Commune of a bourgeois opposition group. Second, the draft Programme of the French Workers'

Party, drawn up by Marx and Engels together with Paul Lafargue and Jules Guesde in May 1880, includes a demand for the right of free expression of opinion and the right of association and assembly. Third, the political organizations to which Marx belonged, the Communist League and the International Workingman's Association, were internally democratic, and gave ordinary members the freedom to criticize leaders and to campaign to remove them from office by majority vote. Fourth, in his first draft for the *Civil War in France*, which was composed at a time when Marx believed that the Commune would spread throughout France, Marx made an assertion which suggests that he assumed that there would be a legal bourgeois opposition. He wrote: 'The commune does not do away with the class struggles, through which the working classes strive to the abolition of all classes . . . but it affords the rational medium in which that class struggle can run through its different phases in the most rational and humane way.'[31]

Richard Hunt suggests that what Marx is referring to in this passage is the existence of a legal bourgeois opposition. Should, however, the bourgeoisie resort to violent opposition to the socialist measures initiated by the workers' state, martial law would be declared, liberties of association and speech would be suspended, and there would be a reversion to dictatorship of the proletariat while the undemocratic insurrection was crushed.

Assuming it to be correct to say that Marx found room for a legal bourgeois opposition party in the workers' state, Marx differs from Lenin who, in 'State and Revolution', wrote: 'Democracy for the vast majority of the people, and suppression by force, i.e. exclusion from democracy, of the exploiters and oppressors of the people – this is the change democracy undergoes during the *transition* from capitalism to communism.'[32]

The position, then, of Marx in relation to the transition to communism from capitalism is this. In non–democratic states, proletarian revolution would be a violent but majority undertaking. The provisional democratically elected government immediately after the proletarian revolution would be a dictatorship of the proletariat because it would rule in an extra-legal setting. It would be a strictly temporary form of government only lasting until the introduction of a constitution when the dictatorship of the proletariat would give way to proletarian rule. During this time, a defence force would still exist to ensure the success of the proletarian revolution against the possibility of violent counter-revolution. In bourgeois democracies, where a working-class socialist government had been elected, there would be immediate rule by the proletariat without dictatorship of the proletariat. However, even in these conditions, the introduction of dictatorship of the proletariat is still possible. This would happen if the minority bourgeois opposition should try to reverse the democratic decisions of the majority by means of violence. The government would then introduce emergency measures and institute martial law. In such conditions, a dictatorship of the proletariat lasts only for the duration of the state of emergency.

In both cases, dictatorship of the proletariat is a strictly temporary measure. Regardless of whether, as in bourgeois oligarchies, proletarian revolution had begun with a dictatorship of the proletariat, or, as in bourgeois democracy, there had been a peaceful transition to worker rule, the first measure of a proletarian government, according to Marx, would be the smashing of the parasite state: the radical deprofessionalization of public life. The coercive functions of the workers' state would gradually disappear along with the need for them. The final state of affairs would be the self-administration of the people. Communist society involves a public authority carrying out necessary administrative functions. But there would no longer be a state for two reasons. First, the administrative functions would no longer be the preserve of a body of professionals separate in identity from the mass of society. Second, there would no longer be coercive agencies, such as an army, police, or prisons, as the need for them would have disappeared.

Marx's ideal polity of the future, then, is a society in which ordinary workers elect from their ranks managers and public officials who administer the economy and society for no more than ordinary levels of remuneration. Among their functions is the formation and execution of a common plan which organizes production in society.

It is time now to turn to criticism of this conception of Marx's of the post-revolutionary polity. There are few who would wish to take issue with the desirability of such a form of association conceived in the abstract. However, many might wish to take issue with its feasibility in practice. There are at least two major problems. First, the sheer magnitude of the administrative task involved would require a large, complex, hierarchically arranged bureaucracy. Planning and administration are specialized, skilled tasks which require expertise that simply could not be supplied by part-time or short-term instantly revocable elected workers' delegates. A large professional bureaucracy would seem to be completely unavoidable in a communist society. And the larger the element of central planning and public services, the larger the bureaucracy that is needed. Second, it seems unrealistic to suppose that, in conditions of material scarcity which must be presumed to continue to exist, most individuals would not continue to seek to maximize their personal incomes just as they do in capitalism. In the early stage of communism, Marx effectively conceded, skilled labour will both demand and be able to secure higher remuneration than unskilled labour (for the same number of hours worked). It seems implausible to suppose that skilled public officials – and, indeed, other managers and professionals – would not seek to secure as large remuneration for the services they provided as they were capable of extracting from society. Assuming that they, indeed, did have superior competence in the necessary administrative functions – and that this superiority is something that would manifest itself quickly were their cooperation withdrawn – then it would not be very long before those with the capacity to administer society demanded higher than average incomes as a condition of performing the tasks. There is no reason to suppose that the income differential between ordinary unskilled manual workers and managers and senior administrators would not be considerable.

It may no doubt be objected that these administrative skills are only as scarce as they are in present society because of present social inequalities that prevent the mass of people from reaching the levels of educational attainment that would enable them to discharge administrative functions as well as those who presently do. This may be so. But so long as society is starting out – as it would be – from a position of initial social and economic inequality, then the families of the better-off would be able to ensure that their children received comparative educational advantages over the children of the less well-off. This would leave these children with superior skills. The technocracy would, thus, be able to perpetuate its comparative advantage over unskilled workers even in conditions of nominal equality of educational opportunity. This is not something that abolition of private schooling would be able to cure. The home as an educational environment is equally important, and income differentials would permit the better-off to give their children a head start. The important managerial and administrative functions would continue to be the preserve of a special élite drawn from other social strata besides the working class, and one which could effectively ensure superior income by virtue of its special skills. Thus, contrary to the impression created by Marx, private ownership of the means of production is by no means the only or even perhaps the main source of inequality in society. Even after the socialization of the means of production, the professional-managerial-administrative élite would continue to enjoy higher incomes, and effectively form a separate social stratum above the workers. It is extremely doubtful, therefore, whether Marx's ideal polity is realizable. First, full-time professionals would be required to administer society. Second, they would be liable to be recruited from strata other than the working labourers who had previously formed the proletariat. As such they would be likely to constitute a new ruling class.

6 Theory of Ideology

1. Outline of the Theory

The term *ideology* is often used today to mean any widely held view of how society is and ought to be. This is not how Marx understood the term. The materialist conception of history and Marx's economic theory together constitute a view of how society is that has very definite implications about how it ought to be. However, Marx did not regard his own theories of history and economics as instances of ideology. This is because Marx believed his view of society to be correct, and, for Marx, a view that is correct is not a case of ideology. Did Marx then simply understand by the term a mistaken view of how society is or ought to be? That comes closer to the truth but still falls somewhat short of it. There are two things wrong with it. First, Marx applied the term 'ideology' to several systems of ideas which are not as such views of how society is and ought to be. Thus, he called religion and morality 'ideology'. Neither is a view of how society is and ought to be. Second, a view of how society is and ought to be could be mistaken, yet not be a case of ideology. An example would be the view that human society is given over to the maximization of the production of razor-blades but ought to maximize the production of soap powder. This view, though evidently mistaken, is not a case of ideology. In order for a system of ideas to be an instance of ideology, as Marx understood the term, the following three conditions must be satisfied by the system. First, the system of ideas has to involve fundamental mistakes concerning the human condition or aspects thereof. Second, the system of ideas has to be accepted by some social group. Third, the system of ideas, by virtue of its acceptance by some social group, has to support exploitative relations of production (and/or associated political institutions).

The view that human society is given over to the maximization of the production of razor-blades but should maximize the production of soap powder is not a case of ideology because it fails to satisfy the second and third conditions. Why morality and religion are cases of ideology for Marx will be explained presently.

The support which an ideology offers exploitative relations of production (and/or associated political institutions) can be either direct or indirect. The support is direct if the system of ideas in question portrays those relations of production (and/or associated political institutions) as maximally conducive to general human well-being and in accordance with the dictates of morality. The support is indirect if the system of ideas in question asserts or implies that general human well-being is wholly dependent upon something other than the establishment of communism in conditions of advanced technology.

Having explained what Marx understood by the term 'ideology', we may now proceed to consider his *theory* of ideology. Marx's theory of ideology consists of an assertion about what sorts of systems of ideas prevail in class-divided societies. This assertion has been called the *Dominant Ideology Thesis*. It maintains that, in all stable class-divided societies, there tends to prevail, among both the ruling and the subordinate class, a shared body of ideology which serves to support the prevailing relations of production (and/or associated political institutions). Stable class-divided societies, therefore, according to Marx, tend to be characterized by the prevalence within them of illusory or mistaken systems of ideas about the human condition.

Further, those belief systems which tend to be prevalent in class-divided societies support the prevailing relations of production (and/or associated political institutions). Thus, in ancient slave society, according to the theory, a system of ideas tended to prevail that supported the institution of slavery; in feudal society, a belief system which supported serfdom. And, in capitalist society, systems of belief tend to prevail that support private ownership of the means of production and private enterprise.

Marx advanced an explanation of that alleged fact which he took the Dominant Ideology Thesis to express. This explanation was that the ruling class in any class-divided society has a material

interest in believing itself, and in having believed by the subordinate class, systems of ideas which support those relations of production (and associated political institutions) which make them the
ruling class. Additionally, the ruling class has the material power
to ensure the widespread promulgation of such systems of ideas.
Thus, the Dominant Ideology Thesis is made true, according to
Marx, by virtue of the alleged fact that the ruling class has both the
inclination and the ability to get universally believed in their society
such systems of ideas as support the relations of production (and
political institutions) favourable to themselves.

Marx identified a number of specific systems of ideas as instances
of ideology. The most important were the philosophical systems
of the Young Hegelians, classical political economy, morality and
religion. It is worth considering in the case of each of these systems
of ideas why Marx regarded it as an instance of ideology. We begin
with the philosopical systems of the Young Hegelians

It was Marx's view that the philosophical systems of the Young
Hegelians were cases of ideology because the following three
things were true of them. First, Marx claimed, these philosophical
systems falsely asserted or implied that the human condition could
be significantly improved simply by philosophers arriving at the
correct philosophical understanding of the world. Second, these
philosophical systems were advanced and accepted by members of
the German middle class. Third, by virtue of what they maintained
to be necessary and sufficient to improve the human condition –
namely, correct philosophical understanding – these philosophical
systems mistakenly implied that universal human well-being was
wholly dependent upon something other than the establishment of
communism in advanced industrial conditions. By virtue of this
mistaken implication, these philosophical systems indirectly supported semi-feudal and petty-bourgeois relations of production
and associated autocratic political institutions. We thus find Marx
writing of the philosophical systems of the Young Hegelians as
follows; 'Since the Young Hegelians consider conceptions,
thoughts, ideas, in fact all the products of consciousness to which
they attribute an independent existence, as the real chains of men,
it is evident that the Young Hegelians have to fight only against
these illusions of consciousness. Since, according to their fantasy,

the relations of men, all their doings, their fetters and their limitations are products of their consciousness, the Young Hegelians logically put to men the moral postulate of exchanging their present consciousness for human, critical or egoistic consciousness, and thus of removing their limitations. This demand to change consciousness amounts to a demand to interpret the existing world in a different way, i.e. to recognize it by means of a different interpretation. The Young-Hegelian ideologists, in spite of all their allegedly "world-shattering" phrases, are the staunchest conservatives . . . They forget . . . that they are in no way combating the real existent world when they are combating solely the phrases of this world."[1]

By *classical political economy*, Marx meant the economic theories of primarily Adam Smith, David Ricardo, Thomas Malthus, Nassau Senior, Thomas McCulloch and John Stuart Mill. Marx regarded their theories to be instances of ideology since their theories satisfied all the conditions required to render a system of ideas ideology in Marx's eyes. First, these theories implied, or, perhaps rather, presupposed – mistakenly in Marx's eyes – that capitalist relations of production were those most conducive to general human well-being. For classical political economy regarded capitalist relations of production as those most consonant with human nature and the human condition. Second, these theories were advanced and widely accepted by members of the capitalist class. Thirdly, these theories directly supported capitalist relations of production by portraying them in so favourable a light.

Before explaining why Marx regarded morality as ideology, it will be necessary to demonstrate first that Marx did regard morality – all morality – to be a case of ideology. (It might be wondered how I can claim that Marx regarded all morality as ideology, given that I have earlier argued that, when Marx claimed that wage-labour involves exploitation of the worker, he was intending to assert that wage-labour involves the perpetration of an injustice against the worker. The answer is that Marx was not entirely consistent in this matter. He called morality ideology, thereby intending to disparage it. This did not stop him from moralizing from time to time. One of those occasions was when he criticized capitalism on grounds of exploitation.) The following quotations from Marx should leave the matter beyond any reasonable doubt. First, there is the evidence from the *German Ideology*. There Marx wrote:'The Communists do not preach *morality* at all . . . They do not put to people the moral demand: love one another, do not be egoists, etc.; on the contrary, they are very well aware that egoism, just as much as selfishness, *is* in definite circumstances a necessary form of the self-assertion of individuals.'[2] Later in the same work Marx writes: 'When it became possible to criticize the conditions of production and intercourse in the hitherto existing world, i.e. when the contradiction between the bourgeoisie and the proletariat had given rise to communist and socialist views, [t]hat shattered the basis of all morality, whether the morality of asceticism or of enjoyment.'[3]

Second, there is the evidence from the *Communist Manifesto*. In that work Marx has an imaginary critic of Marx's form of communism protest that 'Communism abolishes all religion and all morality, instead of constituting them on a new basis.'[4] In replying to this charge, Marx does not deny it. Instead, his reply implies that he accepts the charge. He writes: 'The communist revolution is the most radical rupture with traditional property relations; no wonder that its development involves the most radical rupture with traditional ideas.'[5]

Finally, there is the evidence from the *Critique of the Gotha Programme*. Here Marx writes: 'If I have dealt at some length with the "undiminished proceeds of labour" on the one hand, and "equal right" and "just distribution" on the other, it is in order to show the criminal nature of what is being attempted [by the socialist party whose programme Marx is criticizing]: on the one hand our party is forced to re-accept as dogmas ideas which may have made some sense in a particular time but which are now only a load of obsolete verbal rubbish; on the other hand, the realistic outlook instilled in our party at the cost of immense effort, but now firmly rooted in it, is to be perverted by means of ideological, legal and other humbug so common among the democrats and the French socialists.'[6]

Assuming that Marx may correctly be supposed to have regarded all morality to be a case of ideology, the question arises as to why he did so. Essentially, his reasons were two in number.

First, it was Marx's view that the specific moral norms that were in existence at any given time, and which were the valid moral norms at that time, were those which portrayed as morally right that conduct which harmonized with the relations of production prevailing at that time. Recall Marx's claim in *Capital*, Volume III, that '[t]he content [of legal forms] is just so long as it corresponds to the mode of production and is adequate to it. It is unjust as soon as it contradicts it. Slavery, on the basis of the capitalist mode of production, is unjust.'[7] On this view, morality can and does support exploitative relations of production. This is because morality always endorses such relations of production during such times as they prevail.

Marx's second reason for regarding morality as ideology specifically concerns that area of morality concerned with individual rights and corresponding duties.[8] The view that individuals have rights to which there correspond duties on the part of others presupposes a particular view of the human condition as being one of inherent conflicts of interest between individuals. Rights and duties are necessary for the establishment of order and harmony in such a situation of potential inter-personal conflict. Such conflicts of interest are regarded as endemic because the human condition as conceived by morality is characterized by two facts. The first is the existence of scarcity. The second is the fact that human beings have limited sympathy. Morality is a system of restraint on human conduct to establish conditions for cooperation and harmony. Now, such a view of the human condition implies that communism, as Marx conceived it – with scarcity eradicated and communality established – is an impossible dream. Accordingly, the view of the human condition presupposed by morality is one which Marx believed to be erroneous. It implicitly denied that universal human well-being was wholly dependent upon the establishment of communism in conditions of advanced technology. In so doing, it indirectly supported exploitative relations of production.

Finally, we must consider Marx's reasons for holding religion to be ideology. Essentially there were two reasons: first, in Marx's view, religion gave a fundamentally mistaken account of the human condition. Second, religion implied that human well-being is wholly dependent upon something other than the establishment of communism in conditions of advanced technology. Religion regarded communism plus advanced productive forces as neither a necessary nor a sufficient condition of universal human well-being. Communism is not a necessary condition of human well-being, according to religion, since human well-being is regarded by religion as achievable by man coming into the right relation with the divinity through prayer, piety or grace. Such a state of affairs is independent of political and material conditions. Thus, religion portrays human well-being as attainable independently of what economic structure obtains and of how advanced technology is. Marx regarded such a view as mistaken. Additionally, religion reconciled man with exploitative relations of production and provided man with consolation for his pitiable condition. Religion, also, denied communism plus advanced productive forces to be a sufficient condition of universal human well-being; this is because, in the absence of the appropriate religious orientation of individuals, material conditions and economic institutions would not bring human beings peace of mind. Again, then, religion had the effect of diverting the attention of believers from concern with overcoming exploitative relations of production. Religion is, thus, essentially quietistic. Thus, for Marx, religion had mistaken implications about the human condition and ones which indirectly supported exploitative relations of production. It encouraged human beings to accept such relations and to look elsewhere than to revolution for an improvement of the human condition.

Marx came to this view of religion fairly early on in his life. Thus, he wrote in his 'Introduction to the Critique of Hegel's *Philosophy of Right*': 'The foundation of irreligious criticism is: *Man makes religion*, religion does not make man. Religion is indeed the self-consciousness and self-esteem of man who has either not yet won through to himself or has already lost himself again . . . Religion is the general theory of this world, its encyclopedic compendium, its logic in popular form . . . its solemn complement and its universal basis of consolation and justification. It is the *fantastic realization* of the human essence since the human essence has not yet acquired any true reality. The struggle against religion is therefore indirectly the struggle against *that world* whose spiritual *aroma* is religion..

'*Religious* suffering is at one and the same time the *expression* of real suffering and a protest against real suffering. Religion is the sigh of the oppressed creature, the heart of a heartless world and the soul of soulless conditions. It is the *opium* of the people.

'The abolition of religion as the *illusory* happiness of the people is the demand for their *real* happiness. To call on them to give up their illusions about their condition is to *call on them to give up a condition that requires illusions*. The criticism of religion is therefore in *embryo* the *criticism of that vale of tears* of which religion is the halo.

'Criticism has plucked the imaginary flowers on the chain not in order that man shall continue to bear that chain without fantasy or consolation but so that he shall throw off the chain and pluck the living flower. The criticism of religion disillusions man, so that he will think, act and fashion his reality like a man who has discarded his illusions and regained his senses, so that he will move around himself as his own true sun. Religion is only the illusory sun which revolves around a man so long as he does not revolve around himself.'[9]

We shall now turn to an evaluation of Marx's theory of ideology.

2. The Dominant Ideology Thesis

The Dominant Ideology Thesis is the thesis that, in every stable class-divided society, there tends to prevail, among both the ruling and subordinate class, a shared body of ideology which supports the prevailing relations of production (and/or associated political institutions).

This thesis has been subjected to successful empirical refutation by three sociologists, Nicholas Abercrombie, Stephen Hill and Bryan S. Turner, in their book, *The Dominant Ideology Thesis*. Before surveying the counter-examples to the thesis which the three authors bring forward, it will be necessary, however, first to demonstrate that Marx did subscribe to the thesis. This is because the three authors deny that Marx did subscribe to the thesis. The textual basis for attributing the thesis to Marx is the passage in the *German Ideology* in which Marx states that 'the ideas of the ruling class are in every epoch the ruling ideas'. The three authors identify two different possible interpretations of the passage: a strong and a weak interpretation. The strong interpretation is the thesis that, by virtue of the control exercised by the ruling class over the apparatus for the production and dissemination of ideas, the subordinate class is made subject to the ideas held by the ruling class. This is the Dominant Ideology Thesis which I have attributed to Marx. The weak interpretation is that the only ideas which are conspicuous to an observer of a society are the ideas held by the ruling class. This is because the subordinate class lacks the institutions to make public its own ideas, which can be different from those of the ruling class. The three authors state that '[i]n the *German Ideology* it is not clear which interpretation Marx and Engels favoured'.[10] This claim seems to me simply false. Marx and Engels make it absolutely clear that it is to the stronger interpretation they subscribe. They say: 'The class which is the ruling *material* force of society is at the same time its ruling *intellectual* force. The class which has the means of material production at its disposal, consequently also controls the means of mental production, so that the ideas of those who lack the means of mental production are on the whole subject to it.'[11] It is hard to think of a more explicit way of stating the stronger version of the Dominant Ideology Thesis.

Granted that Marx, like many latter-day Marxists, did subscribe to the Dominant Ideology Thesis in the form in which I have attributed it to him, what is the evidence which Abercrombie, Hill and Turner bring forward against it? The three authors picked out three epochs and compared the sentiments of the subordinate with those of the dominant class to see if they were the same. They found that, whereas the ruling classes in these epochs subscribed to systems of ideas which supported the prevailing economic and political institutions, the subordinate classes in these three epochs did not. There was a marked divergence between the ruling classes and subordinate classes in matters of belief. Indeed, the subordinate classes were not ideologically incorporated into society. These societies were not rendered stable by the subordinate classes accepting ideologies which supported the prevailing relations of production.

Rather, the acquiescence of subordinate classes was based upon coercion or upon pragmatic calculations of what was in their best short-term interest. Subordinate classes did not accept the prevailing relations of production as just.

The three epochs studied were Feudalism (1200–1400), Early Capitalism (1780–1880) and Late Capitalism (1945 onwards). In the case of Feudalism, the ruling class subscribed to Catholicism. The view of the world held by this religion justified a hierarchical social order such as prevailed. Marx, in a footnote in *Capital*, claimed that, in the middle ages, 'Catholicism reigned supreme'. However, the three authors contend, the peasants remained predominantly pagan during this period. They write: 'The peasantry remained incorrigible. They were largely untouched by the civilizing role of the church throughout the Middle Ages and they remained the main vehicle of magical, irrational practices up to the Counter-Reformation and the era of the Protestant evangelical movements of the nineteenth century when the peasantry as a class was transformed into urban wage labourers.'[12]

The reason the peasantry were untouched by Christianity is that the apparatus for transmitting ideology was weak. Contact between the Church and the peasants was minimal. The peasants for the most part were illiterate and did not understand the Latin in which church services were conducted. The peasantry failed to overthrow the feudal lords, but not because the peasants subscribed to Catholicism which legitimated a hierarchical view of the universe, teaching peasants to view their lowly position in society as God-ordained. The peasants failed to rebel for the following reasons. First, poor communications prevented the development of a peasant class consciousness. Second, in virtue of their superior military strength, the landlords enjoyed a monopoly on such means of production as mills and dykes. Third, hunger, disease and drudgery kept the peasantry too preoccupied with scratching a living to have time and energy for radical political action.

During the early period of capitalism in Britain, between 1780 and 1880, the teachings of the classical political economists came to be widely accepted among the ascendant bourgeoisie, and in the latter part of the period by the aristocracy as well. This body of thought portrayed capitalist economic institutions as the best way for advancing the interests of all members of society. However, according to Abercrombie, Hill and Turner, the working class failed to be indoctrinated with this system of ideas. There was much radical working-class opposition to capitalism and bourgeois ideas. This was especially so after 1815 when Tom Paine's egalitarian ideas became popularized. By 1830, an autonomous working-class culture had developed. This culture had its own collectivist and mutualist orientation which was antithetical to bourgeois individualism. The political stability of the mid-Victorian period, the three authors argue, can be explained in other ways than by supporting the view that the working class had come to accept the bourgeois view of capitalism. First, the working class had become exhausted and demoralized after decades of unsuccessful struggle. Second, after 1850 there was an improvement in economic, and later political, conditions. This improvement encouraged the working class to believe that it was possible for them to improve their condition by piecemeal reforms. Third, internal divisons within the working class inhibited collective action against capitalism. Again, it is to be emphasized that the machinery for the transmission of ideology from ruling to working class was relatively undeveloped before the late nineteenth century. As was the case with feudalism, the stability of early British capitalism is not to be accounted for by the supposition that the working class were ideologically incorporated. As the three authors put it: 'Owners had little need to worry about the indoctrination of labour once workers were dependent for their livelihood on industrial work, because the discipline of unemployment and payment by results provided all the compulsion that any owner would ever require . . . The dull compulsion of economic relations . . . provided the discipline and reduced the need for any process of indoctrination.'[13]

But surely, it might be asked, in an age of democracy such as the present, the working class must subscribe to an ideology that favours capitalism. For if they did not share the ideology of the ruling class, why would they not simply vote the system out of existence? It is the view of the three authors that, in late capitalist society (that is, in the case of Britain since the end of the Second World War), there is widespread working-class rejection of capitalism and acceptance of beliefs that portray it as unjust. The authors cite a survey that was carried out in the early 1970s by H. F. Moorhouse and C. Chamberlain into the attitudes of London working-class tenants towards private property. The findings were that tenants rejected the right of individuals to own more than one house, and endorsed squatting and factory occupation. They also attacked the idea that industry should be organized for profit rather than need. It is the view of the three authors that many workers tolerate capitalism, not because they accept beliefs that portray it as just, but because they see no realistic alternative. There is no normative acceptance of capitalism by many members of the working class, only pragmatic acceptance. The authors concluded their study of advanced capitalism by saying: 'Notions such as incorporation via ideological hegemony or integration via common culture need not . . . enter the explanation of why late capitalism survives. There are other satisfactory explanations which make no reference to the ideology of the dominant or subordinate classes, nor to the indoctrination of one by the other.'[14]

The researches of Abercrombie, Hill and Turner, therefore, cast considerable doubt on the validity of the Dominant Ideology Thesis. We shall now turn to consider the validity of Marx's claims that the philosophical systems of the Young Hegelians, classical political economy, morality and religion were all cases of ideology.

3. The Young Hegelians as Ideologists

Most people these days only know about the Young Hegelians from what Marx says about them. They are thus prepared to take Marx's word for it that all the Young Hegelians wished to do was bring about transformations of consciousness, thereby leaving actual economic and political institutions unchanged. This view of them, however, is very much a caricature and misrepresents their position. Their view was that correct philosophical understanding of the world is a necessary precondition of effective change of it. They had great faith in the ability of ideas to change the world. They were not satisfied simply with changing ideas and leaving the world unchanged. I shall provide just one example to illustrate the point. Bruno Bauer, in his *Trumpet of the Last Judgement over Hegel the Atheist and Antichrist* (1841), explains clearly the role which the Young Hegelians assigned to philosophy. Bauer wrote: 'Philosophers are the Lords of this World, and create the destiny of mankind, and their acts are the acts of destiny. They write the executive orders of World History as originally received, and people must obey them, and the King, by acting in accord with their directives, is but a secretary *copying* the directives written originally by philosophers . . . The philosophers . . . direct the whole, and have always the whole in sight, while others have their *particular* interests – this dominion, these riches, this girl.

'But not only when an advance is to occur do philosophers have hands in the affair, but whenever the established order is to be disturbed, and here the positive forms, the institutions, the consitution, and religious statues are to collapse and fall. The philosophers are truly of a singular danger, for they are the most consistent and unrestrained revolutionaries.'[15]

The last quoted sentence might be something of an exaggeration. This is because someone like Blanqui might be thought less restrained a revolutionary than someone content merely to engage in philosophical discourse. Yet Marx has surely misrepresented the Young Hegelians in claiming that all they were interested in doing was effecting changes of consciousness without wanting to change the world. They believed that the most effective way to bring about changes in the world was by changing consciousness. It is not obvious that such a belief satisfies the conditions to render it a case of ideology.

4. Classical Political Economy as Ideology

It was Marx's view that classical political economy is guilty of a major theoretical error. This error suffices to render that body of doctrine an instance of ideology. The error is that of having 'viewed the capitalist order as the absolute and ultimate form of social production, instead of a historically transient stage of development'.[16] Marx also wrote with classical political economy in mind: 'Economists have a singular method of procedure. There are only two kinds of institution for them, artificial and natural. The institutions of feudalism are artificial institutions, those of the bourgeoisie are natural institutions. In this way they resemble the theologians, who likewise establish two kinds of religion. Every religion which is not theirs is an invention of men, while their own is an emanation from God. When the economists say that present-day relations – the relations of bourgeois production – are natural, they imply that these are the relations in which wealth is created and productive forces developed in conformity with the laws of nature. These relations therefore are themselves natural laws independent of the influence of time.'[17]

Now, Marx is undoubtedly correct in claiming that classical political economy did view capitalism in this way. Yet, Marx would only be correct in supposing that classical political economy is thereby ideology if classical political economy was mistaken in having done so. Marx, of course, was sure that socialism would succeed capitalism. He was sure of this because he believed that socialism would be able to make fuller use of technologically advanced productive forces than capitalism. The classical political economists doubted that any other form of economy would be able to make as efficient use of productive forces as capitalism does. If they are right, then they had no reason to suppose that capitalism is a historically transient stage of development, destined to be replaced by socialism. Nor would they have had any reason to doubt that capitalism is the ultimate form of social production. Accordingly, if the classical economists were right in being sceptical of socialism's capacity to match the productive ability of capitalism, then there is no reason to regard classical political economy as ideology. Let us, then, examine classical political economy's reasons for regarding capitalism as the most efficient and productive form of economy.

It is possible to find within the writings of the classical economists two main arguments for the thesis that socialism cannot utilize and develop productive forces as fully as capitalism can. We may call these arguments the *Argument from Self-Interest* and the *Argument from Ignorance* respectively.

The Argument from Self-Interest can be found advanced in the writings of Hume, Bentham and Ricardo. Reduced to its simplest form, the argument goes as follows. Self-interest is the most powerful human motive. (Included within self-interest here is regard for the well-being of a person's loved ones.) The capitalist institutions of private (transferable) property and the market provide individuals with strong self-interested incentives for effort, industry and enterprise. This is because the market tends to reward individuals for effort, enterprise and industry. Socialist forms of society tend to provide individual members with fewer rewards and therefore less incentive for effort, industry and enterprise than capitalism does. Of two different forms of society offering unequal incentives for effort, industry and enterprise, that form of society which offers greater incentives for these qualities will, other things being equal, achieve fuller use and faster development of its productive capacity. Therefore, capitalism, other things being equal, will achieve fuller use and faster development of productive capacity than socialism.

The *Argument from Ignorance* was advanced by Adam Smith. In more recent times, a more elaborate version of the argument has been advanced by F. A. Hayek. The argument runs as follows. No single mind (or collection of human minds) could ever master the volume of information that it would be necessary to master in order to be able to allocate factors of production as efficiently as they are allocated by the market through the pricing system. Therefore, capitalism makes far more efficient use of productive forces than socialism does. Smith wrote: 'The statesman, who should attempt to direct private people in what manner they ought to employ their capitals, would not only load himself with a most unnecessary attention, but assume an authority which could safely be trusted, not only to no single person, but to no council or senate whatever, and which would nowhere be so dangerous as in the hands of a man who had folly and presumption enough to fancy himself fit to exercise it.'[18]

Smith also says of the sovereign that he should not assume the duty of 'superintending the industry of private people, and of directing it towards the employments most suitable to the interest of society – a duty in the attempting of which he must always be exposed to innumerable delusions; and for the proper performance of which no human wisdom or knowledge could ever be sufficient.'[19] It is essentially the same consideration that in recent times has led F. A. Hayek to make the following observation: 'It is becoming progressively less and less imaginable that any one mind or planning authority could picture or survey the millions of connections between the evermore numerous interlocking separate activities which have become indispensable for the efficient use of modern technology and even the maintenance of the standard of life Western man has achieved. That we have been able to have a reasonably high degree of order in our economic lives despite modern complexities is *only* because our affairs have been guided, not by central direction, but by the operation of the market and competition in securing the mutual adjustment of separate efforts. The market system functions because it is able to take account of separate facts and desires, because it reaches with thousands of sensitive feelers into every nook and cranny of the economic world and feeds back the information acquired in coded form to a "public information board" [i.e. the price system]. What the market-place and its prices give most particularly is a continuing updating of the ever-changing relative scarcities of commodities and services. In other words, the complexity of the structure required to produce the real income we are now able to provide for the masses of the Western world . . . could develop *only* because we did *not* attempt to plan it or subject it to any central direction, but left it to be guided by a spontaneous ordering mechanism, or a self-generating order, as modern cybernetics calls it.'[20]

This is a formidable pair of arguments in favour of capitalism. There would appear to be only two ways of defending the superiority of socialism to capitalism in the face of them. The first is by saying that socialism is compatible with a market system which operates through appeal to the self-interest of individual economic agents. The second is by saying that capitalism possesses some major structural deficiency from which socialism does not suffer. This deficiency prevents capitalism from being able to utilize productive capacity as fully as socialism. Let us examine these possible defences of socialism.

The first way of defending socialism is by adopting the line which advocates of workers'-control socialism take. A recent proponent of this form of socialism is David Schweickart.[21] The defining characteristics of such an economic order as proposed by Schweickart are these. First, each firm is managed democratically by its workers. The workers manage but do not own the means of production on which they work. These are owned by society. Workers are not allowed to let the assets in their control deteriorate in value or sell them off for personal gain. The capital stock has to be kept intact. Secondly, the economy is a market economy. The market forces of supply and demand determine the prices of consumer goods and raw materials. Firms try to maximize the difference between their total sales and the total *non-labour* costs. The workers decide how to divide up the resultant revenue democratically. Thus, they have incentive to work hard. Third, it is only *new* investment which the government controls. The government generates funds for investment by taxing the capital assets of firms. Thus, 'capital tax' is the equivalent of interest in a capitalist economy. The government establishes investment banks to decide which proposals for new ventures should be allocated funds.

It is argued that such a system retains the desirable features of capitalism – namely, the allocative efficiency of the pricing system, and reliance upon motivation by self-interest. At the same time, so it is alleged, the system is spared the undesirable features of the capitalist system: namely, unearned incomes and the division of labour between management and workers.

While such a system is undoubtedly an improvement on the inefficient centrally planned socialist economies, there would still appear to be major drawbacks to it. First, workers in such worker-controlled firms, when faced with increased demand for their products, do not have as strong incentives as capitalist firms do to increase their size to expand production. This is because increasing the size of the firm involves taking on additional labour which would reduce the profit share per worker. It pays each member of a worker-controlled firm to keep the size of his firm small, in such conditions, rather than to expand its size. Schweickart thinks that it would be possible to get round this problem. First, he argues, it will be necessary to raise the consciousness of firms as to their social responsibilities. He writes that '[i]f firms do not increase production when demand increases, then the economy will face problems of unnecessary unemployment and a general misallocation of resources. Thus firms must be encouraged to interpret a demand-generated price increase, not as an eternal blessing, but as a temporary compensation for the inconvenience of bringing new workers into the firm to expand production.'[22] Second, because it controls new investment, the government can establish new firms in these areas in which demand has increased.

These two suggested ways of dealing with the problem do not seem to me to meet the difficulty. The first suggested remedy assumes that workers will be persuaded to reduce their potential income through appeal to their 'social responsibilities'. Reference to the Yugoslavian experience of worker cooperatives would tend to suggest that this assumption is unwarranted. One of the major problems with these worker cooperatives has been the unwillingness of workers in highly profitable firms to dilute their profits by taking on additional workers to expand output. The second suggested remedy relies upon government agencies identifying sectors in the economy in which economically viable firms could be set up. However, it is implausible to suppose that officers of state investment banks would have the same incentive as capitalist bankers do to identify profitable areas for expansion. In the case of capitalism, investment bankers' incomes are directly dependent upon how successful they are at identifying profitable areas of investment. Such incentives would have to be lacking in a worker-controlled socialist society otherwise the dreaded non-wage incomes would be reintroduced. This being so, the presumption must be that a worker-controlled economy would be far less responsive to changes in demand than capitalism.

A second drawback with worker-controlled firms in a socialist economy is that, through not owning the assets of their firms, workers have little incentive to engage in long-term investment. This has been a conspicuous failing of Yugoslavian worker-controlled firms.

Finally, there is the objection that making the state responsible for new investment is liable to stifle enterprise and initiative. As Milton Friedman has said: 'It is one thing for an individual by himself, or even for a few individuals who have common tastes and can join together, to undertake a major gamble. It is a very different thing for a large group of workers through a bureaucratic mechanism to justify engaging in risky activities. If one looks at Western capitalist societies, one sees that risky ventures have seldom been financed through banks; they have seldom been financed through major bureaucratic organizations, including the government – except . . . for some risky ventures that are almost sure to fail but have strong political appeal. Risky ventures that seem to hold promise of success but that are also very uncertain have almost invariably been financed by a small group of individuals risking their own funds or the funds of their relatives and friends.'[23]

The conclusion must be that a worker-controlled socialist economy would be less efficient and dynamic than a capitalist one.

We turn now to consider the second way of defending the superiority of socialism to capitalism in the face of the Arguments from Self-Interest and Ignorance. This is by accusing capitalism of some major deficiency from which socialism is free. Since the 1930s, the main candidate has been chronic unemployment arising from so-called *deficiencies in aggregate demand*. With the exception of Malthus, the classical economists all believed that a free capitalist market economy would always tend towards full employment. Keynes argued in the 1930s that capitalism is endemically prone to experience chronic involuntary unemployment. According to Keynes, such unemployment is liable to arise because it is impossible in capitalism to guarantee that all that is saved is invested. The result of an excess of saving over investment is a deficiency in aggregate demand the inevitable consequence of which is unemployment. When savings exceed investment, in Keynes's view, there is bound to be a contraction of economic activity until savings are brought into line with investment. However, such an equilibrium can be obtained at less than full levels of employment. Should this occur, there will be no way in which the market left to itself will be able to generate full employment. If this view of Keynes were correct, there would be a powerful economic case against capitalism, notwithstanding the support lent to it by the Arguments from Self-Interest and Ignorance. A socialist economy can always guarantee full employment by ensuring that investment equals saving. We must, thus, determine whether Keynes's view is correct.

Let us begin by considering why the classical economists thought there could be no (prolonged) involuntary unemployment in a free capitalist economy. Their faith in the ability of capitalism to create and maintain full employment was based upon confidence in the ability of the price mechanism to bring the supply and demand of any commodity into line with each other. For the classical economists, the wage rate is simply the price of labour. This price will be determined on the free market by the interaction of entrepreneurs bidding for labour and labourers seeking work.

A simple model will explain why the classical economists thought there could be no involuntary unemployment in capitalism.[24] Suppose there are 100 potential workers. Suppose that, when the wage rate is £10 per week, only ten workers are willing to work. Suppose that at a wage rate of £20 a week, twenty workers are willing to work; at £30, thirty workers . . . and so on up to £100 per week at which all 100 workers are willing to work. Now, consider the wages which entrepreneurs are willing to pay for labour. Suppose that, at a wage-rate of £100 per week, entrepreneurs are only willing to hire ten workers. Suppose at £90 per week, they are willing to hire twenty; at £80 per week thirty, and so on. When the wage rate is £10 per week, the entrepreneurs are willing to hire all 100. In such circumstances, a wage rate of £50 per week will be established and fifty workers will be employed. At this wage rate and this wage rate alone, all those who are willing to work for this wage will find an employer willing to pay that wage. The fifty potential workers who remain unemployed at this wage rate are not involuntarily unemployed. They are demanding more than £50 per week before they are willing to work. This is more than entrepreneurs are prepared to pay for their labour. This unemployed fifty could find work by reducing their asking price, that is, by being willing to accept a lower wage.

On the classical view, therefore, there can be no such thing as (prolonged) involuntary unemployment. By adjusting his asking price downward – that is, by being willing to accept a lower wage rate – a prospective employee will always be able to find a job – so long, that is, as labour is a scarce factor of production. The size of wage rates, for the classical economists, is a function of the productivity of labour. This, in turn, is a function of how much capital is invested per worker. In a highly technological society such as our own, the productivity of labour is sufficiently high to render the wage rate at which all who are willing to work would find jobs well above subsistence.

In our example, therefore, those who are not working in the economy when the going rate is £50 per week are choosing unemployment in preference to a wage at the going rate.

It may be asked: why are not the entrepreneurs willing to pay more than they do for labour? Why do they not pay £100 per week and thereby provide a job for every potential worker at a wage for which he is willing to work? The answer to this question, on the classical view, is that, at wage rates in excess of £50 a week, an additional worker hired after the first fifty have been employed would cost an employer more than that worker would yield the employer in revenue for him. On the classical view, in a free market, employers will be willing to hire additional labour up to the point where the cost of hiring an extra worker will exceed the revenue which the hire of that worker would bring the employer. In our example, a wage rate of above £50 per week for a worker is not economically worthwhile once fifty workers have been employed for £50 each per week. The fifty-first worker taken on generates less than £50 in revenue for the employer. If the fifty-first worker preferred working for a wage of less than £50 per week to idleness, then, in a free market economy, he would be able to find a job. He could find a job by offering his services for less than £50 per week. An employer would hire him in preference to a worker who demanded £50 before he worked. If all fifty-one workers were willing to work for less than £50 per week, then a new lower equilibrium wage would be established in line with the marginal productivity of the fifty-first worker. Those who remain unemployed in a free capitalist economy, therefore, according to the classical economists, do so of their own choosing. There is a rate of pay at which they could all find work. They are choosing unemployment in preference to working for that rate.

How, then, did Keynes contest this view? Keynes's argument was this. Imagine an economy of 100 potential workers with no foreign trade or government economic activity. Suppose that employers are willing to hire all 100 only when the wage rate is £10 per week. If all 100 were willing to accept this wage rate, the total weekly wages bill would be £1,000. If all these wages are spent by the workers on goods produced by the firms, then the receipts to the firms after the first week will be £1,000. The firms will, thus, have enough revenue to hire all the 100 workers again for the next week at £10 per week. Now, suppose that the workers decide to save 20 per cent of their weekly income. This would mean that, in the week after they made this decision, they would spend only £800 of their total earnings. The receipts of the firms would only be £800. So, assuming that the firms receive no additional source of revenue, the firms will only have £800 to pay on wages in the following week. The 100 potential workers could no longer all be hired by the firms at £10 per week each. The firms would only have enough revenue to hire eighty workers at a wage rate of £10 per week. In such circumstances, twenty workers would become unemployed. If the £200 that has been saved were invested in the firms, then the firms would once again have £1,000 available to hire workers with. The 100 workers could all be hired at the wage rate of £10 per week.

It is natural to suppose that those who save would be prepared to invest their savings for this increases their holdings. If this were so, they would be prepared to invest all their £200 in the firms. But, Keynes was to argue, there is no guarantee in an unregulated capitalist economy that all that is saved will be invested. Should total savings exceed total investment – should, that is, people prefer to hoard money, or, in Keynes's terminology, should they wish to preserve liquidity – then the firms will fail to receive sufficient funds to enable them to hire all the workers previously employed at the accustomed wage rate.

Now, suppose that only £100 of the £200 that is saved is invested. Then, the employers will only have £900 for the payment of wages. The firms would only be able to hire ninety workers at the wage rate of £10 per week. In these circumstances, ten workers would be unemployed. Suppose that the workers in work continue to save 20 per cent of their income and to invest £100 as before. Then, after ninety have been paid £10 for a week's work, there will be a total payroll of £900. Of this £900 paid to workers, 20 per cent, that is, £180, is saved. The remaining £720 is spent by the workers, and £100 of the £180 saved is invested. The firms would thus receive £720 plus £100 = £820. The firms now only have enough to employ eighty-two workers at the rate of £10 per week. A further contraction of the economy will take place. This contraction will continue until only 50 workers are employed. When there are fifty workers employed at £10 per week, then, assuming they still save 20 per cent of their income and still invest £100 per week, all that they save will be invested. The firms will thus receive £400 from spending by the workers and £100 from their investments. The firms now have enough to continue to employ fifty workers at £10 per week. Unemployment will stop growing, but there will be fifty workers out of work who are willing to work for £10 a week, the going rate.

The classical economists' solution to this problem is to say that workers should accept lower wage rates. If they accepted wage reduction, they could price themselves into work. However, Keynes rejects such a solution. According to Keynes, were workers to accept a lower wage rate, they would then have lower incomes to spend. Demand would decline and firms would be obliged to lay off workers. As one Keynesian economist has recently put it: 'For an individual firm, wage cuts might well induce it to increase employment. But if wage cuts are general then the immediate effect is to reduce spending in the economy. Firms will be faced with lower labour costs, but at the same time less demand for their products.'[25]

It looks as if Keynes has identified a fatal flaw in the capitalist economy. But his argument is based upon a number of fallacies. Why cannot workers accept a lower wage when savings exceed investment? Note that the workers would only be accepting a reduced *monetary* wage rate. In the example, the problem begins when £100 is withdrawn from circulation, i.e. saved but not spent. All that this does, however, is reduce the amount of money in circulation. This means that the supply of money will have contracted. Money is a scarce commodity. Like any other commodity, when its supply contracts, its value will go up. In the case of money, its value is represented by the volume of goods and services that can be purchased with it. So, when £100 is saved but not invested, the value of money will rise proportionately. When employers have only £900 to spend on wages, this £900 will be worth as much as £1,000 was worth prior to the withdrawal of £100 from circulation. In that case, were workers to accept £9 per week, they would not experience any decline in real wages, and the firms would have sufficient revenue to employ all 100 workers. The workers will not be any the worse off by accepting £9 per week. For £9 will now be worth what £10 was worth previously. No problems need be caused if savings exceed investment. Full employment can be maintained with no loss of real earnings, provided workers are willing to accept reductions in monetary wage rates.

There can be one and only one cause of unemployment in this situation. This is a refusal on the part of workers to reduce their monetary wage levels in line with the rise in the value of the money produced by the contraction of the amount in circulation. If workers refuse to take a reduction in their monetary wage rates, then they are effectively demanding an increase in their real wage without having increased their productivity. Employers can have no alternative but to lay off workers in this case, since the latter are now asking for more in wages than they generate in revenue by being employed. If the workers demand nothing less than £10 a week after £100 has been withdrawn from circulation, employers will be able to hire no more than ninety workers. Assuming the workers' propensity to save is 20 per cent and that they invest £100 per week, then, as we have seen, unemployment will steadily increase until fifty workers who are willing to work for £10 per week are unemployed.

There can only be two reasons for workers refusing to accept lower monetary wages when the supply of money in circulation contracts. Either potential workers have voluntarily agreed with trade unions not to accept lower monetary wage levels. Alternatively, those in work are able by means of force to prevent those out of work, but who are willing to accept lower monetary wage levels, from accepting such reduced monetary wage rates and displacing them. If the first alternative is the case, then what potential workers have done is to demand an increase in real wages without having increased productivity that alone would be able to fund a wage increase. The unemployment in this case is voluntary. On the second alternative, unions have created involuntary unemployment by preventing potential workers who are willing to accept lower monetary wage rates from accepting these lower rates of pay. Such unemployment, however, is the result of an interference with the workings of the market. It has not been caused by capitalism. It has been caused by something that is preventing voluntary exchange transactions from taking place.

As we have seen, Keynesians respond to the idea that workers should accept cuts in monetary wage rates when savings exceed investment by saying such wage cuts simply depress demand further and would do nothing to lower unemployment. This response, however, rests upon a confusion between wage rates and total payroll. Thus, suppose there are fifty workers employed at £10 per week. The total payroll will be £500 per week. Suppose that workers were willing to accept a cut of 10 per cent in their wages, and by so doing increase the total number of employed to sixty. There would, then, be a weekly payroll of £9 × 60 = £540. Wage rates would have declined but total payroll would have increased. There would thus have been generated an increase in demand by wage rate cuts.

The Keynesian argument is, as Henry Hazlitt has said, a 'tissue of fallacies'. Its widespread acceptance has been responsible for persisting unemployment in Britain in recent years as well as for inflation. It has been responsible for the latter since governments, under the spell of Keynes, have thought that they could cure unemployment by increasing demand through credit expansion. The source of the problem, however, has been the ability of trade unions to maintain monetary wage levels above the rate to which they would fall in a free market.[26]

There is simply no basis in logic or fact for the contention that in capitalism, there is an inherent tendency towards chronic unemployment. Consequently, there is no reason to reject the view of the classical political economists that capitalism secures fuller use and faster development of productive capacity than any other economic system. Consequently, there is no reason to believe that classical political economy is ideology. This body of theory may have been accepted by the capitalist class. It may also have supported capitalist relations of production. But it is not ideology, since the account of those aspects of the human condition of which it treats is substantially correct.

5. Morality as Ideology

It has been argued earlier in this chapter that Marx regarded morality as ideology. It was maintained that he did this for two reasons. First, as he saw it, the conduct that morality enjoins at any time is that which harmonizes with the relations of production prevailing at that time. Thus, morality can support exploitative relations of production. Second, in ascribing rights to individuals, morality presupposes a view of the human condition that sees it as inherently one of conflict. Thus, morality implicitly denies that communism, as Marx conceived it, is possible.

We consider first the thesis that morality is ideology because, for any given society at any given time, morality enjoins conduct which harmonizes with the prevailing mode of production. This is a view of morality which Allen Wood ascribes to Marx. Wood writes: '[Marx] sees moral norms as having no better foundation than their serviceability to transient forms of human social intercourse, and most fundamentally, to the social requirements of a given mode of production . . . He does so because such norms are for him only the juridical and ideological devices by which a given mode of production enforces its social relations, or a class attempts to promote its own interests.'[27]

Wood observes that Marx offers no argument in support of this conception of morality. However, Wood supplies an argument which he says is probably the reasoning behind Marx's conception of morality. This argument proceeds from the premise that, according to historical materialism, the moral standards which prevail in a society at any time are those which sanction the relations of production that favour the full use of that society's productive forces. Wood writes: 'If a society adopted standards of justice different from its actual ones, treating as just what it currently treats as unjust, then production under the existing conditions could not function as smoothly or efficiently as it does, and as it must tend to do if the postulates of historical materialism are to hold.'[28]

Wood then writes as follows: 'It is only in so far as moral standards serve the function of sanctioning social relations that they exist. Standards which are at odds with the prevailing relations do not fulfil the function proper to moral standards. Hence they must be not only socially impotent but also wrong, because they are at odds with the proper social function of morality. Material production thus provides a basis for moral standards, the only real basis Marx thinks they can have. For Marx . . . the morally rational is determined by the socially actual.'[29]

Wood is maintaining in this argument that the only moral standards that are correct for a given period are those which sanction the relations of production prevailing during that period. This is because only such standards fulfil the proper function of moral standards which is to sanction prevailing relations. Why should it be accepted, however, that the proper function of moral standards is to sanction prevailing social relations? The fact that this is what moral standards invariably do does not mean that it is morally right that they should do so. The fact that moral standards invariably sanction prevailing relations of production does not make such moral standards the correct ones. Why cannot it be maintained instead that the proper function of moral standards is to prescribe morally right conduct? Unless one holds that what makes acts morally right is the fact that they help bring about full use of productive forces, one has no reason to agree that morally right conduct is that which harmonizes with prevailing relations of production.

In *Anti-Dühring*, Engels does appear to argue that that conduct is morally right which brings about full use of productive forces. (This was a work which Engels read to Marx in manuscript and which Marx may be presumed to have agreed with.) Engels argues this in connection with the institution of slavery. He writes: 'It is very easy to inveigh against slavery and similar things in general terms, and to give vent to high moral indignation at such infamies. Unfortunately, all that this conveys is only what everyone knows, namely, that these institutions of antiquity are no longer in accord with our present conditions and our sentiments, which these conditions determine. But it does not tell us one word as to how these conditions arose, why they existed, and what role they played in history. And when we examine these questions, we are compelled to say – however contradictory and heretical it may sound – that the introduction of slavery under the conditions prevailing at that time was a great step forward. For it is a fact that man sprang from the beasts, and had consequently to use barbaric and almost bestial means to extricate himself from barbarism . . . It is clear that so long as human labour was still so little productive that it provided but a small surplus over and above the necessary means of subsistence, any increase of the productive forces, extension of trade, development of the state and law, or foundation of art and science, was possible only by means of greater division of labour. And the necessary basis for this was the great division of labour between the masses discharging simple manual labour and the few privileged persons directing labour, conducting trade and public affairs, and, at a later stage, occupying themselves with art and science. The simplest and most natural form of this division of labour was in fact slavery . . . This was an advance even for the slaves; the prisoners of war, from whom the mass of slaves was recruited, now at least saved their lives, instead of being killed as they had been before, or even roasted, as at a still earlier period.'[30]

The fact that the vanquished in battle preferred enslavement to being killed does not make past slavery morally right. Nor does the fact that slavery enabled culture to flourish. There is absolutely no reason for supposing that, because a set of institutions promotes maximum use of productive forces, this set of institutions is morally right. Nor is there any reason to suppose that moral standards which serve to support such institutions are morally correct. It may be the function of morality to sanction prevailing relations of production in the sense that this is what morality invariably does. It does not mean that this function of morality is proper in the sense that it is in accord with correct moral standards. I can see no reason for accepting the view which Wood attributes to Marx that those moral standards are correct which sanction prevailing social relations. Wood says such standards are correct because this is the function which moral standards invariably perform and must perform in order that full use be made of productive forces. This does not seem to be a compelling reason. Suppose, *per impossibile*, that modern productive forces could be most fully used by means of slavery. Suppose, further, that slavery was imposed on the majority by a powerful minority. Suppose, further still, that the prevailing moral standards in such a society were to sanction slavery. Would it follow from the fact that the prevailing moral standards in such a society sanctioned slavery that slavery was, not simply accepted there as morally right, but actually morally right? Of course not. The fact that a set of moral standards prevails in a society does not make those standards correct. Nor does the fact that those standards sanction social relations which promote full use of productive forces. The sole proper function of moral standards is to specify what conduct is morally right. Marx's first reason for supposing morality to be ideology does not stand up to critical examination.

We turn now to consider Marx's second reason for supposing morality is ideology. This is that morality, as a system specifying individuals' rights and correlative obligations, presupposes a view of the human condition as one of endemic conflict between individuals. Such conflict is presumed to arise from material scarcity in the presence of limited sympathies. Moral requirements, sanctioned by law and public opinion, on this view, are necessary to secure from individuals a degree of other-regardingness that would otherwise be unforthcoming. Now, Marx believed that, in communism, there will be neither scarcity nor limited sympathies. Thus, he believed, there would be no need for moral requirements in communism.

The view that the institution of morality could be dispensed with in a system of communism rests on two assumptions. The first is that scarcity can be abolished. The second is that human sympathy need not be limited. Neither of these assumptions seems warranted. As human productive capacity has grown, so have the wants of individuals for material goods. Thus, scarcity continues amidst affluence. There is no reason to suppose that this will not continue for the indefinite future. At the same time, it would seem to be the case that human beings, as a rule, are disposed to be self-centred in their concerns and to have only strictly limited sympathy. Scarcity together with limited sympathy necessitates the institution of private property as a means for avoiding inter-personal conflict. The need for the institution of private property entails the need for a system of rules which specify what makes a scarce material good the rightful property of an individual. Social peace and cooperation are possible among the predominantly self-interested beings we are, in the face of scarcity, only where it is generally acknowledged to be the duty of everyone to abstain from taking what belongs to another without his or her consent. The existence of scarcity and the limitations of sympathy, therefore, create the need for a system of justice, specifying rights and duties. The suggestion that morality could be dispensed with, therefore, is unrealistic. There is no reason to reject the view of the human condition presupposed by morality. Therefore, there is no reason to regard morality as ideology.

6. Religion as Ideology

For anyone who does not believe in the existence of God, it would seem that Marx's thesis that religion is a case of ideology is unassailable. Yet that is not so. On the one hand, not all religions are clearly committed to the existence of any supernatural beings. The most notable example of a religion without supernatural ontological commitments is Buddhism. On the other hand, even in the case of religions committed to the existence of the supernatural, assertions about the supernatural may have an allegorical as well as a literal significance. In their allegorical sense, even theistic religions may express profound truths about the human condition.

The nineteenth-century philosopher, Arthur Schopenhauer, maintained that the fundamental difference between religions is not whether they are monotheistic, polytheistic, pantheistic, or atheistic. Rather, it is whether they are optimistic or pessimistic. That is, for Schopenhauer, the fundamental difference between religions is 'whether they present the existence of this world as justified by itself, and consequently praise and commend it, or consider it as something which can be conceived only as the consequence of our guilt, and thus really ought not to be'.[31]

Schopenhauer classifies Judaism and Islam as optimistic religions, and Christianity, Brahmanism, and Buddhism as pessimistic. He dismisses the optimistic religions as instances of wish-fulfilment. His opinion of these religions is not altogether dissimilar to Marx's. But Schopenhauer maintains that the pessimistic religions express a fundamental truth about the human condition. If Schopenhauer is correct about this, then, contrary to Marx, such religions cannot be dismissed as mere instances of ideology.

The great truth expressed by the pessimistic religions, according to Schopenhauer, is that of man's 'need for salvation from an existence given up to suffering and death, and its [salvation's] attainability through the denial of the will, hence by a decided opposition to nature'.[32] Schopenhauer says of this proposition that it is 'beyond all comparison the most important truth there can be'.[33] The function of the pessimistic religions is to express this profound truth in a way that is accessible to the masses who are not capable of deep thought. Religions express this truth in the form of myths and mysteries. These pessimistic religions are thus, for Schopenhauer, 'sacred vessels in which the great truth, recognized and expressed for thousands of years . . . and yet remaining in itself an esoteric doctrine as regards the great mass of mankind, is made accessible to them according to their powers, and preserved and passed on through the centuries'.[34]

It may be wondered what right Schopenhauer has to call the esoteric doctrine contained in the pessimistic religions a profound truth. The explanation of his doing so is that Schopenhauer believed that this truth is also the lesson of philosophy. Philosophy differs from religion in two ways however. First, philosophy teaches this truth purely by reflection upon the nature of experience and without reliance upon revelation. Second, philosophy states this truth literally rather than through allegory. Schopenhauer saw philosophy and religion as having a common source: the need of man for metaphysics. This is the need to understand why the world is like it is, given that it contains suffering and death.

Schopenhauer's own philosophy is an account of the world which portrays it as one in which human suffering can only be terminated by denial of the will. I will now attempt to offer a brief summary of the essential steps in his argument. After that, we shall return to the question of whether all religion is ideology.

The book in which Schopenhauer presented his philosophy is entitled *The World as Will and Representation*. The world as representation refers to the world as we perceive it by sense in space and time. The world as will refers to the inner essence of the world. It is Schopenhauer's thesis that the inner essence of all things in the world is will to existence. He arrives at this conclusion as follows. We have, he says, two forms of awareness of ourselves. First, there is sense-perception. Through this form of awareness our bodies are revealed to us as one among a number of other bodies in the universe, some animate, others inanimate. Second, there is inner sense or introspection. This offers us an immediate awareness of ourselves from the inside. Inner sense presents us to ourselves as striving, desirous beings: in short, as will. The outward manifestations of our acts of will are our various bodily actions.

Schopenhauer observes that our will operates below as well as above the threshold of consciousness. First, our will unconsciously governs our thinking. For example, we repress painful memories. Second, our will regulates our metabolic processes like digestion and the beating of the heart. Cases such as these reveal that the will can be active even when it is not guided by any knowledge. The will is ultimately a will to life. It manifests itself as a will to self-preservation and to reproduction, the latter in the form of sexual desire.

By means of analogy, we are able to see that all living beings are similarly animated by will at varying levels of development. In animals, will stands behind instinctive action. For example, a one-year-old bird has no notion of the eggs for which it builds its nest. Once it is accepted that will can operate without being guided by an idea of the purpose for which the activity is being undertaken, Schopenhauer believes that there will be no objection to extending the notion of will to processes in which there is no consciousness at all. Thus, for example, we shall see will active in the formation of a snail's shell.

The major difference between plants and animals is that, by virtue of the more manifold physical needs of animal organisms as compared with plants, animals need to be able to move around and be aware of what is in their environment. Animals need to be able to become aware of that which they need when it is at a distance from them, and must be able to move towards it. Accordingly, animals possess brains and nervous systems the purpose of which is to allow for the recognition of needed objects in the environment. The brain or intellect has, for Schopenhauer, an essentially practical function. Schopenhauer extends his understanding of things as manifestations of will to inorganic nature. The forces of nature like gravity and solidity are regarded as manifestations of will at the lowest levels of development.

The next major thesis of Schopenhauer's is that, because our essence and that of everything else is will, life is suffering. He offers three main reasons for this thesis. First, satisfaction can only be momentary. Unsatisfied want is experienced as painful. Pleasure is the cessation of the suffering bound up with wanting. Pleasure comes with the attainment of the wanted object. But satiation is pleasant only by contrast with the prior unpleasurable state of wanting. Once the preceding state of unpleasure is no longer vividly remembered, satisfaction of desire ceases to be pleasurable. It gives way to the state of boredom and forms the starting-point of fresh discontent. Satisfaction, therefore, can only ever be strictly temporary. Schopenhauer writes: 'Human endeavours and desires . . . buoy us up with the vain hope that their fulfilment is always the final goal of willing. But as soon as they are attained, they no longer look the same, and so are soon forgotten, become antiquated, and are really, although not admittedly, always laid aside as vanished illusions.'[35]

Schopenhauer's second main reason for the thesis that life is suffering is that life is war, competition and conflict. Since there is only will that exists, and since will signifies lack, what is lacked and striven for must also be something that is will. So the will is in conflict with itself.

'Everywhere in nature we see contest, struggle, and the fluctuation of victory, . . . that variance with itself essential to will. Every grade of the will's objectification fights for the matter, the space, and the time of another . . . This universal conflict is to be seen most clearly in the animal kingdom. Animals have the vegetable kingdom for their nourishment, and within the animal kingdom again every animal is the prey and food of some other.'[36]

The conflict of will with itself shows itself most clearly in the case of man. The will's striving reflects itself in the individual egoism. We are motivated predominantly by a self-regard which puts us into opposition with everyone else. The state is a device created by man for restraining egoism. But egoism is always ready to break out.

The third main reason for the thesis that life is suffering is that death awaits every individual as an inevitable fate.

Art offers a temporary escape from striving and hence from suffering. This is why we take such delight in works of art. They temporarily bring an end to striving and give us temporary respite from willing. However, a more permanent form of respite is needed, and this brings us to religion.

The beginnings of the turn away from willing lie in moral virtue. The morally good man is he who intuitively perceives that all individuals are in essence one: namely, will. This realization produces compassion in place of egoism. The compassionate man identifies himself with others and takes their suffering upon himself. Because the compassionate man has reduced his concern for himself, he no longer feels such anxiety, and so tends to be calm and serene.

The process of ceasing to will is carried to completion in the transition from virtue to holiness. The holy man or saint is the person who, having identified with all suffering beings and having seen suffering everywhere, turns away from life, which he now recognizes as bound up with suffering. The holy man ceases to will. The first stage on the road to denial of will is celibacy. The holy man or saint will voluntarily and deliberately renounce worldly possessions. He will seek poverty so as to mortify the will and in order to prevent himself from being seduced by life's pleasures into willing. The state of mind of the holy man is not, however, unpleasant. He enjoys tranquillity and serenity because he is no longer preoccupied with any desire.

'How blessed must be the life of a man whose will is silenced not for a few moments, as in the enjoyment of the beautiful, but for ever, indeed completely extinguished, except for the last glimmering spark that maintains the body and is extinguished with it. Such a man who, after many bitter struggles with his own nature, has at last completely conquered, is then left only as pure knowing being, as the undimmed mirror of the world. Nothing can distress or alarm him any more, . . . for he has cut all the thousand threads of willing which as craving, fear, envy, and anger drag us here and there in constant pain.'[37]

In the light of this account of the human condition, it is possible to appreciate why Schopenhauer maintains that the three great pessimistic religions express the profoundest truth there is about the human condition in allegorical form. It is as allegories of the truth that they are to be understood. Thus, Schopenhauer interprets Christianity in the following terms: 'The doctrine of original sin (affirmation of the will) and of salvation (denial of the will) is really the great truth which constitutes the kernel of Christianity, while the rest is in the main only clothing and covering, or something accessory. Accordingly, we should interpret Jesus Christ always in the universal, as the symbol or personification of the denial of the will-to-live, but not in the individual.'[38]

If one finds the account of the human condition which Schopenhauer presents in his philosophy plausible, and if one interprets the doctrines of these pessimistic religions allegorically, then these religions turn out not to be a case of ideology. Rather, they express the most profound truth about the human condition that there is. Once again, we must judge Marx's theory of ideology to be unsatisfactory.

7 Conclusion

It was remarked in the first chapter that Marx's main contribution to ideas consists of a pair of doctrines. The first is that capitalism is inferior to communism as a form of organization of society. The second is that capitalism is historically destined to give way to communism. The preceding chapters have considered Marx's grounds for these two doctrines. It was seen that for the first Marx offered three reasons. First, capitalism causes alienation. Second, capitalism involves exploitation. Third, capitalism produces periodic crises and unemployment. The other main doctrine of Marx's was supported by two claims which he advances. The first of these is a constituent thesis of historical materialism. It is the thesis that societies tend to adopt economic structures that make fullest possible use of their productive forces. The second is that capitalism fetters highly developed productive forces, whereas communism facilitates their full use.

These various contentions of Marx have been examined and found not to survive critical scrutiny. Marx's claim that capitalism causes alienation we found to be based on a certain conception of human nature together with a certain view of how capitalism affects that nature. Marx equated human nature with a set of three potentialities unique to members of a human species. These were the potentialities for autonomy, sociality and aesthetic experience. Marx contended that capitalism prevents the actualization of these potentialities to any marked degree, whereas communism facilitates their full actualization. The absence of central planning together with the adoption of the division of labour were alleged by Marx to be the main features of capitalism which prevent the actualization of the capacity for autonomy. The fact that capitalism is a form of market society is claimed by Marx to be responsible for capitalism's stultifying the capacity for sociality and aesthetic experience.

Critical scrutiny of these claims has led us to withhold our assent from them. We have remained sceptical of the possibility of communism's providing ordinary members of society with more control of their lives than capitalism does. We have denied that capitalism prevents workers from being able to engage in more meaningful work than that in which they do engage under capitalism. If there is rigid division of labour in capitalism, this is because such labour is more productive. Capitalist employers would be willing to provide workers with more meaningful work if the latter were willing to accept lower wages in line with the resultant lower productivity. If, as they do, workers tend to opt for less meaningful work in return for a higher wage than they would be able to receive were their work divided into more mean-ingful segments, their autonomy has not thereby been impugned. If anything, it has been enhanced through their being offered such a choice.

The claim that capitalism stultifies the actualization of the pot-entialities for sociality and aesthetic experience was based on the contention that a market form of economy encourages egoistic attitudes which inhibit the formation of other-regarding senti-ments and the aesthetic attitude. This claim was rejected on the grounds that acquisitiveness and egoism long antedated capital-ism as central features of human make-up and may be presumed to be endemic. In opposition to Marx, we maintained that human beings tend to be egocentric by nature. Given this central fact about human nature, communism would not promote greater other-regardingness among human beings than capitalism does.

Marx's claim that capitalism involves exploitation rested upon the assertion that capitalist employers render no service to their employees when they make available to them means of pro-duction to work on plus their wages. Against this assertion, we defended the traditional view that capitalists serve the useful and indispensable functions of saving and risk-taking. These func-tions, it was argued, morally entitle capitalists to part of (the value of) the product of labour. The institution of private property in means of production was defended on the grounds that it need violate no one's rights. In practice, it was argued, this institution has made workers better off than they would have been in the absence of the institution.

Marx's claim that capitalism produces periodic crises and unemployment was examined and rejected. A capitalist economy that was uninterfered with by government (and by the state – conferring coercive power upon trade unions) would tend to generate full employment and no overall economic fluctuations. Economic crises, it was argued, have been the product of government interference with the workings of the capitalist order. The Keynesian claim that capitalism produces chronic unemployment because of under-investment or over-saving was likewise examined and found to be fallacious.

In Chapter 6, consideration was given to two arguments advanced by the classical political economists to the effect that capitalism is superior to communism as an economic system. The first of these arguments was that capitalism is conducive to greater enterprise and effort than communism because it provides greater incentive for these things. The second was that the pricing mechanism of the market constitutes a much more efficient way of allocating resources than the system of central planning. These two arguments were endorsed. It was further argued that worker-controlled socialism, although superior to a form of socialism that makes use of central planning, would not be as productively efficient and dynamic as capitalism.

Our conclusions with respect to the relative efficiency of capitalism and communism mean that we reject Marx's claim that capitalism fetters highly developed productive forces. This in turn means that we would not accept Marx's thesis that capitalism is destined to give way to communism, even if we accepted Marx's thesis that societies tend to acquire economic structures that are conducive to the full utilization of their productive forces. This latter thesis was rejected in Chapter 3 because it was there found to be reliant upon two assumptions for which Marx had no good reason. The first of these unwarranted assumptions was that members of a class who have an interest in replacing an economic structure that fetters the use of forces of production with one that promotes their use would always be willing to embark on revolutionary action. The second unwarranted assumption is that a class whose members have an interest and the will to replace such a use-fettering economic structure would have the capacity to overthrow such an economic structure.

The upshot of our examination of Marx's theories, therefore, is that they are fundamentally flawed. In fact, so flawed are they that we have no alternative but to conclude that the time has come when they should be discarded and consigned to the lumber-room of intellectual history.

Many will resist my conclusions by saying that many of my objections to Marx rest upon attributing to human nature a pre-dominantly self-interested character. It will be argued against me that such a view represents an instance of bourgeois ideology. It will be argued against me that human nature is not constant. What man is like, it will be said, is a function of the economic structure of his society. It will be contended that it is capitalism that makes man acquisitive and self-centred. 'Bring man up in communist society and you will find he becomes altruistic,' it will be said. I deny that Marx or anyone else provides any good reason for accepting this claim about the malleableness of human nature. It is sometimes contended, in support of it, that members of so-called 'primitive societies' display towards each other the kind of empathy and altruism that communism both requires and would call forth. Such societies, however, do not prove that human beings could be as communism requires them to be in order to have a chance of success. Granted that members of such societies display an endearing propensity towards altruism and mutual aid *vis-á-vis* other members. But such altruism is confined to a very small number of other people all of whom are very well known to everyone. Moreover, such altruism is typically conjoined with extreme hostility or else indifference towards those who are not members of the society. Communism, to be effective, requires that individual members be disposed to regard anonymous, unknown others with as much regard as close relations and kin. How is it possible to identify closely with people whom one does not even know? It is true that saints manage to do something like this. But can we and should we pin our trust upon the possibility that all could become as saints?

Marx once wrote: 'The criticism of religion disillusions man, so that he will think, act and fashion his reality like a man who has discarded his illusions and regained his senses, so that he will move around himself as his own true sun.'[1] Our final verdict on Marx must be that he never fully freed himself from optimistic illusions about human nature. Where Marx failed, we can succeed. And, through succeeding, we shall avoid being misled into discarding the one economic system that has been responsible for such prosperity and happiness as the ordinary man and woman have been able to enjoy.

Notes

Introduction*

1. Among the best introductory books on Marx are P. Singer, *Marx*, Oxford, 1980; and A. Callinicos, *The Revolutionary Ideas of Marx*, London, 1983.

Philosophical Anthropology

1. K. Marx, 'Communism and the Augsburg *Allgemeine Zeitung*', in K. Marx and F. Engels, *Collected Works*, Vol. 1, London, 1975, p. 220.
2. K. Marx, 'Debates on Freedom of the Press', in K. Marx and F. Engels, *Collected Works*, Vol. 1, London, 1975, p. 162.
3. K. Marx, 'Leading Article in No. 179 of *Kölnische Zeitung*', in K. Marx and F. Engels, *Collected Works*, Vol. 1, London, 1975, p. 202.
4. L. Feuerbach, *The Essence of Christianity*, trans. G. Eliot, New York, 1957, p. 14.
5. *ibid.*, p. 274.
6. *ibid.*, p. 1.
7. *ibid.*, p. 171.
8. K. Marx, 'Debates on the Law of Thefts of Wood', in K. Marx and F. Engels, *Collected Works*, Vol. 1, London, 1975, p. 236.
9. *ibid.*, p. 259.
10. K. Marx, 'Letters from the Franco–German Yearbooks', in K. Marx, *Early Writings*, trans. R. Livingstone and G. Benton, London, 1975, pp. 201–2.
11. See CHPR, p. 108.
12. CHPR, p. 184.
13. CHPR, p. 145.
14. See CHPR, p. 89.
15. OJQ, pp. 225–6.

* See Abbreviated Titles of Works by Marx, p. 220.

16. OJQ, p. 234.
17. ICHPR, p. 251.
18. EPM, p. 348.
19. EPM, p. 328.
20. EPM, p. 329.
21. G, p. 611.
22. *ibid*.
23. CI, p. 284.
24. G, p. 612.
25. EPM, p. 328.
26. EPM, p. 350.
27. EPM, pp. 352–3.
28. K. Marx, 'Theses on Feuerbach', in Karl Marx, *Early Writings*, London, 1975, p. 423.
29. See A. Wood, *Karl Marx*, London, 1981, p. 8.
30. ICHPR, p. 244.
31. GI, pp. 47–8.
32. CI, p. 799.
33. EPM, p. 326.
34. EJMEPE, p. 265.
35. OJQ, p. 240.
36. EJMEPE, p. 275.
37. EPM, p. 331.
38. EPM, p. 366.
39. EPM, pp. 351–2.
40. EPM, p. 361.
41. EPM, p. 353.
42. EPM, p. 359.
43. EPM, pp. 359–60.
44. EPM, p. 348.
45. GI, p. 48.
46. CI, p. 173.
47. GI, p. 47.
48. G, pp. 611–12.
49. CIII, p. 959.
50. EJMEPE, p. 278.
51. EPM, p. 365.
52. EJMEPE, pp. 277–8.
53. EPM, p. 352.
54. GI, p. 394.

Notes

55. I have taken this argument from Robert Nozick, *Anarchy, State and Utopia*, New York, 1974, pp. 246–50.
56. M. Friedman and R. Friedman, *Free to Choose*, London, 1980, p. 234.

The Materialist Conception of History

1. The interpretation of historical materialism given here owes a great deal to the work of G. A. Cohen. See G. A. Cohen, *Karl Marx's Theory of History: A Defence*, Oxford, 1978; and G. A. Cohen, 'Forces and Relations of Production', in B. Matthews (ed.), *Marx: A Hundred Years On*, London, 1983, pp. 111–34.
2. G, p. 831.
3. CI, p. 344.
4. GI, p. 90.
5. CM, p. 87.
6. CIII, p. 929.
7. GI, p. 59.
8. GI, pp. 36–7.
9. PP, p. 114.
10. GI, p. 74.
11. CCPE, pp. 425–6.
12. Quoted in R. N. Hunt, *The Political Ideas of Marx and Engels*, II, *Classical Marxism, 1850–1895*, London, 1984, p. 304.
13. 'Marx to the Editorial Board of the Otechestvenniye Zapiski (Fatherland Notes)', November 1977, in L. S. Feuer (ed.), *Marx and Engels: Basic Writings on Politics and Philosophy*, London, 1959, p. 477.
14. *ibid.*, p. 478.
15. *ibid.*, p. 479.
16. *ibid.*, p. 477.
x17. K. Marx and F. Engels, *The Russian Menace to Europe*, P. W. Blackstock and B. F. Hoselitz (eds.), London, 1953, pp. 278–9.
18. *ibid.*, p. 311.
19. *ibid.*, pp. 311–12.
20. Marx to Annekov, December 1846, in PP, p. 166.
21. PP, p. 102.
22. GI, pp. 53–4.
23. F. Engels, 'The End of German Classical Philosophy', in L. S. Feuer (ed.), *Marx and Engels: Basic Writings on Philosophy and Politics*, London, 1959, pp. 279–80.

24. G. R. Elton, *Reformation Europe*, London, 1963, p. 318.

25. G. A. Cohen, *Karl Marx's Theory of History: A Defence*, Oxford, 1978.

26. T. Honderich, 'Against Teleological Historical Materialism', *Inquiry*, Vol. 25, 1982, pp. 451–69.

27. G. A. Cohen, *Karl Marx's Theory of History: A Defence*, Oxford, 1978, p. 152.

28. I owe this point to J. N. Gray, 'Philosophy, Science and Myth in Marxism', in G. H. R. Parkinson (ed.), *Marx and Marxisms*, Royal Institute of Philosophy Series 14, Cambridge, 1982.

29. J. Cohen, 'Review of G. A. Cohen's *Karl Marx's Theory of History*', *Journal of Philosophy*, Vol. LXXIX, 1982, p. 268.

30. G. A. Cohen, *Karl Marx's Theory of History: A Defence*, Oxford, 1978, p. 292.

31. A. Levine and E. O. Wright, 'Rationality and Class Struggle', *New Left Review*, No. 123, Sept/Oct 1980, p. 59.

32. A. E. Buchanan, *Marx and Justice*, London, 1982, p. 89.

33. F. Engels, Funeral Oration, March 1883, in P. S. Foner (ed.), *When Marx Died*, New York, 1973, p. 39.

Economic Theory

1. CI, p. 129.

2. *ibid.*

3. CI, p. 135.

4. *ibid.*

5. I derive this term from L. von Mises, 'Remarks on the Fundamental Problem of the Subjective Theory of Value', in L. von Mises, *Epistemological Problems of Economics*, New York, 1981, pp. 167–82.

6. CI, pp. 127–8.

7. CI, p. 127.

8. The objections that follow were first advanced by Eugen von Böhm-Bawerk. See E. Böhm-Bawerk, *The Exploitation Theory of Socialism-Communism*, third revised edition, South Holland, Illinois, 1975.

9. CI, p. 135.

10. The account of the Subjective Theory of Value offered here owes much to M. Rothbard, *Man, Economy, and State*, Los Angeles, 1962.

11. CI, p. 326.

12. Proponents of the justice interpretation of exploitation include Z. I. Husami, 'Marx on Distributive Justice', in M. Cohen, T. Nagel

and T. Scanlon (eds), *Marx, Justice, and History*, Princeton, NJ, 1980, pp. 42–79; G. A. Cohen, 'The Labour Theory of Value and the Concept of Exploitation', in M. Cohen, T. Nagel and T. Scanlon (eds), *op. cit.*, pp. 135–57; G. A. Cohen, 'More on Exploitation and the Labour Theory of Value', *Inquiry*, Vol. 26, 1983, pp. 309–31; and G. Young, 'Justice and Capitalist Production: Marx and Bourgeois Ideology', *Canadian Journal of Philosophy*, Vol. VIII, No. 3, September 1978, pp. 421–55.

13. The leading proponent of the coercion interpretation is A. W. Wood, 'The Marxian Critique of Justice', in M. Cohen, T. Nagel and T. Scanlon (eds), *op. cit.*, pp. 3–41; and 'Marx on Right and Justice: A Reply to Husami', in *ibid.*, pp. 107–35; and A. W. Wood, *Karl Marx*, London, 1981.

14. CI, p. 301.

15. CIII, pp. 460–61.

16. CGP, p. 344.

17. Marx, 'Critical Notes to Adolph Wagner's Textbook', quoted in A. Wood, 'Marx on Right and Justice: A Reply to Husami', in M. Cohen, T. Nagel and T. Scanlon (eds), *op. cit.*, p. 115.

18. A. W. Wood, *Karl Marx*, London, 1981, p. 149.

19. CGP, p. 347.

20. G. A. Cohen, 'Review of A. W. Wood, *Karl Marx*', *Mind*, Vol. XCII, No. 367, 1983, pp. 440–45.

21. G, p. 705.

22. CI, p. 743.

23. CI, p. 728.

24. CGP, p. 347.

25. See A. E. Buchanan, *Marx and Justice*, London, 1982, Ch. 5. especially p. 59.

26. J. S. Mill, *Principles of Political Economy*, D. Winch (ed.), London, 1970, pp. 368–9.

27. CI, p. 202.

28. A. Wood, *Karl Marx*, London, 1981, p. 233.

29. CI, p. 874.

30. CI, p. 915.

31. CI, p. 744.

32. CI, pp. 744–5.

33. See R. Cameron, *Banking in the Early Stages of Industralization*, New York, 1967, pp. 38–9.

34. F. Heaton, 'Financing the Industrial Revolution', in F. Crouzet

(ed.), *Capital Formation in the Industrial Revolution*, London, 1972, pp. 88–9.

35. R. Cameron, *Banking in the Early Stages of Industrialization*, New York, 1967, p. 39.

36. F. Crouzet, 'Capital Formation in Great Britain during the Industrial Revolution', in F. Crouzet (ed.), *op. cit*, pp. 176–7.

37. D. Friedman, *The Machinery of Freedom*, New Rochelle, NY, 1973, pp. 61–2.

38. See S. Scheffler, 'Natural Rights, Equality, and the Minimal State', in J. Paul (ed.), *Reading Nozick*, London, 1982, pp. 148–68, see esp. p. 153.

39. CI, p. 908.

40. See CI, Chapters 27 and 28.

41. CI, p. 895.

42. J. D. Chambers and G. E. Mingay, *The Agricultural Revolution*, London, 1966, p. 91.

43. *ibid.*, p. 99.

44. F. A. Hayek (ed.), *Capitalism and the Historians*, London, 1954, pp. 16–17.

45. CM, p. 72.

46. CM, p. 70.

47. CI, p. 617.

48. CI, p. 480.

49. CI, p. 739.

50. CI, p. 777.

51. *ibid.*

52. CI, p. 780.

53. CI, p. 782.

54. CI, p. 784.

55. *ibid.*

56. CI, p. 763.

57. CI, p. 791.

58. CI, p. 771.

59. CI, p. 790.

60. CI, pp. 789–90.

61. CI, p. 799.

62. *ibid.*

63. CI, p. 798. Marx's emphasis.

64. VPP, p. 92.

65. CM, p. 74.

66. P. T. Bauer, *Equality, the Third World, and Economic Delusion*, London, 1981, p. 70.
67. WLC, p. 259.
68. See CI, p. 806.
69. CIII, pp. 318–19.
70. G, p. 748.
71. G, p. 749.
72. CIII, p. 343. My italics.
73. P. Sweezy, *The Theory of Capitalist Development*, New York, 1970, p. 104.
74. CI, p. 785.
75. CM, pp. 72–3.
76. G, pp. 749–50.
77. CIII, p. 615.
78. CIII, p. 367.
79. CIII, pp. 360–63.
80. CIII, p. 347.
81. See P. M. Sweezy, *The Theory of Capitalist Development*, London, 1942, Ch. 9; and K. Uno, *Principles of Political Economy*, Brighton, 1980, Part III, Section 1.
82. M. C. Howard and J. E. King, *The Political Economy of Marx*, London, 1975, p. 215.
83. See C. Harman, *Explaining the Crisis*, London, 1984, p. 124.
84. See L. von Mises, *Human Action*, Third Edition, Chicago, 1963, Ch. XX; M. N. Rothbard, *America's Great Depression*, Kansas City, 1963; and M. N. Rothbard, *For a New Liberty*, Revised Edition, London, 1978, Ch. 9.
85. CIII, p. 742.
86. CI, p. 786.

Politics

1. P. S. Foner (ed.), *When Marx Died*, New York, 1973, pp. 39–40.
2. Mao Tse-tung, 'Problems of War and Strategy', *Selected Works*, Peking, 1965–77, Vol. 2, pp. 224–5.
3. S. Moore, *Three Tactics: The Background in Marx*, New York, 1963, p. 22.
4. CM, p. 98.
5. *ibid.*
6. R. Hunt, *The Political Ideas of Marx and Engels*, Vol. 1, London, 1975, Ch. 6.

7. MA, p. 322.
8. MA, pp. 323–4.
9. MA, p. 330.
10. Quoted in R. N. Hunt, *The Political Ideas of Marx and Engels*, Vol. 1, London, 1975, p. 241.
11. MCCM, p. 341.
12. VCV, p. 176.
13. K. Marx, Editorial in *Neue Rheinische Zeitung* No. 301, 19 May 1849, in K. Marx and F. Engels, *Articles from the Neue Rheinische Zeitung*, London, 1972, p. 254.
14. Review from *Neue Rheinische Zeitung Politisch-Ökonomische Revue*, No. 4, April 1850; K. Marx, 'Review of *Les Conspirateurs* by A. Chenu, and *La Naissance de la Republique en Février 1848* by Lucien de La Hodde', in K. Marx and F. Engels, *Collected Works*, Vol. 10, London, 1978, pp. 318 and 319–20.
15. CSF, p. 131.
16. CM, p. 78.
17. CM, p. 86.
18. CCR, p. 161.
19. CH, p. 264.
20. K. Marx, Interview, *New York World*, 18 July 1871, in K. Marx, *First International and After*, D. Fernbach (ed.), Harmondsworth, 1974, p. 395.
21. SHC, p. 324.
22. K. Marx, Interview, *New York World*, 18 July 1871, in K. Marx, *First International and After*, D. Fernbach (ed.), Harmondsworth, 1974, p. 400.
23. CM, p. 69.
24. CM, p. 87.
25. See R. Miliband, 'Marx and the State', in T. Bottomore (ed.), *Karl Marx*, Oxford, 1973, pp. 128–50.
26. EBLB, pp. 237–8.
27. CWF, p. 212.
28. CWF, p. 209.
29. CWF, p. 210.
30. CWF, p. 209.
31. K. Marx, 'First Draft of *Civil War in France*', in K. Marx, *The First International and After*, D. Fernbach (ed.), London, 1974, p. 253.
32. V. I. Lenin, 'State and Revolution', *Selected Works*, Vol. 2, Moscow, 1975, p. 302.

Theory of Ideology

1. GI, p. 30.
2. GI, p. 247.
3. GI, p. 419.
4. CM, p. 86.
5. *ibid.*
6. CGP, pp. 347–8.
7. CIII, p. 461.
8. That Marx holds morality to be ideology for this reason is argued in S. Lukes, *Marxism and Morality*, Oxford, 1985.
9. ICHPR, p. 244.
10. N. Abercrombie, S. Hill, and B. S. Turner, *The Dominant Ideology Thesis*, London, 1984, p. 8.
11. GI, p. 59.
12. N. Abercrombie, S. Hill and B. S. Turner, *The Dominant Ideology Thesis*, London, 1984, pp. 69–70.
13. *ibid.*, pp. 124–5.
14. *ibid.*, p. 155.
15. B. Bauer, 'The Trumpet of the Last Judgement over Hegel the Atheist and Antichrist', in L. S. Stepelevich (ed.), *The Young Hegelians: An Anthology*, Cambridge, 1983, p. 182.
16. CI, p. 96.
17. PP, p. 112.
18. A. Smith quoted in Lord Robbins, *The Theory of Economic Policy in English Classical Political Economy*, Second Edition, London, 1978, pp. 17–18.
19. *ibid.*, pp. 116–17.
20. F. A. Hayek, 'The New Confusion about "Planning" ', in F. A. Hayek, *New Studies in Philosophy, Politics, Economics and History of Ideas*, London, 1978, p. 237.
21. David Schweickart, *Capitalism or Worker Control?*, New York, 1980.
22. *ibid.*, p. 73.
23. M. Friedman, *Market Mechanisms and Central Economic Planning*, Washington, 1981, p. 19.
24. The model and associated Keynesian argument is set out more fully in P. Donaldson, *Economics of the Real World*, Harmondsworth, 1978, Ch. 3.
25. P. Donaldson, *A Question of Economics*, Harmondsworth, 1985, p. 111.
26. The fallacies of Keynesian economics are well set out in M.

Rothbard, *Man, Economy, and State*, Los Angeles, 1962, pp. 679–93. For a more extended critique of Keynesian economics, see H. Hazlitt, *The Failure of the 'New Economics'*, Lanham and London, 1959.

27. A. Wood, *Karl Marx*, London, 1981, p. 128.
28. *ibid.*, p. 132.
29. *ibid.*
30. F. Engels, *Anti-Dühring* (1878), London, 1975, pp. 216–17.
31. A. Schopenhauer, *The World as Will and Representation*, Volume II, trans. E. F. J. Payne, New York, 1958, p. 170.
32. *ibid.*, p. 628.
33. *ibid.*
34. *ibid.*, p. 629.
35. A. Schopenhauer, *The World as Will and Representation*, Volume I, trans. E. F. J. Payne, New York, 1958, p. 164.
36. *ibid.*, pp. 146–7.
37. *ibid.*, p. 390.
38. *ibid.*, p. 405.

Conclusion

1. ICHPR, p. 244.

Abbreviated Titles of Works by Marx

CI	*Capital*, Volume I
CII	*Capital*, Volume II
CIII	*Capital*, Volume III
CCPE	*Contribution to the Critique of Political Economy*
CCR	'The Crisis and the Counter-Revolution'
CGP	*Critique of the Gotha Programme*
CH	'The Chartists'
CHPR	'Critique of Hegel's *Philosophy of Right*'
CM	*Communist Manifesto*
CSF	*Class Struggles in France*
CWF	*Civil War in France*
EBLB	*Eighteenth Brumaire of Louis Bonaparte*
EJMEPE	'Excerpts from James Mill's *Elements of Political Economy*'
EPM	*Economic and Philosophical Manuscripts*
G	*Grundrisse*
GI	*German Ideology*
ICHPR	Introduction to the *Critique of Hegel's Philosophy of Right*
MA	Address of the Central Committee to the Communist League, March 1850
MCCM	Minutes of the Central Committee Meeting 15 September 1850
OJQ	'On the Jewish Question'
PP	*Poverty of Philosophy*
SHC	Speech on the Hague Congress, 8 September 1872
VCV	'Victory of the Counter-Revolution in Vienna'
VPP	*Value, Price and Profit*
WLC	*Wage-Labour and Capital*

References

Works by Marx

Address of the Central Committee to the Communist League (March 1850) in K. Marx, *The Revolutions of 1848*, Harmondsworth, 1973.

Capital, Volume I (1867), Harmondsworth, 1976.

Capital, Volume II (1885), Harmondsworth, 1978.

Capital, Volume III (1894), Harmondsworth, 1981.

'The Chartists' (1852) in K. Marx, *Surveys from Exile*, Harmondsworth, 1973.

Civil War in France (1871) in K. Marx, *The First International and After*, Harmondsworth, 1974.

Class Struggles in France (1850) in K. Marx, *Surveys from Exile*, Harmondsworth, 1973.

'Communism and the Augsburg *Allgemeine Zeitung*' (1842) in K. Marx and F. Engels, *Collected Works*, Volume 1, London, 1975.

Communist Manifesto (1848) in K. Marx, *The Revolutions of 1848*, Harmondsworth, 1973.

Contribution to the Critique of Political Economy (1859), Moscow, 1970.

'The Crisis and the Counter-Revolution' (1848) in K. Marx, *The Revolutions of 1848*, Harmondsworth, 1973.

Critique of the Gotha Programme (1875) in K. Marx, *The First International and After*, Harmondsworth, 1974.

Critique of Hegel's Philosophy of Right (1843) in K. Marx, *Early Writings*, Harmondsworth, 1975.

'Debates on Freedom of the Press' in K. Marx and F. Engels, *Collected Works*, Volume 1, London, 1975.

'Debates on the Law of Thefts of Wood' in K. Marx and F. Engels, *Collected Works*, Volume 1, London, 1975.

Economic and Philosophical Manuscripts (1844) in K. Marx, *Early Writings*, Harmondsworth, 1975.

Eighteenth Brumaire of Louis Bonaparte (1852) in K. Marx, *Surveys from Exile*, Harmondsworth, 1973.

'Excerpts from James Mill's *Elements of Political Economy*' (1844) in K. Marx, *Early Writings*, Harmondsworth, 1975.

References

German Ideology (1845) in K. Marx and F. Engels, *Collected Works*, London, 1976.

Grundrisse (1857–8), Harmondsworth, 1973.

'Introduction to a Contribution to the Critique of Hegel's *Philosophy of Right*' (1843) in K. Marx, *Early Writings*, Harmondsworth, 1975.

'Leading Article in No. 179 *Kölnische Zeitung*' in K. Marx and F. Engels, *Collected Works*, Vol. 1, London, 1975.

Minutes of the Central Committee Meeting of 15 September 1850 in K. Marx, *The Revolutions of 1848*, Harmondsworth, 1973.

'On the Jewish Question' (1843) in K. Marx, *Early Writings*, Harmondsworth, 1975.

The Poverty of Philosophy (1847), Moscow, 1975.

Review of *Les Conspirateurs* by A. Chenu and *La Naissance de la Republique en Février 1848* by Lucien de La Hodde in K. Marx and F. Engels, *Collected Works*, Volume 10, London, 1978.

The Russian Menace to Europe, P. W. Blackstock and B. F. Hoselitz (eds.), London, 1953.

Speech on the Hague Congress (8 September 1872) in K. Marx, *The First International and After*, Harmondsworth, 1974.

'Theses on Feuerbach' (1845) in K. Marx, *Early Writings*, London, 1975.

Value, Price and Profit (1865), London, 1899.

'The Victory of the Counter-Revolution in Vienna' (1848) in K. Marx, *The Revolutions of 1848*, Harmondsworth, 1973.

'Wage-Labour and Capital' (1849) in K. Marx, *Selected Writings*, D. McLellan (ed.), Oxford, 1977.

Works by Others

ABERCROMBIE, N., HILL, S. and TURNER, B. S., *The Dominant Ideology Thesis*, London, 1984.

BAUER, B. 'The Trumpet of the Last Judgement over Hegel the Atheist and Antichrist', in L. S. Stepelevich (ed.), *The Young Hegelians: An Anthology*, Cambridge, 1983.

BAUER, P. T., *Equality, the Third World, and Economic Delusion*, London, 1981.

BÖHM-BAWERK, E., *The Exploitation Theory of Socialism-Communism*, third revised edition, South Holland, Illinois, 1975.

BUCHANAN, A. E., *Marx and Justice*, London, 1982.

CALLINICOS, A., *The Revolutionary Ideas of Marx*, London, 1983.

CAMERON, R., *Banking in the Early Stages of Industrialization*, New York, 1967.

CHAMBERS, J. D. and MINGAY, G. E., *The Agricultural Revolution*, London, 1966.

COHEN, G. A., 'Forces and Relations of Production', in B. Matthews (ed.), *Marx: A Hundred Years On*, London, 1983.

COHEN, G. A., *Karl Marx's Theory of History: A Defence*, Oxford, 1978.

COHEN, G. A., 'The Labour Theory of Value and the Concept of Exploitation', in M. Cohen, T. Nagel and T. Scanlon (eds.), *op. cit.*, pp. 135–57.

COHEN, G. A., 'More on Exploitation and the Labour Theory of Value', *Inquiry*, Vol. 26, 1984, pp. 309–31.

COHEN, J., Review of G. A. Cohen's *Karl Marx's Theory of History*, *Journal of Philosophy*, Vol. LXXIX, 1982, pp. 253–73.

COHEN, M., NAGEL, T. and SCANLON, T. (eds.), *Marx, Justice and History*, Princeton, NJ, 1980.

CROUZET, F., *Capital Formation in the Industrial Revolution*, London, 1972.

DONALDSON, P., *Economics of the Real World*, second edition, Harmondsworth, 1978.

DONALDSON, P., *A Question of Economics*, Harmondsworth, 1985.

ELTON, G. R., *Reformation Europe*, London, 1963.

ENGELS, F., 'The End of German Classical Philosophy', in L. S. Feuer (ed.), *Marx and Engels: Basic Writings on Philosophy and Politics*, London, 1959.

ENGELS, F., *Anti-Dühring* (1878), London, 1975.

FEUERBACH, L., *The Essence of Christianity*, trans. G. Eliot, New York, 1951.

FONER, P. S., *When Marx Died*, New York, 1973.

FRIEDMAN, D., *The Machinery of Freedom*, New Rochelle, NY, 1973.

FRIEDMAN, M. and FRIEDMAN, R., *Free to Choose*, London, 1980.

FRIEDMAN, M., *Market Mechanisms and Central Economic Planning*, Washington, 1981.

GRAY, J., 'Philosophy, Science and Myth in Marxism', in G. H. R. Parkinson (ed.), *Marx and Marxisms*, Royal Institute of Philosophy, Series 14, Cambridge, 1982.

HARMAN, C., *Explaining the Crisis*, London, 1984.

HAYEK, F. A. (ed.), *Capitalism and the Historians*, London, 1954.

HAYEK, F. A., 'The New Confusion about "Planning" ', in F. A. Hayek, *New Studies in Philosophy, Politics, Economics and History of Ideas*, London, 1978.

HAZLITT, H., *The Failure of the 'New Economics'*, Lanham and London, 1959.

HEATON, H., 'Financing the Industrial Revolution', in F. Crouzet (ed.), *Capital Formation in the Industrial Revolution*, London, 1972.

HONDERICH, T., 'Against Teleological Historical Materialism', *Inquiry*, Vol. 25, 1982, pp. 451–69.

References

HOWARD, M. C. and KING, J. E., *The Political Economy of Marx*, London, 1975.

HUNT, R. N., *The Political Ideas of Marx and Engels*, Vol. 1, London, 1975.

HUNT, R. N., *The Political Ideas of Marx and Engels*, Vol. 2, London, 1984.

HUSAMI, Z. I., 'Marx on Distributive Justice', in M. Cohen, T. Nagel and T. Scanlon (eds.), *op. cit.*, pp. 42–79.

LENIN, V. I., 'State and Revolution', in *Selected Works*, Vol. 2, Moscow, 1975.

LEVINE, A. and WRIGHT, E. O., 'Rationality and Class Struggle', *New Left Review*, No. 123, Sept./Oct. 1980, pp. 47–68.

LUKES, S., *Marxism and Morality*, Oxford, 1985.

MAO TSE-TUNG, 'Problems of War and Strategy', *Selected Works*, Peking, 1965–77, Vol. 2.

MILIBAND, R., 'Marx and the State', in T. Bottomore (ed.), *Karl Marx*, Oxford, 1973, pp. 128–50.

MILL, J. S., *Principles of Political Economy*, D. Winch (ed.), Harmondsworth, 1970.

MISES, L. VON, *Human Action*, third edition, Chicago, 1963.

MOORE, S., *Three Tactics: The Background in Marx*, New York, 1963.

NOZICK, R., *Anarchy, State and Utopia*, New York, 1974.

ROBBINS, Lord, *The Theory of Economic Policy in English Classical Political Economy*, second edition, London, 1978.

ROTHBARD, M. N., *America's Great Depression*, third edition, Kansas City, 1975.

ROTHBARD, M. N., *For a New Liberty*, New York, 1978.

ROTHBARD, M. N., *Man, Economy, and State*, Los Angeles, 1962.

SCHEFFLER, S., 'Natural Rights, Equality, and the Minimal State', in J. Paul (ed.), *Reading Nozick*, London, 1982, pp. 148–68.

SCHOPENHAUER, A., *The World as Will and Representation*, trans. E. F. J. Payne, New York, 1958.

SCHWEICKART, D., *Capitalism or Worker Control?*, New York, 1980.

SINGER, P., *Marx*, Oxford, 1980.

SWEEZY, P. M., *The Theory of Capitalist Development*, New York, 1970.

UNO, K., *Principles of Political Economy*, trans. T. T. Sekine, Brighton, 1980.

WOOD, A. W., *Karl Marx*, London, 1981.

WOOD, A. W., 'The Marxian Critique of Justice', in M. Cohen, T. Nagel and T. Scanlon (eds.), *op. cit.*, pp. 3–41.

WOOD, A. W., 'Marx on Right and Justice: A Reply to Husami', in M. Cohen, T. Nagel and T. Scanlon (eds.), *op. cit.*, pp. 106–35.

Name Index

Subject Index

Aesthetic experience, 33, 39–40, 44–5, 203
Alienation, 13, 21, 34–41, 45–51
Autonomy, 31–2, 41–3, 46–9

Bureaucracy
    Hegel's view of, 24
    Marx's view of, 23
    Need for in communism, 46, 168
Business Cycle, 137–142

Capital
    centralization of, 126–8
    circuit of, 93, 134–5
    concentration of, 126–7
    constant, 95, 136
    organic composition of, 133–7
    technical composition of, 134–7
    variable, 95
Capitalism, 35–41, 49–50, 124–42
Civil society, 24, 25, 68
Class
    capacities, 79
    consciousness, 156
    defined, 55
    Hegel's view of, 24
    ruling, 55–7, 61

Classical political economy, 173, 182–5, 188–194
Commodity, 82
Communism, 27, 29–30, 41–5, 163–9
Communist League, 144–8, 166
Cyclical crises; see Business Cycle

Democracy, 25–7, 159–160, 164–7
Dictatorship of the proletariat, 145, 156–8, 165–7
Division of labour, 37
Dominant Ideology Thesis, 171–2, 177–181

Egoism, 21–2, 24–5, 33, 38, 50, 174, 203
Enclosures, 122
Exchange-value, 82
Exploitation, 13, 98–124
Forces of production, 53, 60, 69, 77–8, 124
Functional explanation, 72–7

Human nature, 30–34, 205, 208–9
Historical materialism: see Materialist conception of history

227

Acknowledgements

Our thanks are due to the following for their kind permission to reproduce material in this book:

N. Abercrombie, S. Hill and B. S. Turner, *The Dominant Ideology Thesis*, Allen & Unwin, 1984, London.

K. Marx and F. Engels, *The Russian Menace to Europe* (ed. P. W. Blackstock and B. F. Hoselitz), Allen & Unwin, 1953, London.

M. Friedman, *Market Mechanisms and Central Economic Planning*, American Enterprise Institute for Public Policy Research, 1981, Washington D.C.

J. D. Chambers and G. E. Mingay, *The Agricultural Revolution*, B. T. Batsford Ltd, 1966, London.

L. S. Stepelevich (ed.), *The Young Hegelians: An Anthology*, Cambridge University Press, 1983, Cambridge.

G. A. Cohen, *Karl Marx's Theory of History: A Defence*, Clarendon Press, 1978, London.

G. R. Elton, *Reformation Europe 1517–1559*, Fontana, Collins, 1963, London.

P. S. Foner (ed.), *When Marx Died*, International Publishers, 1973, New York.

Joshua Cohen, *Review of Karl Marx's Theory of History: A Defence by G. A. Cohen*, in the *Journal of Philosophy*, Vol. LXXXIX No. 5, 1982, New York.

F. Engels, *Anti-Dühring*, Lawrence & Wishart Ltd, 1975, London.

V. I. Lenin, *Selected Works, Vol. 2*, Progress Publishers, 1975, Moscow, Lawrence & Wishart, London.

K. Marx, *The Poverty of Philosophy*, Progress Publishers, 1975, Moscow, Lawrence & Wishart, London.

Acknowledgements

K. Marx and F. Engels, *Collected Works, Vol. 1*, Lawrence & Wishart, 1975, London.

K. Marx and F. Engels, *Collected Works, Vol. 5*, Lawrence & Wishart, 1976, London.

K. Marx and F. Engels, *Collected Works, Vol. 10*, Lawrence & Wishart, 1978, London.

M. C. Howard and J. E. King, *The Political Economy of Marx*, Longman, 1975, London.

R. N. Hunt, *The Political Ideas of Marx and Engels; I. Marxism and Totalitarian Democracy*, Macmillan, 1975, London.

R. N. Hunt, *The Political Ideas of Marx and Engels; II. Classical Marxism 1850–1895*, Macmillan, 1984, London and Basingstoke.

M. and R. Friedman, *Free to Choose*, Martin Secker & Warburg Limited, 1980, London.

F. Crouzet (ed.), *Capital Formation in the Industrial Revolution*, Methuen and Co. Ltd, 1972, London.

S. Moore, *Three Tactics: The Background in Marx*, Monthly Review Foundation, 1963, New York.

A. Levine and E. O. Wright, *Rationality and the Class Struggle*, New Left Review, No. 123, Sept.–Oct. 1980.

K. Marx, *Selected Writings* (ed. D. McLellan), Oxford University Press, 1977, London.

P. Donaldson, *A Question of Economics*, Pelican Books, 1985, London.

D. Schweickart, *Capitalism or Worker Control?*, Praeger, 1980, New York.

L. Feuerbach, *The Essence of Christianity*, Routledge and Kegan Paul, 1957, London.

F. A. Hayek, *Capitalism and the Historians*, Routledge and Kegan Paul, 1954, London.

F. A. Hayek, *New Studies in Philosophy, Politics, Economics, and History of Ideas*, Routledge and Kegan Paul, 1978, London.

A. Wood, *Karl Marx*, Routledge and Kegan Paul, 1981, London.

P. T. Bauer, *Equality, the Third World and Economic Delusion*, Weidenfeld and Nicolson, 1981, London.

My thanks are also due to Penguin Books and Random House, Inc., for their kind permission to reproduce material from the following:

Karl Marx, *Capital, Vol. I*, Introduction by Ernest Mandel, translated by Ben Fowkes, Pelican Marx Library, 1976; edition copyright © New Left Review, 1976, translation copyright © Ben Fowkes, 1976.

Karl Marx, *Capital, Vol. III*, Introduction by Ernest Mandel, translated by David Fernbach, Pelican Marx Library, 1981; edition copyright © New Left Review, 1981, translation copyright © David Fernbach, 1981.

Karl Marx, *Grundrisse*, translated by Martin Nicolaus, Pelican Marx Library, 1973; translation copyright © Martin Nicolaus, 1973.

Karl Marx, *The Revolutions of 1848*, edited and introduced by David Fernbach, Pelican Marx Library, 1973; selection copyright © New Left Review, 1973, articles from the *Neue Rheinische Zeitung* copyright © Ben Fowkes, 1983, 'Address of the Central Committee to the Communist League' copyright © Paul Jackson, 1973, 'Minutes of the Central Committee Meeting of 15 September 1850' copyright © Joris de Bres, 1973.

Karl Marx, *Surveys From Exile*, edited and introduced by David Fernbach, Pelican Marx Library, 1973; selection copyright © New Left Review, 1973, 'The Class Struggle in France 1848–1850' copyright © Paul Jackson, 1973, 'The Eighteenth Brumaire of Louis Bonaparte' copyright © Ben Fowkes, 1973, articles on Britain copyright © Paul Jackson, 1973.

Karl Marx, *Early Writings*, introduced by Lucio Colletti, Pelican Marx Library, 1975; selection copyright © New Left Review, 1975, 'Critique of Hegel's Doctrine of the State,' 'Letters from the *Franco-German Yearbook*,' copyright © Rodney Livingstone, 1975, 'On The Jewish Question', 'A Contribution to the Critique of Hegel's Philosophy of Right. Introduction', 'Excerpts from James Mill's *Elements of Political Economy*', 'Economic and Philosophical Manuscripts' copyright © Gregor Benton, 1975.

Karl Marx, *The First International and After*, edited and introduced by David Fernbach, Pelican Marx Library, 1974; selection copyright © New Left Review, 1974, 'Speech on the Hague Congress' copyright © Paul Jackson, 1974, 'Critique of the Gotha Programme' copyright © Joris de Bres, 1974.

FOR THE BEST IN PAPERBACKS, LOOK FOR THE

In every corner of the world, on every subject under the sun, Penguin represents quality and variety – the very best in publishing today.

For complete information about books available from Penguin – including Pelicans, Puffins, Peregrines and Penguin Classics – and how to order them, write to us at the appropriate address below. Please note that for copyright reasons the selection of books varies from country to country.

In the United Kingdom: For a complete list of books available from Penguin in the U.K., please write to *Dept E.P., Penguin Books Ltd, Harmondsworth, Middlesex, UB7 0DA*

In the United States: For a complete list of books available from Penguin in the U.S., please write to *Dept BA, Penguin, 299 Murray Hill Parkway, East Rutherford, New Jersey 07073*

In Canada: For a complete list of books available from Penguin in Canada, please write to *Penguin Books Canada Ltd, 2801 John Street, Markham, Ontario L3R 1B4*

In Australia: For a complete list of books available from Penguin in Australia, please write to the *Marketing Department, Penguin Books Australia Ltd, P.O. Box 257, Ringwood, Victoria 3134*

In New Zealand: For a complete list of books available from Penguin in New Zealand, please write to the *Marketing Department, Penguin Books (NZ) Ltd, Private Bag, Takapuna, Auckland 9*

In India: For a complete list of books available from Penguin, please write to *Penguin Overseas Ltd, 706 Eros Apartments, 56 Nehru Place, New Delhi, 110019*

In Holland: For a complete list of books available from Penguin in Holland, please write to *Penguin Books Nederland B.V., Postbus 195, NL–1380AD Weesp, Netherlands*

In Germany: For a complete list of books available from Penguin, please write to *Penguin Books Ltd, Friedrichstrasse 10 – 12, D–6000 Frankfurt Main 1, Federal Republic of Germany*

In Spain: For a complete list of books available from Penguin in Spain, please write to *Longman Penguin España, Calle San Nicolas 15, E–28013 Madrid, Spain*

The Second World War (6 volumes) Winston S. Churchill

The definitive history of the cataclysm which swept the world for the second time in thirty years.

1917: The Russian Revolutions and the Origins of Present-Day Communism
Leonard Schapiro

A superb narrative history of one of the greatest episodes in modern history by one of our greatest historians.

Imperial Spain 1496–1716 J. H. Elliot

A brilliant modern study of the sudden rise of a barren and isolated country to be the greatest power on earth, and of its equally sudden decline. 'Outstandingly good' – *Daily Telegraph*

Joan of Arc: The Image of Female Heroism Marina Warner

'A profound book, about human history in general and the place of women in it' – Christopher Hill

Man and the Natural World: Changing Attitudes in England 1500–1800
Keith Thomas

'A delight to read and a pleasure to own' – Auberon Waugh in the *Sunday Telegraph*

The Making of the English Working Class E. P. Thompson

Probably the most imaginative – and the most famous – post-war work of English social history.

A CHOICE OF PENGUINS AND PELICANS

The French Revolution   Christopher Hibbert

'One of the best accounts of the Revolution that I know . . . Mr Hibbert is outstanding' – J. H. Plumb in the *Sunday Telegraph*

The Germans   Gordon A. Craig

An intimate study of a complex and fascinating nation by 'one of the ablest and most distinguished American historians of modern Germany' – Hugh Trevor-Roper

Ireland: A Positive Proposal   Kevin Boyle and Tom Hadden

A timely and realistic book on Northern Ireland which explains the historical context – and offers a practical and coherent set of proposals which could actually work.

A History of Venice   John Julius Norwich

'Lord Norwich has loved and understood Venice as well as any other Englishman has ever done' – Peter Levi in the *Sunday Times*

Montaillou: Cathars and Catholics in a French Village 1294–1324
Emmanuel Le Roy Ladurie

'A classic adventure in eavesdropping across time' – Michael Ratcliffe in *The Times*

Star Wars   E. P. Thompson and others

Is Star Wars a serious defence strategy or just a science fiction fantasy? This major book sets out all the arguments and makes an unanswerable case *against* Star Wars.

FOR THE BEST IN PAPERBACKS, LOOK FOR THE 🐧

A CHOICE OF PENGUINS AND PELICANS

The Apartheid Handbook Roger Omond

This book provides the essential hard information about how apartheid actually works from day to day and fills in the details behind the headlines.

The World Turned Upside Down Christopher Hill

This classic study of radical ideas during the English Revolution 'will stand as a notable monument to . . . one of the finest historians of the present age' – *The Times Literary Supplement*

Islam in the World Malise Ruthven

'His exposition of "the Qurenic world view" is the most convincing, and the most appealing, that I have read' – Edward Mortimer in *The Times*

The Knight, the Lady and the Priest Georges Duby

'A very fine book' (Philippe Aries) that traces back to its medieval origin one of our most important institutions, modern marriage.

A Social History of England New Edition Asa Briggs

'A treasure house of scholarly knowledge . . . beautifully written and full of the author's love of his country, its people and its landscape' – John Keegan in the *Sunday Times*, Books of the Year

The Second World War A. J. P. Taylor

A brilliant and detailed illustrated history, enlivened by all Professor Taylor's customary iconoclasm and wit.

A CHOICE OF PENGUINS AND PELICANS

Adieux   Simone de Beauvoir

This 'farewell to Sartre' by his life-long companion is a 'true labour of love' (the *Listener*) and 'an extraordinary achievement' (*New Statesman*).

British Society 1914–45   John Stevenson

A major contribution to the Pelican Social History of Britain, which 'will undoubtedly be the standard work for students of modern Britain for many years to come' – *The Times Educational Supplement*

The Pelican History of Greek Literature   Peter Levi

A remarkable survey covering all the major writers from Homer to Plutarch, with brilliant translations by the author, one of the leading poets of today.

Art and Literature   Sigmund Freud

Volume 14 of the Pelican Freud Library contains Freud's major essays on Leonardo, Michelangelo and Dostoevsky, plus shorter pieces on Shakespeare, the nature of creativity and much more.

A History of the Crusades   Sir Steven Runciman

This three-volume history of the events which transferred world power to Western Europe – and founded Modern History – has been universally acclaimed as a masterpiece.

A Night to Remember   Walter Lord

The classic account of the sinking of the *Titanic*. 'A stunning book, incomparably the best on its subject and one of the most exciting books of this or any year' – *The New York Times*

FOR THE BEST IN PAPERBACKS, LOOK FOR THE

A CHOICE OF PENGUINS AND PELICANS

The Informed Heart   Bruno Bettelheim

Bettelheim draws on his experience in concentration camps to illuminate the dangers inherent in all mass societies in this profound and moving masterpiece.

God and the New Physics   Paul Davies

Can science, now come of age, offer a surer path to God than religion? This 'very interesting' (*New Scientist*) book suggests it can.

Modernism   Malcolm Bradbury and James McFarlane (eds.)

A brilliant collection of essays dealing with all aspects of literature and culture for the period 1890–1930 – from Apollinaire and Brecht to Yeats and Zola.

Rise to Globalism   Stephen E. Ambrose

A clear, up-to-date and well-researched history of American foreign policy since 1938, Volume 8 of the Pelican History of the United States.

The Waning of the Middle Ages   Johan Huizinga

A magnificent study of life, thought and art in 14th and 15th century France and the Netherlands, long established as a classic.

The Penguin Dictionary of Psychology   Arthur S. Reber

Over 17,000 terms from psychology, psychiatry and related fields are given clear, concise and modern definitions.

FOR THE BEST IN PAPERBACKS, LOOK FOR THE

A CHOICE OF PENGUINS AND PELICANS

The Literature of the United States   Marcus Cunliffe

The fourth edition of a masterly one-volume survey, described by D. W. Brogan in the *Guardian* as 'a very good book indeed'.

The Sceptical Feminist   Janet Radcliffe Richards

A rigorously argued but sympathetic consideration of feminist claims. 'A triumph' – *Sunday Times*

The Enlightenment   Norman Hampson

A classic survey of the age of Diderot and Voltaire, Goethe and Hume, which forms part of the Pelican History of European Thought.

Defoe to the Victorians   David Skilton

A 'Learned and stimulating' (*The Times Educational Supplement*) survey of two centuries of the English novel.

Reformation to Industrial Revolution   Christopher Hill

This 'formidable little book' (Peter Laslett in the *Guardian*) by one of our leading historians is Volume 2 of the Pelican Economic History of Britain.

The New Pelican Guide to English Literature   Boris Ford (ed.)
Volume 8: The Present

This book brings a major series up to date with important essays on Ted Hughes and Nadine Gordimer, Philip Larkin and V. S. Naipaul, and all the other leading writers of today.